Praise for
The Selected Letters of Mark Twain

"Twain's letters are as much a pleasure as his books."—**Anthony Burgess**, *The Observer* (London)

"Twain's letters are just as fresh, witty and penetrating as the day he wrote them. Charles Neider has made an intelligent selection that shows as many aspects as possible of this many-sided genius."—*Houston Chronicle*

"If the 'Letter to the Editor' ever gets recognized as a literary genre, Mark Twain will head the list as a past master of glorious griping. He was also very good at epistolary blasts at the Gas Company, Western Union, publishers who got out of line, and opportunists. . . . Readers interested in Twain's life will be grateful to Neider for culling this selection."—*Chicago Tribune Book World*

"[A] delightful book. The letters are fascinating. It's wonderful to have available this further evidence of Twain's genius."—*Christian Science Monitor*

"[This collection] gives us an incomparable view of a complex personality, and the unparalleled opportunity to see one of America's best writers at work. . . . Twain's letters gave him space to vent his spleen, a podium for his unorthodox beliefs, and room to grieve privately. They helped him practice his own craft, sharpen his wit, and try out new ideas. . . . Some of his finest writing can be found in these letters."—*Philadelphia Inquirer*

"Twain the private man and philosopher-at-large looms vividly in these pages. . . . *The Selected Letters* will arouse the sympathies and tickle the funny bone of even the most casual reader."—*Kansas City Star*

"These letters make us laugh, cry, and marvel at the enduring vitality of a master of the language."—*Publishers Weekly*

"[A] full, entertaining, often poignant, and decidedly valuable book."—*St. Louis Post-Dispatch*

"Through these letters we see Twain as he himself might have liked us to see him, not without flaws, but nearly always purposeful, witty and gifted. . . . [This book] makes absorbing reading, for Neider is a sympathetic and skillful editor."
—*Baltimore Sun*

"Even in the most casual correspondence, there is a transcendent joy in the way Twain uses English. . . . Thank goodness there weren't many telephones back then."—*People Weekly*

"To open a letter from Mark Twain must have been a heady experience. . . . More than eighty years after his death they are still eminently readable and perhaps even more enjoyable."—*The Times Higher Education Supplement*

"Twain's letters give an intimate account of the man behind the myth."—*Arizona Daily Star*

"*The Selected Letters* provides a fascinating and delightful overview of Twain's life and work. . . . An excellent choice for Twain enthusiasts."—*Booklist*

"According to the evidence of even his earliest extant letters, Twain was a writer from the very start, having already acquired the warm, familiar, humorous style and the comprehensive understanding of human nature that inform his most famous works."—*Smithsonian*

The Selected Letters of
MARK TWAIN

edited with an introduction and commentary
by CHARLES NEIDER

Cooper Square Press

To Kate (Kathlyn) Harris

Copyright © 1982 by Charles Neider
First Cooper Square Press edition 1999

This Cooper Square Press paperback edition of *The Selected Letters of Mark Twain* is an unabridged republication of the edition first published in New York in 1982. It is reprinted by arrangement with the editor.

The work contains selections from *Mark Twain's Letters*, volumes I and II, edited by Albert Bigelow Paine. Copyright © 1917 by The Mark Twain Company. Copyright renewed © 1945 by Clara Clemens Samossoud. Published by Harper & Row Publishers, Inc., and reprinted by arrangement with the Mark Twain Foundation.

Published by Cooper Square Press,
An Imprint of Rowman & Littlefield Publishers, Inc.
150 Fifth Avenue, Suite 911
New York, New York 10011

Distributed by National Book Network

Library of Congress Cataloging-in-Publication Data

Twain, Mark, 1835–1910.
   [Correspondence. Selections]
   The selected letters of Mark Twain / edited with an introduction and commentary by Charles Neider. —1st Cooper Square Press ed.
     p.   cm.
   Includes index.
   ISBN 0-8154-1011-5 (pbk. : alk. paper)
   1. Twain, Mark, 1835–1910 Correspondence. 2. Humorists, American—19th century—Correspondence. 4. Journalists—United States Correspondence.   I. Neider, Charles, 1915- .
II. Title.
PS1331.A4   1999
818'.409—dc21   99–35026
[B]   CIP

♾™ The paper used in this publication meets the minimum requirements of American National Standard for Information Sciences—Permanence of Paper for Printed Library Materials, ANSI/NISO Z39.48-1992.
Manufactured in the United States of America.

Contents

Acknowledgments

I want to thank Carlos Noreña, Joseph Silverman and Paul and Nancy Spriggs of Stevenson College, University of California at Santa Cruz, for kindnesses extended to me during the preparation of this book. I also wish to thank my wife, Joan Merrick Neider, for valuable suggestions connected with the inception of the volume.

Above all I am indebted to Jeanie Jordan of the McHenry Library, UCSC, for help of many kinds.

—C.N.

Mark Twain: A Biographical Sketch

by Albert Bigelow Paine

Samuel Langhorne Clemens, for nearly half a century known and celebrated as "Mark Twain," was born in Florida, Missouri, on November 30, 1835. He was one of the foremost American philosophers of his day. He was the world's most famous humorist of any day. During the later years of his life he ranked not only as America's chief man of letters but also as her best known and best loved citizen.

The beginnings of that life were sufficiently unpromising. The family was a good one, of old Virginia and Kentucky stock, but its circumstances were reduced, its environment meager and disheartening. The father, John Marshall Clemens—a lawyer by profession, a merchant by vocation—had brought his household to Florida from Jamestown, Tennessee, somewhat after the manner of Judge Hawkins as pictured in *The Gilded Age*. Florida was a small town then, a mere village of twenty-one houses located on Salt River, but Judge Clemens, as he was usually called, optimistic and speculative in his temperament, believed in its future. Salt River would be made navigable, Florida would become a metropolis. He established a small business there and located his family in the simple frame cottage where, five months later, was born a baby boy to whom they gave the name of Samuel—a family name—and added Langhorne, after an old Virginia friend of his father.

The child was puny and did not make a very sturdy fight for life. Still, he weathered along season after season and survived two stronger children, Margaret and Benjamin. By 1839 Judge Clemens had lost faith in Florida. He removed his family to Hannibal, and in this Mississippi River town the little lad whom the world was to know as Mark Twain spent his early life. In *Tom Sawyer* we have a picture of the Hannibal of those days and the atmosphere of his boyhood there.

His schooling was brief and of a desultory kind. It ended one day in 1847, when his father died and it became necessary that each one should help in the domestic crisis. His brother Orion, ten years his senior, was already a printer by trade. Pamela, his sister, also considerably older, had acquired music, and now took a few pupils. The little boy Sam, at twelve, was apprenticed to a printer named Ament. His wages consisted of his board and clothes—"more board than clothes," as he once remarked to the writer.

He remained with Ament until his brother Orion bought out a small paper in Hannibal in 1850. The paper, in time, was moved into a part of the Clemens home and the two brothers ran it, the younger setting most of the type. A still younger brother, Henry, entered the office as an apprentice. The Hannibal *Journal* was no great paper from the beginning and it did not improve with time. Still, it managed to survive—country papers nearly always manage to survive—year after year, bringing in some sort of return. It was on this paper that young Sam Clemens began his writings—burlesque, as a rule, of local characters and conditions— usually published in his brother's absence, generally resulting in trouble on his return. Yet they made the paper sell, and if Orion had but realized his brother's talent he might have turned it into capital even then.

In 1853 (he was not yet eighteen) Sam Clemens grew tired of his limitations and pined for the wider horizon of the world. He gave out to his family that he was going to St. Louis but he kept on to New York, where a World's Fair was going on. In New York he found employment at his trade, and during the hot months of 1853 worked in a printing office in Cliff Street. By and by he went to Philadelphia, where he worked a brief time, made a trip to Washington, and presently set out for the West again, after an absence of more than a year.

Orion meanwhile had established himself at Muscatine, Iowa, but soon after removed to Keokuk, where the brothers were once more together, still following their trade. Young Sam Clemens remained in Keokuk until the winter of 1856–57, when he caught a touch of the South American fever then prevalent and decided to go to Brazil. He left Keokuk for Cincinnati, worked that winter in a printing office there, and in April took the little steamer, *Paul Jones*, for New Orleans, where he expected to find a South American vessel. In *Life on the Mississippi* we have his story of how he met Horace Bixby and decided to become a pilot instead of a South American adventurer, jauntily setting himself the stupendous task of learning the twelve hundred miles of the Mississippi River between St. Louis and New Orleans, of knowing it as exactly and as unfailingly, even in the dark, as one knows the way to his own features. It seems incredible to those who knew Mark Twain in his later years—dreamy, unpractical and indifferent to details—that he could have acquired so vast a store of minute facts as were required by that task. Yet within eighteen months he had become not only a pilot but one of the best and most careful pilots on the river, entrusted with some of the largest and most valuable steamers. He continued in that profession for two and a half years longer, and during that time met with no disaster that cost his owners a single dollar for damage.

Then the war broke out. South Carolina seceded in December, 1860, and other States followed. Clemens was in New Orleans in January, 1861, when Louisiana seceded, and his boat was put into the Confederate service and sent up the Red River. His occupation gone, he took steamer for the North—the last one before the blockade closed. A blank cartridge was fired at them from Jefferson Barracks when they reached St. Louis but they did not understand the signal and kept on. Presently a shell carried away part of the pilot house and considerably disturbed its inmates. They realized then that war had really begun.

In those days Clemens's sympathies were with the South. He hurried up to Hannibal and enlisted with a company of young fellows who were recruiting with the avowed purpose of "throwing off the yoke of the invader." They were ready for the field, presently, and set out in good order, a sort of nondescript cavalry detachment, mounted on animals more picturesque than beautiful. Still, it was a resolute band and might have done very well, only it rained a good deal, which made soldiering disagreeable and hard. Lieutenant Clemens resigned at the end of two weeks and decided to go to Nevada with Orion, who was a Union abolitionist and had received an appointment from Lincoln as Secretary of the new Territory.

In *Roughing It* Mark Twain gives us the story of the overland journey made by the two brothers, and a picture of experiences at the other end— true in aspect, even if here and there elaborated in detail. He was Orion's private secretary but there was no private secretary work to do and no salary attached to the position. The incumbent presently went to mining, adding that to his other trades.

He became a professional miner but not a rich one. He was at Aurora, California, in the Esmeralda district, skimping along, with not much to eat and less to wear, when he was summoned by Joe Goodman, owner and editor of the Virginia City *Enterprise*, to come up and take the local editorship of that paper. He had been contributing sketches to it now and then under the penname of "Josh," and Goodman, a man of fine literary instincts, recognized a talent full of possibilities. This was in the late summer of 1862. Clemens walked one hundred and thirty miles over very bad roads to take the job and arrived way-worn and travel-stained. He began on a salary of twenty-five dollars a week, picking up news items here and there and contributing occasional sketches—burlesques, hoaxes and the like. When the Legislature convened at Carson City he was sent down to report it, and then, for the first time, began signing his articles "Mark Twain," a river term used in making soundings, recalled from his piloting days. The name presently became known up and down the Pacific coast. His articles were copied and commented upon. He was recognized as one of the foremost among a little coterie of overland writers, two of whom, Mark Twain and Bret Harte, were soon to acquire a world-wide fame.

He left Carson City one day after becoming involved in a duel, the result of an editorial squib written in Goodman's absence, and went across the Sierras to San Francisco. The duel turned out farcically enough but the Nevada law, which regarded even a challenge or its acceptance as a felony, was an inducement to his departure. Furthermore, he had already aspired to a wider field of literary effort. He attached himself to the

Morning Call and wrote occasionally for one or two literary papers, the *Golden Era* and the *Californian*, prospering well enough during the better part of the year. Bret Harte and the rest of the little Pacific-slope group were also on the staff of these papers, and for a time at least the new school of American humor mustered in San Francisco.

The connection with the *Call* was not congenial. In due course it came to a natural end and Mark Twain arranged to do a daily San Francisco letter for his old paper, the *Enterprise*. The *Enterprise* letters stirred up trouble. They criticized the police of San Francisco so severely that the officials found means of making the writer's life there difficult and comfortless. With Jim Gillis, brother of a printer of whom he was fond, and who had been the indirect cause of his troubles, he went up into Calaveras County, to a cabin on Jackass Hill. Jim Gillis, a lovable, picturesque character (the Truthful James of Bret Harte), owned mining claims. Mark Twain decided to spend his vacation in pocket mining and soon added that science to his store of knowledge. It was a halcyon, happy three months that he lingered there but did not make his fortune, he only laid the cornerstone.

They tried their fortune at Angel's Camp, a place well known to readers of Bret Harte. But it rained pretty steadily and they put in most of their time huddled around the single stove of the dingy hotel of Angel's, telling yarns. Among the stories was one told by a dreary narrator named Ben Coon. It was about a frog that had been trained to jump but failed to win a wager because the owner of a rival frog had surreptitiously loaded him with shot. The story had been circulated among the camps, but Mark Twain had never heard it until then. The tale and the tiresome fashion of its telling amused him. He made notes to remember it.

Their stay in Angel's Camp came presently to an end. One day, when the mining partners were following the specks of gold that led to a pocket somewhere up the hill, a chill, dreary rain set in. Jim as usual was washing and Clemens was carrying water. The "color" became better and better as they ascended, and Gillis, possessed with the mining passion, would have gone on, regardless of the rain. Clemens, however, protested, and declared that each pail of water was his last. Finally he said, in his deliberate drawl:

"Jim, I won't carry any more water. This work is too disagreeable. Let's go to the house and wait till it clears up."

Gillis had just taken out a pan of earth. "Bring one more pail, Sam," he pleaded.

"I won't do it, Jim! Not a drop! Not if I knew there was a million dollars in that pan!"

They left the pan standing there and went back to Angel's Camp. The rain continued and they returned to Jackass Hill without visiting their claim again. Meantime the rain had washed away the top of the pan of earth left standing on the slope above Angel's, and exposed a handful of nuggets—pure gold. Two strangers came along and, observing it, had sat down to wait until the thirty-day claim notice posted by Jim Gillis should expire. They did not mind the rain—not with that gold in sight—and the minute the thirty days were up they followed the lead a few pans further and took out—some say ten, some say twenty, thousand dollars. It was a good pocket. Mark Twain missed it by one pail of water. Still, it is just as well, perhaps, when one remembers *The Jumping Frog.*

Matters having quieted down in San Francisco, he returned and took up his work again. Artemus Ward, whom he had met in Virginia City, wrote him for something to use in his (Ward's) new book. Clemens sent the frog story but he had been dilatory in preparing it and when it reached New York, Carleton, the publisher, had Ward's book about ready for the press. It did not seem worthwhile to Carleton to include the frog story, and he handed it over to Henry Clapp, editor of the *Saturday Press,* a perishing sheet, saying:

"Here, Clapp, here's something you can use."

The story appeared in the *Saturday Press* of November 18, 1865. According to the accounts of that time, it set all New York in a roar, which annoyed rather than gratified its author. He had thought very little of it, indeed, yet had been wondering why some of his more highly regarded work had not found fuller recognition.

But *The Jumping Frog* did not die. Papers printed it and reprinted it, and it was translated into foreign tongues. The name of "Mark Twain" became known as the author of that sketch, and the two were permanently associated from the day of its publication.

Such fame as it brought did not yield heavy financial return. Its author continued to win a more or less precarious livelihood doing miscellaneous work until March, 1866, when he was employed by the Sacramento *Union* to contribute a series of letters from the Sandwich Islands. They were notable letters, widely read and freely copied, and the sojourn there was a generally fortunate one. It was during his stay in the islands that the survivors of the wrecked vessel, the *Hornet,* came in after long privation at sea. Clemens was sick at the time but Anson Burlingame, who was in Honolulu, on the way to China, had him carried in a cot to the hospital, where he could interview the surviving sailors and take down their story. It proved a great "beat" for the *Union* and added considerably to its author's prestige. On his return to San Francisco he contributed an article on the *Hornet* disaster to *Harper's Magazine* and looked forward to its publication as a beginning of a real career. But alas! when it appeared the printer and the proofreader had somehow converted "Mark Twain" into "Mark Swain" and his dreams perished.

Undecided as to his plans, he was one day advised by a friend to deliver a lecture. He was already known as an entertaining talker, and his adviser judged his possibilities well. In *Roughing It* we find the story of that first lecture and its success. He followed it with other lectures up and down the Coast. He had added one more profession to his intellectual stock in trade.

Mark Twain, now provided with money, decided to pay a visit to his people. He set out for the East in December, 1866, via Panama, arriving in New York in January. A few days later he was with his mother, then living with his sister in St. Louis. A little later he lectured in Keokuk, and in Hannibal, his old home.

It was about this time that the first great Mediterranean steamship excursion began to be exploited. No such ocean picnic had ever been planned before and it created a good deal of interest East and West. Mark Twain heard of it and wanted to go. He wrote to friends on the *Alta-California* of San Francisco, and the publishers of that paper had sufficient faith to advance the money for his passage, on the understanding that he was to contribute frequent letters at twenty dollars apiece. It was a liberal offer as rates went in those days, and a godsend in the fullest sense of the word to Mark Twain.

Clemens now hurried to New York in order to be there in good season for the sailing date, which was in June. In New York he met Frank Fuller, whom he had known as territorial Governor of Utah, an energetic and enthusiastic admirer of the Western humorist. Fuller immediately proposed that Clemens give a lecture in order to establish his reputation on the Atlantic coast. Clemens demurred but Fuller insisted and engaged Cooper Union for the occasion. Not many tickets were sold. Fuller, however, always ready for an emergency, sent out a flood of complimentaries to the school teachers of New York and adjacent territory, and the house was crammed. It turned out to be a notable event. Mark Twain was at his best that night. The audience laughed until, as some of them declared when the lecture was over, they were too weak to leave their seats. His success as a lecturer was assured.

The *Quaker City* was the steamer selected for the great Oriental tour. It sailed as advertised, June 8, 1867, and was absent five months, during which Mark Twain contributed regularly to the *Alta-California* and wrote several letters for the New York *Tribune*. They were read and copied everywhere. They preached a new gospel in travel literature, a gospel of seeing with an overflowing honesty; a gospel of sincerity in according praise to whatever he considered genuine, and ridicule to the things believed to be shams. It was a gospel that Mark Twain continued to preach during his whole career. It became, in fact, his chief literary message to the world, a world ready for that message.

He returned to find himself famous. Publishers were ready with plans for collecting the letters in book form. The American Publishing Company of Hartford proposed a volume, elaborately illustrated, to be sold by subscription. He agreed with them as to terms and went to Washington to prepare copy. But he could not work quietly there and presently was back in San Francisco, putting his book together, lecturing occasionally, always to crowded houses. He returned in August, 1868, with the manuscript of the *Innocents Abroad*, and that winter, while his book was being manufactured, lectured throughout the East and Middle West, making his headquarters in Hartford, and in Elmira, New York.

He had an especial reason for going to Elmira. On the *Quaker City* he had met a young man by the name of Charles Langdon, and one day, in the Bay of Smyrna, had seen a miniature of the boy's sister, Olivia Langdon, then a girl of about twenty-two. He fell in love with that picture and still more deeply in love with the original when he met her in New York on his return. The Langdon home was in Elmira, and it was for this reason that as time passed he frequently sojourned there. When the proofs of the *Innocents Abroad* were sent him he took them along, and he and sweet Livy Langdon read them together. What he lacked in those days in literary delicacy she detected, and together they pruned it away. She became his editor that winter, a position which she held until her death.

The book was published in July, 1869, and its success was immediate and abundant. On his wedding day, February 2, 1870, Clemens received a check from his publishers for more than four thousand dollars, royalty accumulated during the three months preceding. The sales soon amounted to more than fifty thousand copies, and had increased to very nearly one hundred thousand at the end of the first three years. It was a book of travel, its lowest price three dollars and fifty cents. Even with our increased reading population no such sale is found for a book of that description today. And the *Innocents Abroad* holds its place, still outsells every other book in its particular field.

Mark Twain now decided to settle down. He had bought an interest in the *Express* of Buffalo, New York, and took up his residence in that city in a house presented to the young couple by Livy's father. It did not prove a fortunate beginning. Sickness, death and trouble of many kinds put a blight on the happiness of their first married year and gave them a distaste for the home in which they had made such a promising start. A baby boy, Langdon, came along in November but he was never a strong child. By the end of the following year the Clemenses had arranged for a residence in Hartford, temporary at first, later made permanent. It was in Hartford that little Langdon died, in 1872.

Clemens meanwhile had sold out his interest in the *Express*, severed his connection with the *Galaxy*, a magazine for which he was doing a department each month, and had written a second book for the American Publishing Company, *Roughing It*, published in 1872. In August of the same year he made a trip to London to get material for a book on England but was too much sought after, too continuously fêted, to do any work. He went alone but in November returned with the purpose of taking Livy and the new baby, Susy, to England the following spring. They sailed in April, 1873, and spent a good portion of the year in England and Scotland. They returned to America in November, and Clemens hurried back to London alone to deliver a notable series of lectures under the management of George Dolby, formerly managing agent for Charles Dickens. For two months Mark Twain lectured steadily to London audiences, the big Hanover Square rooms always filled. He returned to his family in January, 1874.

Meantime a home was being built for them in Hartford, and in the autumn of 1874 they took up residence in it, a happy residence, continued through seventeen years, well-nigh perfect years. Their summers they spent in Elmira, on Quarry Farm, a beautiful hilltop, the home of Livy's sister. It was in Elmira that much of Mark Twain's literary work was done. He had a special study there some distance from the house, where he loved to work out his fancies and put them into visible form.

It was not so easy to work at Hartford. There was too much going on. The Clemens home was a sort of general headquarters for literary folk near and far, and for distinguished foreign visitors of every sort. Howells and Aldrich used it as their half-way station between Boston and New York, and almost every foreign notable who visited America made a pilgrimage to Hartford to see Mark Twain. Some even went as far as Elmira, among them Rudyard Kipling, who recorded his visit in a chapter of his *American Notes*. Kipling declared he had come all the way from India to see Mark Twain.

Hartford had its own literary group. Harriet Beecher Stowe lived near the Clemens home; also Charles Dudley Warner. The Clemens and Warner families were constantly associated, and *The Gilded Age*, published in 1873, resulted from the friendship of Warner and Mark Twain. The character of Colonel Sellers in that book has become immortal. It is a character that only Mark Twain could create, for, though drawn from his mother's cousin, James Lampton, it embodies, and in no very exaggerated degree, characteristics that were his own. The tendency to make millions was always imminent, temptation was always hard to resist. Money making schemes are continually being placed before men of means and prominence, and Mark Twain to the day of his death found such schemes fatally attractive.

It was because of the Sellers characteristics in him that he invested in a typesetting machine which cost him nearly two hundred thousand dollars and helped to wreck his fortunes by and by. It was because of this characteristic that he invested in numberless schemes of lesser importance but no less disastrous in the end. His one successful commercial venture was his association with Charles L. Webster in the publication of the *Grant Memoirs*, of which enough copies were sold to pay a royalty of more than four hundred thousand dollars to Grant's widow, the largest royalty ever paid from any single publication. It saved the Grant family from poverty. Yet even this triumph was a misfortune to Mark Twain, for it led to scores of less profitable book ventures and eventual disaster.

Meanwhile he had written and published a number of books. *Tom Sawyer, The Prince and the Pauper, Life on the Mississippi, Huckleberry Finn,* and *A Connecticut Yankee in King Arthur's Court* were among the volumes that had entertained the world and inspired it with admiration and love for their author. In 1878–79 he had taken his family to Europe, where they spent their time in traveling over the Continent. It was during this period that he was joined by his intimate friend, the Rev. Joseph H. Twichell of Hartford, and the two made a journey, the story of which is told in *A Tramp Abroad.*

In 1891 the Hartford house was again closed, this time indefinitely, and the family, now five in number, took up residence in Berlin. The typesetting machine and the unfortunate publishing venture were drawing heavily on the family finances at this period, and the cost of the Hartford establishment was too great to be maintained. During the next three years he was distracted by the financial struggle which ended in April 1894, with the failure of Charles L. Webster & Co. Mark Twain now found himself bankrupt and nearly one hundred thousand dollars in debt. It had been a losing fight, with this bitter ending always in view, yet during this period of hard, hopeless effort he had written a large portion of the book which of all his works will perhaps survive the longest—his tender and beautiful story of Joan of Arc. All his life Joan had been his favorite character in the world's history, and during those trying months and years of the early nineties—in Berlin, in Florence, in Paris—he was conceiving and putting his picture of that gentle girl-warrior into perfect literary form. It was published in *Harper's Magazine*—anonymously, because, as he said, it would not have been received seriously had it appeared over his own name. The authorship was presently recognized. Exquisitely, reverently, as the story was told, it had in it the touch of quaint and gentle humor which could only have been given to it by Mark Twain.

It was only now and then that Mark Twain lectured during these years. He had made a reading tour with George W. Cable during the winter of 1884–85 but he abominated the lecture platform and often vowed he would never appear before an audience again. Yet in 1895, when he was sixty years old, he decided to rebuild his fortunes by making a reading tour around the world. It was not required of him to pay his debts in full. The creditors were willing to accept fifty per cent of the liabilities and had agreed to a settlement on that basis. But this did not satisfy Livy, and it did not satisfy him. They decided to pay dollar for dollar. They sailed for America, and in July, 1895, set out from Elmira on the long trail across land and sea. Livy, and Clara, their daughter, joined this pilgrim-

age, Susy and Jean remaining at Elmira with their aunt. Looking out of
the car windows, the travelers saw Susy waving them a goodbye. It was a
picture they would long remember.

The reading tour was one of triumph. High prices and crowded houses
prevailed everywhere. The author-reader visited Australia, New Zealand,
India, Ceylon and South Africa, arriving in England at last with the money and material which would pay off the heavy burden of debt and make
him once more free before the world. And in that hour of triumph came
the heavy blow. Susy Clemens, never very strong, had been struck down.
The first cable announced her illness. Livy and Clara sailed at once. Before they were half-way across the ocean a second cable announced that
Susy was dead. Mark Twain had to meet and endure the heartbreak
alone. He could not reach America in time for the burial. He remained in
England, and was joined there by the sorrowing family.

They passed that winter in London, where he worked at the story of
his travels, *Following the Equator*, the proofs of which he read the next
summer in Switzerland. The returns from it and from his reading venture
wiped away his indebtedness and made him free. He could go back to
America, as he said, able to look any man in the face again.

Yet he did not go immediately. He could live more economically
abroad, and economy was still necessary. The family spent two winters in
Vienna, and their apartments there constituted a veritable court where
the world's notables gathered. Another winter in England followed and
then, in the latter part of 1900, they went home—that is, to America.
Livy never could bring herself to return to Hartford, and never saw their
home there again.

Mark Twain's return to America was in the nature of a national event.
Wherever he appeared throngs turned out to bid him welcome. Mighty
banquets were planned in his honor.

In a house at 14 West Tenth Street in New York, and in a beautiful
place at Riverdale on the Hudson, most of the next three years were
passed. Then Livy's health failed, and in the autumn of 1903 the family
went to Florence for her benefit. There, on the 5th of June, 1904, she
died. They brought her back and laid her beside Susy at Elmira. That
winter the family took up residence at 21 Fifth Avenue, New York, and
remained there until the completion of Stormfield, at Redding, Connecticut, in 1908.

In his later life Mark Twain was accorded high academic honors. Already, in 1888, he had received from Yale College the degree of Master
of Arts, and the same college made him a Doctor of Literature in 1901. A
year later the university of his own State, at Columbia, Missouri, conferred the same degree, and then, in 1907, came the crowning honor,
when venerable Oxford tendered him the doctor's robe.

"I don't know why they should give me a degree like that," he said quaintly. "I never doctored any literature. I wouldn't know how."

He had thought never to cross the ocean again but he declared he would travel to Mars and back, if necessary, to get that Oxford degree. He appreciated its full meaning—recognition by the world's foremost institution of learning of the achievements of one who had no learning of the institutionary kind. He sailed in June, and his sojourn in England was marked by a continuous ovation. His hotel was besieged by callers. Two secretaries were busy nearly twenty hours a day attending to visitors and mail. When he appeared on the street his name went echoing in every direction and the multitudes gathered. On the day when he rose, in his scarlet robe and black mortar-board, to receive his degree (he must have made a splendid picture in that dress, with his crown of silver hair), the vast assembly went wild. What a triumph, indeed, for the little Missouri printer-boy! It was the climax of a great career.

Mark Twain's work was always of a kind to make people talk, always important, even when it was mere humor. Yet it was seldom that. There was always wisdom under it, and purpose, and these things gave it dynamic force and enduring life. Some of his aphorisms, so quaint in form as to invite laughter, are yet fairly startling in their purport. His paraphrase, "When in doubt, tell the truth," is of this sort. "Frankness is a jewel. Only the young can afford it," he once said to the writer, apropos of a little girl's remark. His daily speech was full of such things. The secret of his great charm was his great humanity and the gentle quaintness and sincerity of his utterance.

His work did not cease when the pressing need of money came to an end. He was full of ideas, and likely to begin a new article or story at any time. He wrote and published a number of notable sketches, articles, stories, even books, during these later years, among them that marvelous short story, "The Man That Corrupted Hadleyburg." In that story, as in most of his later work, he proved to the world that he was much more than a humorist, that he was, in fact, a great teacher, moralist, philosopher—the greatest, perhaps, of his age.

His life at Stormfield—he had never seen the place until the day of his arrival, June 18, 1908—was a peaceful and serene old age. Not that he was really old. He never was that. His step, his manner, his point of view were all and always young. He was fond of children and frequently had them about him. He delighted in games, especially in billiards, and in building the house at Stormfield the billiard room was first considered. He had a genuine passion for the sport. Without it his afternoon was not complete. His mornings he was likely to pass in bed, smoking (he was always smoking) and attending to his correspondence and reading. History and the sciences interested him, and his bed was strewn with biographies and stories of astronomical and geological research. The vastness of distances and periods always impressed him. He had no head for figures but he would labor for hours over scientific calculations, trying to compass them and to grasp their gigantic import. I remember once finding him highly elated over the fact that he had figured out for himself the length in hours and minutes of a "light year." He showed me the pages covered with figures, and was more proud of them than if they had been the pages of an immortal story. Then we played billiards, but even his favorite game could not make him altogether forget his splendid achievement.[*]

It was on the day before Christmas, 1909, that heavy bereavement once more came into the life of Mark Twain. His daughter Jean, long subject to epileptic attacks, was seized with a convulsion while in her bath and died before assistance reached her. He was dazed by the suddenness of the blow. His philosophy sustained him. He was glad, deeply glad, for the beautiful girl that had been released.

"I never greatly envied anybody but the dead," he said when he had looked at her. "I always envy the dead."

The coveted estate of silence, time's only absolute gift, was the one benefaction he had ever considered worth while.

Yet the years were not unkind to Mark Twain. They brought him sorrow, but they brought him also the capacity and opportunity for large enjoyment, and at the last they laid upon him a kind of benediction. Naturally impatient, he grew always more gentle, more generous, more tractable and considerate as the seasons passed. His final days may be said to have been spent in the tranquil light of a summer afternoon.

His own end followed by a few months that of his daughter. There were already indications that his heart was seriously affected, and soon after Jean's death he sought the warm climate of Bermuda. But his malady made rapid progress, and in April he returned to Stormfield. He died there just a week later, April 21, 1910.

Any attempt to designate Mark Twain's place in the world's literary history would be presumptuous now. Yet I cannot help thinking that he will maintain his supremacy in the century that produced him. I think so because, of all the writers of that hundred years, his work was the most human, his utterances went most surely to the mark. In the long analysis of the ages it is the truth that counts, and he never approximated, never compromised, but pronounced those absolute verities to which every human being of whatever rank must instantly respond.

His understanding of subjective human nature, the vast, unwritten life

[*] Judging by the fact that Clemens made many calculations, I assume that Paine misunderstood this. It would be too easy to calculate the number of hours in a year: 24 x 365. A light year is the distance traveled by light, moving at approximately 186,000 miles per second, in a year. This is no doubt what Clemens had calculated. 186,000 x 60 (seconds) x 60 (minutes) x 24 (hours) x 365 (days) = 5,865,696,000,000 miles, or almost six trillion miles.—C.N.

within, was simply amazing. Such knowledge he acquired at the fountain-head—that is, from himself. He recognized in himself an extreme example of the human being with all the attributes of power and of weakness, and he made his exposition complete.

The world will long miss Mark Twain. His example and his teaching will be neither ignored nor forgotten. Genius defies the laws of perspective and looms larger as it recedes. The memory of Mark Twain remains to us a living and intimate presence that today, even more than in life, constitutes a stately moral bulwark reared against hypocrisy and superstition—a mighty national menace to sham.

Introduction

by Charles Neider

The other day a friend of mine read aloud "The Story of the Old Ram" from Mark Twain's *Roughing It*. It is no exaggeration to say we both howled and that tears came to our eyes. This is the kind of very tall tale, a fiction, that Clemens characteristically threw into a book of nonfiction as if it belonged exactly there. Later he made the old ram even more famous on the lecture platform under the title of "His Grandfather's Old Ram."

Near the end of his life he discussed this story in his autobiography, retelling it precisely as he remembered it from the platform and pointing up the great and crucial differences between the printed version and the spoken one. That this particular yarn was very important to him is proven by the fact it occupies more than six pages of the autobiography.

It's the one that Jim Blaine, the drunken miner, tells in frontier surroundings: cabin; bunks, powder-kegs and candle-boxes for chairs; a candle flickering on a pine table; "the boys" sitting here and there. The one in which Blaine meanders until he nods off without getting to the point, so that nobody ever learns what happened to his grandfather's ram; in which Mark Twain is "sold," taken in, by his companions, who know in advance what will happen, or rather what won't. The joke is that Blaine is victimized by such a fantastic memory for idle details that he can never reach the nub of his story.

As in this tale, laughing with Mark Twain (or with Samuel L. Clemens; in the letters we'll encounter both the very private man and his very public persona) can sometimes be a strange and complex experience. I was embarrassed to find something funny in the image of Miss Wagner, an old spinster who had one eye, one leg and was "as bald as a jug," and in addition "was considerable on the borrow, she was," which is to say she was a seasoned borrower of glass eye, wooden leg and wig. Clemens understood profoundly the comedy inherent in other people's misfortunes, for example the laughter caused by seeing someone slip on a banana peel.

A glass eye and a wooden leg in themselves are hardly funny. It is the astonishing things that Clemens does with them that lifts the story above the level of stupid frontier cruelty. His comic invention is marvelous and unflagging. He piles up an incredible array and variety of details, to the extent that we realize he is exercising a remarkable gift and not simply being realistic and cruel. Furthermore, in the printed version of this story he hides behind the figure of Blaine. In the platform story he discarded him, or rather acted him, using the Western dialect and mannerisms and his own inimitable deadpan and drawl and making important use of improvised timing and pauses, varying them subtly to suit each audience.

In *Roughing It* it was old Miss Jefferson who used to lend her glass eye to Miss Wagner, "that hadn't any, to receive company in; it warn't big enough, and when Miss Wagner warn't noticing, it would get twisted around in the socket, and look up, maybe, or out to one side, and every which way, while t'other one was looking as straight ahead as a spy-glass. Grown people didn't mind it, but it 'most always made the children cry, it was so sort of scary. She tried packing it in raw cotton, but it wouldn't work, somehow—the cotton would get loose and stick out and look so kind of awful that the children couldn't stand it no way. She was always dropping it out, and turning up her old deadlight on the company empty, and making them oncomfortable, becuz *she* could never tell when it hopped out, being blind on that side, you see. So somebody would have to hunch her and say, 'Your game leg has fetched loose, Miss Wagner, dear'—and then all of them would have to sit and wait till she jammed it in again—wrong side before, as a general thing, and green as a bird's egg, being a bashful cretur and easy sot back before company. But being wrong side before warn't much difference, anyway, becuz her own eye was sky-blue and the glass one was yaller on the front side, so whichever way she turned it it didn't match nohow."

The reason Clemens gets away with all this is that his invention is so freewheeling, wild, that it distances him (and us) from the reality and therefore from simple bad taste. At the same time it releases something in us, perhaps some powerful repression, taboo. The glass eye is an instrument gone haywire, a machine with a life of its own. Designed to help Miss Wagner, it victimizes her, in this respect being a bit like the society she lives in. Meanwhile Clemens's invention is so gifted we are lost in admiration, and our own good taste nods.

Clemens's audacity is an important aspect of his comic genius. He can stretch a yarn until you hold your breath. You feel sure the tale will collapse—but it doesn't. His taste can be audacious too. Making jokes about a person with a glass eye is obviously not something one does in polite society. But of course the frontier society of *Roughing It* was not polite. Frontier humor could be rough, and often it was directed at minorities. In the present case the minority is woman, about whom the men could be endlessly sentimental as well as thickly insensitive: not a far cry from Clemens's own attitude toward women, especially those in his immediate family (mother, wife, daughters) and his literary imagination (for example Joan of Arc, about whom he wrote quite a poor novel). Is there really a truly live female in any of his literary creations?

Clemens's relations with women is a theme for a potentially fascinating study. So little is known about his sexual life. Was he in fact a virgin when he married Livy at thirty-four, as Dixon Wechter, a close student of his early years, has strongly suggested? If true it would be, at the least, quite odd, given his opportunities: a well-paid, even glamorous job as a Mississippi pilot while he was still in the hot flush of youth; New Orleans, St. Louis; the silver-mining frontier; San Francisco, the Hawaiian Islands; New York and Washington when he was already nationally famous. If he indulged sexually how was he able to cover his tracks so well? If one were to judge solely by the evidence of his early sex life one might conclude he had never existed. And what about his relations with Livy, the poor woman who was often in fragile psychological and physiological health and who was at times physically and entirely removed from him for months though she lived in the same house? Reading the letters in the present volume, one finds many such questions rising in one's mind.

Clemens's literary high jinks are remarkable—his love of mugging, monologue, dialect, caricature. He is a great proponent of the tall story, piling on details until we are breathless with admiration and amazement. At his best he is uproarious, a great comic virtuoso who delights in sharing the pyrotechnics of his genius. It is a large part of his greatness that he heard so well. His dialogue is extraordinary. One sometimes wonders if he had a phonographic memory. His ability to imitate styles of speech, with an array of accurate details, is rare indeed.

Returning to "The Story of the Old Ram": There was also Maria, who "married a missionary and died in grace—et up by the savages. They et *him*, too, poor feller—biled him. It warn't the custom, so they say, but they explained to friends of his'n that went down there to bring away his things, that they'd tried missionaries every other way and never could get any good out of 'em—and so it annoyed all his relations to find out that that man's life was fooled away just out of a dern'd experiment, so to speak. But mind you, there ain't anything ever reely lost; everything that people can't understand and don't see the reason of does good if you only hold on and give it a fair shake; Prov'dence don't fire no blank ca'tridges, boys. That there missionary's substance, unbeknowns to himself, actu'ly converted every last one of them heathens that took a chance at the barbecue. Nothing ever fetched them but that."

A great deal of Clemens's humor, as well as his essential, larger genius (which includes that of the great novelist), depends on his alive language, strongly idiomatic, and flavored with the vernacular. His language dates less than that of any other American writer I can think of. The simple, spoken English language holds up much better than the literary one. It is a hardier instrument, and actually more difficult to manage, for it quickly reveals false tones, unsteady ones, and the least touch of strutting, cakewalking, putting on the dog. Clemens understood instinctively, as did Charles Darwin, the virtues of sober English prose, unadorned with literary sequins, and why the four-letter words have lasted for centuries, only in our own most recent time being debased by overuse. In addition, his wild effects often stem from his extraordinarily rich and wide-ranging vocabulary and his vigorous and unexpected use of verbs, all usually proffered deadpan.

A brilliant showpiece contrasting a formal language with an earthy one can be found in "Buck Fanshaw's Funeral" in *Roughing It*. It is a wonderful dialogue between a veteran of the frontier and a young minister, in which there is a total breakdown of communication because the two are speaking in different tongues. Scotty Briggs, the frontiersman, says in one of his exchanges, "Well, you've ruther got the bulge on me. Or maybe we've both got the bulge, somehow. You don't smoke me and I don't smoke you. You see, one of the boys has passed in his checks and we want to give him a good send-off, and so the thing I'm on now is to roust out somebody to jerk a little chin-music for us and waltz him through handsome."

The minister replies, "My friend, I seem to grow more and more bewildered. Your observations are wholly incomprehensible to me. Cannot you simplify them in some way? At first I thought perhaps I understood you, but I grope now. Would it not expedite matters if you restricted yourself to categorical statements of fact unencumbered with obstructing accumulations of metaphor and allegory?"

After another pause and some reflection, Scotty says, "I'll have to pass, I judge. . . . You've raised me out, pard. . . . Why, that last lead of yourn is too many for me—that's the idea. I can't neither trump nor follow suit."

Roughing It by no means has a monopoly of wild episodes and incidents in Clemens's nonfiction books. "Keelboat Talk and Manners" in *Life on the Mississippi* is a fabulous set piece about "low" life on the great river, especially about the antics of types who used to be called, in the days of Davy Crockett, "ring-tailed roarers" (great and colorful braggarts and/or yarn-spinners). "Keelboat" was robbed from *Huckleberry Finn*, which Clemens was working on at the time he wrote the river book. The novel never regained this wonderful invention. Another wild favorite of mine in the Mississippi book is "The Art of Inhumation," an extravagant yarn about the piles of money to be made in the undertaking business, good times or bad.

Clemens had a very proper side too but even when he was being proper and even when he was largely divorcing himself from his Western roots, as he was when he wrote *A Tramp Abroad*, another travel book, he could be irresistibly funny. There are few things in any literature, probably, as astonishingly comic and sustained as "Ascending the Riffelberg" and "The Awful German Language" in that book. To be a comic virtuoso in so sustained a way meant that he was also a comic architect of genius.

I have been reading Mark Twain a long time, but there is so much of him that is absolutely first-rate on a wild and gut comic level, that stands up decade after decade and generation after generation, that I still often react to him in a very fresh way, with a sense of surprise. He is a healing force, a literary medicine, an international health treasure of incalculable worth. I bless his memory once again for the endless chuckles and belly laughs he has given me—for more than half a century, I now realize.

In humor I don't believe anyone else in American literature, and possibly any other literature, can touch him. His friend William Dean Howells, in a moving small volume written soon after Clemens's death in the spring of 1910, called him "the Lincoln of our literature." I would add, "And the Shakespeare of our humor."

The letters in the present volume span the major portion of Clemens's life. The first is from his eighteenth year, the last was written four months before his death at seventy-four. What an incomparable purview we get of his psyche and genius in reading them, and how suggestive some of the details are. In the first letter, he mentions having a poor memory. One wonders, for he had a fine one by the time he became a pilot. In the second, he writes, "I shall ask favors from no one, and endeavor to be (and shall be) as 'independent as a wood-sawyer's clerk.'" One thinks: and so he had personal independence on his mind this early, which he achieved in unusual measure: as pilot, frontier silver-miner, newspaper correspondent, eminently successful lecturer and author.

And one realizes that very early, when he was fresh from the great river basin and the country's interior (the nation was seventy-seven years old) and was brand-new to the eastern metropolis with its international flavor, he had a xenophobic view of foreigners. Writing to his older brother, Orion, from Philadelphia two days before his eighteenth birthday, he noted, ". . . but there are so many abominable foreigners here (and among printers, too) who hate everything American. . . . I was in Franklin's old office this morning . . . and there was at least one foreigner for every American at work there." One senses job rivalry. This jaundiced view of foreigners, perhaps having its genesis during his first visits to New York and Philadelphia (or was it only inflamed by them?) would reward him handsomely through his *Innocents Abroad,* published sixteen years later, the remarkable travel book in which he repaid with interest but with the ameliorating power of humor the debt he felt America owed those visitors from overseas who had criticized his own country too archly, glibly. The Missouri upstart would some day become an Anglophile, a Germanophile, a Francophobe and, in terms of length of time spent abroad, one of the nation's early literary expatriates.

When he was in his twenty-third year he revealed an extraordinary ability to write with great force and accuracy about a devastating event extremely close to him, an ability suggesting a strange kind of psychic split. This was in his letter about his younger brother Henry's death, written to Orion's wife, Mollie, June 18, 1858. Later we'll see him writing with even greater power about the death of his favorite child, Susy, the death of his wife, Livy, and finally about the death of his daughter, Jean. And we see in the letter to Mollie what an overactive conscience he has, for he insists on blaming himself for Henry's terrible death in the explosion of the *Pennsylvania's* boilers. He himself, Sam Clemens, had been spared by a trifle. But part of his guilt is common to survivors of a calamity, the haunting question being, "Why was *I* spared, I who didn't deserve to be?" Nine years later, also in June, in a letter to his mother and family written in New York on the eve of that *Quaker City* excursion which was to make him prosperous and famous, he feels guilty toward Orion for not having "gouged an office" in the Federal government for him, and his mind "is stored full of unworthy conduct toward Orion and towards you all."

There is not much humor in his early letters. But his writing flows; he's articulate, bursting with language and life. A large difference in content and style is noticeable when he begins writing from Nevada. His style now is freewheeling, his humor increasingly evident. It's as if his imagination exploded with the experience of plains, mountains, alkali desert and the get-rich-quick society of the silver-mining frontier. In his letter of February 8, 1862, to his mother and his sister Pamela, written in Carson City, we encounter a talent which is almost full-blown: the gift of gab, of phrase, the richness of material (really the richness of mind), the ageless gusto, the wild or understated Western humor. All is possible in the American West, for good or bad, he seems to be suggesting between the lines.

In August 1863, when he was not yet twenty-eight, he was feeling his oats even though presumably he was not sowing them. "You think that picture looks old?" he asked his mother and Pamela. "Well, I can't help it—in reality I am not as old as I was when I was eighteen." About his writing habits, he wrote to them roughly a year later, "I work as I always did—by fits and starts." In January 1866 he wrote, again to them, "I wish I was back there piloting up and down the river again. Verily, all is vanity and little worth—save piloting." This is not only an indication that he was reaching the end of his Western period as far as actual experience was concerned. It is also an early hint of that river nostalgia which was later to possess him powerfully and to find expression both in fiction and nonfiction.

The present letters are like a second but even more intimate autobiography. Of course, not all his letters are equally good. Many of this period deal with mining business, money matters, chore transactions. I have selected with care, my chief concern being that the letters be lively and interesting. It is doubtful that any but a handful were written with the thought of publication in mind.

"We chase phantoms half the days of our lives," he wrote to Orion from Washington the third week of February 1868. "It is well if we learn wisdom even then, and save the other half. I am in for it. I must go on chasing them—until I marry—*then* I am done with literature and all other bosh—that is, literature wherewith to please the general public. I shall write to please myself then. . . . To be *busy* is a man's only happiness—and I *am*—otherwise I should die."

His letter of October 11, 1869, to the New York Society of California Pioneers (he was almost thirty-four) is one of my favorites. In addition to striking very strongly and aptly the note that would be orchestrated in *Roughing It,* it evidences his unsurpassed, instinctive understatement and timing. All the tones are so right: wryness, irony, his manner of poking fun at himself. Here, even though the text is relatively brief, we touch the humorist as genius, opening new psychological corridors for us, changing us permanently by an exposure to comic subtleties, the ballet of the humorous mind. What a fertile imagination, and what metaphors. "I ran tunnels till I tapped the Arctic Ocean and I sunk shafts till I broke through the roof of perdition. . . ." One wonders: where did he learn it all? But of course on the whole he didn't. We are observing the unexplainable, the possession of a wondrous gift.

The letter is not without surprises. It keeps you off balance. It begins soberly, quietly, with no humor. It grows riotous with comedy. It ends with the pathos of aging and human change. At the conclusion there are no jokes, only a marvelous humanity and wisdom expressed by haunting prose. ". . . and close this screed with the sincere hope that your visit here will be a happy one and not embittered by the sorrowful surprises that absence and lapse of years are wont to prepare for wanderers; surprises which come in the form of old friends missed from their places; silence where familiar voices should be; the young grown old; change and decay everywhere . . ." and so on.

Reading his letters, one understands that rarely if ever did he have to strain for humor. It seems to flow from his pores, and apparently he could afford to throw it away on even minor business mail, as in his letter to his lecture agent of August 8, 1871, written in Hartford. "I am different from other women. My mind changes oftener. People who have no mind can easily be steadfast and firm, but when a man is loaded down to the guards with it, as I am, every heavy sea of foreboding or inclination, maybe of indolence, shifts the cargo. . . . You must try to keep the run of my mind, Redpath, it is your business being the agent, and it always was too many for me. It appears to me to be one of the finest pieces of mechanism I have ever met with."

Some of the letters I have not selected have parts that are particularly fine, such as his letter to Howells from Munich dated November 17, 1878, in which he wrote, "She [Susy Clemens] is sorely badgered with dreams, and her stock dream is that she is being eaten up by bears. She is a grave and thoughtful child, as you will remember. Last night she had the usual dream. This morning she stood apart (after telling it) for some time, look-ing vacantly at the floor and absorbed in meditation. At last she looked up, and with the pathos of one who feels he has not been dealt by with even-handed fairness, said, 'But Mamma, the trouble is that I am never the *bear*, but always the *person*.'" In his letter to Howells of November 28, 1879, he noted, ". . . reminds me of Susy's newest and very earnest longing—to have crooked teeth and glasses—'like Mamma.' I would like to look into a child's head once and see what its processes are."

Other letters included here remind us, in case we had forgotten, that Clemens could use humor with deadly intent and effect, that his power of invective was awesome, perhaps especially in his unmailed replies to cer-tain correspondence, as when he wrote, "Dear Sir, What is the trouble with you? If it is your viscera, you cannot have them taken out and reor-ganized a moment too soon. I mean, if they are inside. But if you are composed of them, that is another matter. Is it your brain? But it could not be your brain. Possibly it is your skull: you want to look out for that. Some people, when they get an idea, it pries the structure apart."

Perhaps the epitome of this kind of writing was his priceless lulu of September 8, 1887, which reached the pitch of: "Why the pale doubt that flitteth dim and nebulous athwart the forecastle of your third sentence?"

During the last four years of Clemens's life, Albert Bigelow Paine, twenty-six years his junior and destined to live about the same length of time as Clemens, became his official biographer and closest companion. Upon Clemens's death he was named literary editor of the Mark Twain estate. He published his biography of Clemens in 1912, about two years after the humorist's death. Compared with subsequent biographers of Clemens, he had the great advantage of having known Clemens, two of the latter's children and many of Clemens's friends, and the considerable advantage of having access to both Clemens's papers and related ones before many were scattered through various sales, gifts and the vagaries of time.

He had certain shortcomings as a biographer and an editor of Clemens. He was not trained as a literary scholar, and his literary tastes were uncer-tain. He called Clemens's novel about Joan of Arc "the book which of all his works will perhaps survive the longest," a remark which unhappily indicates a damaged crystal ball. It is not surprising that in these current times of more precise, more pedantic and more costly literary scholarship, scholarship increasingly leaning on computers, he is underestimated in the contribution he made to our knowledge of Clemens and the latter's works.

When he edited *Mark Twain's Letters*, published in 1917, he had be-fore him not only Clemens's papers but letters which some of Clemens's correspondents had loaned to him and whose present whereabouts, speak-ing of the originals, are unknown. He had a grasp of the biography and an overall view of the correspondence which in my opinion have not been equalled since. To undertake to do a selected letters at this time without depending heavily on him would be an immense task, for Clemens was an almost tireless and voluminous correspondent. Consequently the present selection, with few exceptions, is based on his 1917 two-volume edition, and I am very glad to take this opportunity to note my great indebtedness to him.

I have selected letters primarily but not exclusively for their humor, their autobiographical interest, their literary quality and the degree to which they discuss literary matters. I have omitted those which are obviously dated, which are trivial and which were half-hearted responses to fan letters. I have also excluded letters in which Clemens indulged his penchant for philosophical determinism, a humorless belief in man as a piece of mechanical clockwork about which Clemens was dogmatic, even fanatical, and which was usually associated with his personal pessimism. Our country does not need to be taught lessons in pessimism at this time. It does need to have its mood lifted by great humor. I trust I am not confusing pessimism with tragedy. There is plenty of tragedy in the present work, which mirrors the human condition in a remarkable way. In brief, wherever possible I have favored the comic and humane sides of Clemens.

I have carefully avoided trying to provide a "representative" or "balanced" collection. For example, I have omitted his courtship letters to Livy, which I find overly sentimental, and the false, strident, self-abasing letters to Mrs. Fairbanks. The present volume is frankly idiosyncratic, it was formed essentially to please me, I wanted above all to enjoy it myself. I worked in the belief that my own taste would find many sympathetic readers, as it has in the past, say, with my edition of Clemens's autobiography.

Some of the letters are fragmentary. In others I have not hesitated to delete portions which I consider boring. One senses that Clemens wrote the present letters quickly and that he often used punctuation to satisfy his ear, to slow down the pace, to suggest how the prose should sound. Such guidemarks are unnecessary when the prose is in print. The printed language and the eye's response have conventions of their own. Furthermore, our own punctuation is different from that of his time. Once again I have modernized his and his printer's punctuation, chopping through thickets of ampersands, commas, semicolons and dashes. It was an arduous task but well worth it, for the result, to the modern eye and ear, is a wonderful airiness, a streamlined freedom from typogenic (to coin a word) claustrophobia.

Princeton, New Jersey
May 3, 1981

ONE

[[1853-61]]

New York — "I have taken a liking to the abominable place" — Philadelphia — "Unlike New York, I like this Philadelphia amazingly" — piloting on the Mississippi — the tragic death of Henry Clemens — "Pray for me, Mollie, and pray for my poor sinless brother" — visit to a female clairvoyant

In his eighteenth year Clemens left Hannibal, Missouri, taking the night boat to St. Louis, where he visited his sister Pamela, the wife of William A. Moffett, and worked briefly in the composing room of the *Evening News*. Then he proceeded to New York.

In the following, which is fragmentary, he described a visit to New York's Crystal Palace Fair, in progress at Forty-Second Street and Sixth Avenue, the site of what was later to be Bryant Park. He was earning $4 a week in a printing shop on Cliff Street and lodging in a boarding house on Duane.

To Pamela Moffett, St. Louis

[New York, *summer, 1853*]

... From the gallery (second floor) you have a glorious sight—the flags of the different countries represented, the lofty dome, glittering jewelry, gaudy tapestry, &c, with the busy crowd passing to and fro—tis a perfect fairy palace—beautiful beyond description.

The Machinery department is on the main floor but I cannot enumerate any of it on account of the lateness of the hour (past 8 o'clock.) It would take more than a week to examine everything on exhibition, and as I was only in a little over two hours tonight, I only glanced at about one-third of the articles, and having a poor memory, I have enumerated scarcely any of even the principal objects. The visitors to the Palace average 6,000 daily—double the population of Hannibal. The price of admission being 50 cents, they take in about $3,000.

The Latting Observatory (height about 280 feet) is near the Palace. From it you can obtain a grand view of the city and the country round. The Croton Aqueduct, to supply the city with water, is the greatest wonder yet. Immense sewers are laid across the bed of the Hudson River, and pass through the country to Westchester county, where a whole river is turned from its course and brought to New York. From the reservoir in the city to the Westchester county reservoir, the distance is *thirty-eight* miles! And if necessary they could supply every family in New York with *one hundred barrels of water per day!*

I am very sorry to learn that Henry has been sick. He ought to go to the country and take exercise, for he is not half so healthy as Ma thinks he is. If he had my walking to do he would be another boy entirely. Four times every day I walk a little over one mile. And working hard all day and walking four miles *is* exercise. I am used to it now, though, and it is no trouble. Where is it Orion's going to? Tell Ma my promises are faithfully kept, and if I have my health I will take her to Ky. in the spring. I shall save money for this. Tell Jim and all the rest of them to write and give me all the news. I am sorry to hear such bad news from Will and Captain Bowen. I shall write to Will soon. The Chatham Square Post Office and the Broadway office too are out of my way and I always go to the General Post Office, so you must write the direction of my letters plain, "New York City, N. Y.," without giving the street or anything of the kind or they may go to some of the other offices. (It has just struck 2 A.M. and I always get up at 6 and am at work at 7.) You ask me where I spend my evenings. Where would you suppose, with a free printers' library containing more than 4,000 volumes within a quarter of a mile of me and nobody at home to talk to? I shall write to Ella soon. Write soon.

Truly your Brother
Sam

P. S. I have written this by a light so dim that you nor Ma could not read by it.

Henry was Clemens's brother, three years his junior. Orion (with the accent on the first syllable) was his older brother, ten years older than himself. Jim was Jim Wolfe, an apprentice in Orion's printing shop. Will was Will Bowen, a Hannibal childhood friend who was studying Mississippi piloting with an older brother, the "Captain." Ella was Ella Creel, Clemens's cousin. "Tell Ma my promises are faithfully kept" referred to Clemens's promise to his mother that he would not throw a card or drink a drop of liquor while he was away from home.

To Pamela Moffett, St. Louis

New York, *Oct. Saturday* '53

My dear Sister,

I have not written to any of the family for some time, from the fact, *firstly,* that I didn't know where they were, and *secondly,* because I have been fooling myself with the idea that I was going to leave New York every day for the last two weeks. I have taken a liking to the abominable place, and every time I get ready to leave I put it off a day or so from some unaccountable cause. It is as hard on my conscience to leave New York as it was easy to leave Hannibal. I think I shall get off Tuesday, though.

Edwin Forrest has been playing for the last sixteen days at the Broadway Theatre but I never went to see him till last night. The play was the "Gladiator." I did not like parts of it much but other portions were really splendid. In the latter part of the last act, where the "Gladiator" (Forrest) dies at his brother's feet (in all the fierce pleasure of gratified revenge), the man's whole soul seems absorbed in the part he is playing, and it is really startling to see him. I am sorry I did not see him play "Damon and Pythias," the former character being his greatest. He appears in Philadelphia on Monday night.

I have not received a letter from home lately but got a *Journal* the other day, in which I see the office has been sold. I suppose Ma, Orion and Henry are in St. Louis now. If Orion has no other project in his head he ought to take the contract for getting out some weekly paper if he cannot get a foremanship. Now, for such a paper as the *Presbyterian* (containing about 60,000) he could get $20 or $25 per week, and he and Henry could easily do the work. Nothing to do but set the type and make up the forms....

If my letters do not come often you need not bother yourself about me, for if you have a brother nearly eighteen years of age who is not able to take care of himself a few miles from home, such a brother is not worth one's thoughts, and if I don't manage to take care of *No. I,* be assured you will never know it. I am not afraid, however. I shall ask favors from no one, and endeavor to be (and shall be) as "independent as a wood-sawyer's clerk."

I never saw such a place for military companies as New York. Go on the street when you will, you are sure to meet a company in full uniform, with all the usual appendages of drums, fifes, &c. I saw a large company of soldiers of 1812 the other day, with a '76 veteran scattered here and there in the ranks. And as I passed through one of the parks lately I came upon a company of *boys* on parade. Their uniforms were neat and their muskets about half the common size. Some of them were not more than seven or eight years of age but had evidently been well drilled.

Passage to Albany (160 miles) on the finest steamers that ply the Hudson is now 25 cents—cheap enough, but is generally cheaper than that in the summer.

I want you to write as soon as I tell you where to direct your letter. I would let you know now if I knew myself. I may perhaps be here a week longer but I cannot tell. When you write tell me the whereabouts of the family. My love to Mr. Moffett and Ella. Tell Ella I intend to write to her soon, whether she wants me to nor not.

Truly your Brother,
Saml L. Clemens

The *Journal* referred to was Orion's paper, the Hannibal *Journal,* on which Clemens had worked. The number 60,000 refers to 60,000 ems (type measurement).

To Orion Clemens, Hannibal

Philadelphia, Pa. Oct. 26, 1853

My dear Brother,

It was at least two weeks before I left New York that I received my last letter from home, and since then not a word have I heard from any of you. And now, since I think of it, it wasn't a letter either but the last number of the "Daily Journal," saying that that paper was sold, and I very naturally supposed from that that the family had disbanded and taken up winter quarters in St. Louis. Therefore I have been writing to Pamela till I've tired of it, and have received no answer. I have been writing for the last two or three weeks to send Ma some money but devil take me if I knew where she was, and so the money has slipped out of my pocket somehow or other, but I have a dollar left and a good deal owing to me, which will be paid next Monday. I shall enclose the dollar in this letter and you can hand it to her. I know it's a small amount but then it will buy her a handkerchief and at the same time serve as a specimen of the kind of stuff we are paid with in Philadelphia, for you see it's against the law, in Pennsylvania, to keep or pass a bill of less denomination than $5. I have only seen two or three bank bills since I have been in the State. On Monday the hands are paid off in sparkling gold, fresh from the Mint, so your dreams are not troubled with the fear of having doubtful money in your pocket.

I am subbing at the *Inquirer* office. One man has engaged me to work for him every Sunday till the first of next April, when I shall return home to take Ma to Ky, and another has engaged my services for the 24th of next month, and if I want it I can get subbing *every night* of the week. I go to work at 7 o'clock in the evening and work till 3 o'clock the next morning. I can go to the theatre and stay till 12 o'clock and then go to the office and get work from that till 3 the next morning, when I go to bed and sleep till 11 o'clock, then get up and loaf the rest of the day. The type is mostly agate and minion, with some bourgeois, and when one gets a good agate take° he is sure to make money. I made $2.50 last Sunday and was laughed at by all the hands, the poorest of whom sets 11,000 on Sunday. And if I don't set 10,000, at least, next Sunday, I'll give them leave to laugh as much as they want to. Out of the 22 compositors in this office, 12 at least set 15,000 on Sunday.

Unlike New York, I like this Philadelphia amazingly and the people in it. There is only one thing that gets my "dander" up and that

---

° "Agate," "minion," etc., sizes of type; "take," a piece of work. Type measurement is by ems, meaning the width of the letter m.—A.B.P.

is the hands are always *encouraging* me, telling me, "It's no use to get discouraged, no use to be down-hearted, for there is more work here than you can do!" "Down-hearted" the devil! I have not had a particle of such a feeling since I left Hannibal more than four months ago. I fancy they'll have to wait some time till they see me down-hearted or afraid of starving while I have strength to work and am in a city of 400,000 inhabitants. When I was in Hannibal, before I had scarcely stepped out of the town limits nothing could have convinced me that I would starve as soon as I got a little way from home. . . .

The grave of Franklin is in Christ Church yard, cor. of Fifth and Arch Streets. They keep the gates locked, and one can only see the flat slab that lies over his remains and that of his wife. But you cannot see the inscription distinctly enough to read it. The inscription, I believe, reads thus:

$$\left. \begin{array}{c} \text{Benjamin} \\ \text{and} \\ \text{Deborah} \end{array} \right\} \text{Franklin}$$

I counted 27 cannons (6 pounders) planted in the edge of the sidewalk in Water St. the other day. They are driven into the ground about a foot, with the mouth end upwards. A ball is driven fast into the mouth of each to exclude the water. They look like so many posts. They were put there during the war. I have also seen them planted in this manner round the old churches in N.Y. . . .

There is one fine custom observed in Phila. A gentleman is always expected to hand up a lady's money for her. Yesterday I sat in the front end of the bus, directly under the driver's box. A lady sat opposite me. She handed me her money, which was right. But Lord! a St. Louis lady would think herself ruined if she should be so familiar with a stranger. In St. Louis a man will sit in the front end of the stage and see a lady stagger from the far end to pay her fare. The Phila. bus drivers cannot cheat. In the front of the stage is a thing like an office clock, with figures from 0 to 40 marked on its face. When the stage starts, the hand of the clock is turned toward the 0. When you get in and pay your fare the driver strikes a bell, and the hand moves to the figure 1—that is, "one fare, and paid for," and there is your receipt, as good as if you had it in your pocket. When a passenger pays his fare and the driver does not strike the bell immediately, he is greeted, "Strike that bell! Will you?"

I must close now. I intend visiting the Navy Yard, Mint, etc., before I write again. You must write often. You see I have nothing to write interesting to you, while you can write nothing that will not interest me. Don't say my letters are not *long* enough. Tell Jim Wolfe to write. Tell all the boys where I am, and to write. Jim Robinson, particularly. I wrote to him from N.Y. Tell me all that is going on in H—l.

Truly your brother
Sam

The dubious money, known as wildcat, was paper issued by private banks. "H—l" was Clemens's abbreviation for Hannibal and an allusion to its use in the title of a poem. "To Mary in H—l," which he had printed in the *Journal* during one of Orion's periodic absences. The next letter is also to Orion, now living in Iowa, where he had just founded a new paper with an old title, *The Journal.*

To Orion Clemens, Muscatine, Iowa

Philadelphia, *Nov. 28th, 1853*

My dear Brother,

I received your letter today. I think Ma ought to spend the winter in St. Louis. I don't believe in that climate—it's too cold for her.

The printers' annual ball and supper came off the other night. The proceeds amounted to about $1,000. The printers, as well as other people, are endeavoring to raise money to erect a monument to Franklin but there are so many abominable foreigners here (and among printers too) who hate everything American that I am very certain as much money for such a purpose could be raised in St. Louis as in Philadelphia. I was in Franklin's old office this morning, the "North American" (formerly "Philadelphia Gazette"), and there was at least one foreigner for every American at work there.

How many subscribers has the *Journal* got? What does the Job-work pay, and what does the whole concern pay?. . .

I will try to write for the paper occasionally but I fear my letters will be very uninteresting, for this incessant night work dulls one's ideas amazingly.

From some cause, I cannot set type nearly so fast as when I was at home. Sunday is a long day, and while others set 12 and 15,000, yesterday I only set 10,000. However, I will shake this laziness off soon, I reckon. . . .

How do you like "free soil?" I would like amazingly to see a good old-fashioned negro.

> My love to all
> Truly your brother
> Sam

Late in the summer of 1854 Clemens headed back for St. Louis, sitting up three days and nights in a smoking car. After visiting Pamela for several hours, he caught the river packet for Muscatine, where his mother and two brothers were now living. The boat trip took thirty-six hours. He slept in his berth all the way. On his return to St. Louis he worked again for the *Evening News*. When Orion got married in Keokuk, Iowa, and set up a printing shop there, Clemens eventually joined him and became partners with him in the venture.

To Henry Clemens

Keokuk, *August 5th, '56*

My dear Brother,

. . . Ward and I held a long consultation Sunday morning and the result was that we two have determined to start to Brazil, if possible, in *six weeks* from now in order to look carefully into matters there and report to Dr. Martin in time for him to follow on the first of March. We propose going *via* New York. Now, between you and I and the fence you must say nothing about this to *Orion*, for he thinks that Ward is to go clear through alone and that I am to stop at New York or New Orleans until he reports. But that don't suit me. My confidence in human nature does not extend quite that far. I won't depend upon Ward's judgment or anybody's else. I want to see with my own eyes and form my own opinion. But you know what

Orion is. When he gets a notion into his head, and more especially if it is an erroneous one, the Devil can't get it out again. So I know better than to combat his arguments long, but apparently yielded, inwardly determined to go clear through. Ma knows my determination but *even she* counsels me to keep it from Orion. She says I can treat him as I did her when I started to St. Louis and went to New York—I can start to New York and go to South America! Although Orion talks grandly about furnishing me with fifty or a hundred dollars in six weeks, I could not depend upon him for ten dollars, so I have "feelers" out in several directions and have already asked for a hundred dollars from one source (keep it to yourself.) I will lay on my oars for awhile and see how the wind sets, when I may probably try to get more. Mrs. Creel is a great friend of mine and has some influence with Ma and Orion, though I reckon they would not acknowledge it. I am going up there tomorrow to press her into my service. I shall take care that Ma and Orion are plentifully supplied with South American books. They have Herndon's Report now. Ward and the Dr. and myself will hold a grand consultation tonight at the office. We have agreed that no more shall be admitted into our company.

I believe the Guards went down to Quincy today to escort *our first locomotive* home.

Write soon.
Your Brother,
Sam

Clemens worked at the printer's trade in Cincinnati awhile. During this period he had the Amazon much on his mind. In his autobiography he wrote, "I had been reading Lieutenant Herndon's account of his explorations of the Amazon and had been mightily attracted by what he said of coca. I made up my mind that I would go to the head-waters of the Amazon and collect coca and trade in it and make a fortune. I left for New Orleans in the steamer *Paul Jones* with this great idea filling my mind. One of the pilots of that boat was Horace Bixby. Little by little I got acquainted with him and pretty soon I was doing a lot of steering for him in his daylight watches. When I got to New Orleans I inquired about ships leaving for Pará and discovered that there weren't any and learned that there probably wouldn't be any during that century. It had not occurred to me to inquire about these particulars before leaving Cincinnati, so there I was. I couldn't get to the Amazon. I had no friends in New Orleans and no money to speak of. I went to Horace Bixby and asked him to make a pilot out of me. He said he would do it for five hundred dollars, one hundred dollars cash in advance. So I steered for him up to St. Louis, borrowed the money from my brother-in-law, and closed the bargain. . . . Within eighteen months I was become a competent pilot, and I served that office until the Mississippi River traffic was brought to a standstill by the breaking out of the Civil War."

To Orion Clemens and wife Mollie, Keokuk, Iowa

Saint Louis, *March 9th, 1858*

Dear Brother and Sister,

I must take advantage of the opportunity now presented to write you but I shall necessarily be dull, as I feel uncommonly stupid. We have had a hard trip this time. Left Saint Louis three weeks ago on the *Pennsylvania*. The weather was very cold and the ice running densely. We got 15 miles below town, landed the boat and then one pilot. Second Mate and four deck hands took the sounding boat and shoved out in the ice to hunt the channel. They failed to find it, and the ice drifted them ashore. The pilot left the men with the boat and walked back to us, a mile and a half. Then the other pilot and myself, with a larger crew of men, started out and met with the same fate. We drifted ashore just below the other boat. Then the fun commenced. We made fast a line 20 fathoms long to the bow of the yawl and put the men (both crews) to it like horses, on the shore. Brown, the pilot, stood in the bow with an oar to keep her head out, and I took the tiller. We would start the men and all would go well till the yawl would bring up on a heavy cake of ice, and then the men would drop like so many tenpins, while Brown assumed the horizontal in the bottom of the boat. After an hour's hard work we got back, with ice half an inch thick on the oars. Sent back and warped up the other yawl and then George (the first mentioned pilot) and myself took a double crew of fresh men and tried it again. This time we found the channel in less than half an hour and landed on an island till the *Pennsylvania* came along and took us off.

The next day was colder still. I was out in the yawl twice and then we got through but the infernal steamboat came near running over us. We went ten miles further, landed, and George and I cleared out again—found the channel first trial but got caught in the gorge and drifted helplessly down the river. The *Ocean Spray* came along and started into the ice after us but although she didn't succeed in her kind intention of taking us aboard, her waves washed us out and that was all we wanted. We landed on an island, built a big fire and waited for the boat. She started and ran aground! It commenced raining and sleeting, and a very interesting time we had on that barren sandbar for the next four hours, when the boat got off and took us aboard.

The next day was terribly cold. We sounded Hat Island, warped up around a bar and sounded again, but in order to understand our situation you will have to read Dr. Kane. It would have been impossible to get back to the boat. But the *Maria Denning* was aground at the head of the island—they hailed us—we ran alongside and they hoisted us in and thawed us out. We had then been out in the yawl from 4 o'clock in the morning till half past 9 without being near a fire. There was a thick coating of ice over men, yawl, ropes and everything else, and we looked like rock-candy statuary. We got to Saint Louis this morning after an absence of 3 weeks. That boat generally makes the trip in 2.

Henry was doing little or nothing here, and I sent him to our clerk to work his way for a trip by measuring wood piles, counting coal boxes, and other clerkly duties, which he performed satisfactorily. He may go down with us again, for I expect he likes our bill of fare better than that of his boarding house.

I got your letter at Memphis as I went down. That is the best place to write me at. The post office here is always out of my route, somehow or other. Remember the direction: "S.L.C., Steamer *Pennsylvania* Care Duval & Algeo, Wharfboat, Memphis." I cannot correspond with a paper, because when one is learning the river he is not allowed to do or think about anything else.

I am glad to see you in such high spirits about the land, and I hope you will remain so, if you never get richer. I seldom venture to think about our landed wealth, for "hope deferred maketh the heart sick."

I *did* intend to *answer* your letter but I am too lazy and too sleepy now. We have had a rough time during the last 24 hours working through the ice between Cairo and Saint Louis, and I have had but little rest.

I got here too late to see the funeral of the 10 victims by the burning of the Pacific hotel in 7th street. Ma says there were 10 hearses with the fire companies (their engines in mourning, firemen in uniform), the various benevolent societies in uniform and mourning, and a multitude of citizens and strangers, forming altogether a procession of 30,000 persons! One steam fire engine was drawn by four white horses, with crape festoons on their heads.

> Well, I am—just—about—asleep—
> Your brother
> Sam

Dr. Kane was Elisha Kent Kane, an American Arctic explorer. The references to "the land" and "our landed wealth" are to the very large tract of land in eastern Tennessee which Clemens's father had bought as a heritage for his heirs, a heritage that never materialized and which Clemens used imaginatively when he co-authored *The Gilded Age* with Charles Dudley Warner.

To Mollie Clemens

Memphis, Tenn., *Friday, June 18th, 1858*

Dear Sister Mollie,

Long before this reaches you, my poor Henry, my darling, my pride, my glory, my all, will have finished his blameless career, and the light of my life will have gone out in utter darkness. O, God! this is hard to bear. Hardened, hopeless—aye, lost—lost—lost and ruined sinner as I am—*I*, even *I*, have humbled myself to the ground and prayed as never man prayed before that the great God might let this cup pass from me, that he would strike me to the earth but spare my brother, that he would pour out the fulness of his just wrath upon my wicked head but have mercy, mercy, mercy upon that unoffending boy. The horrors of three days have swept over me. They have blasted my youth and left me an old man before my time. Mollie, there are gray hairs in my head tonight. For forty-eight hours I labored at the bedside of my poor burned and bruised but uncomplaining brother, and then the star of my hope went out and left me in the gloom of despair. Men take me by the hand and *congratulate* me and call me "lucky" because I was not on the *Pennsylvania* when she blew up! May God forgive them, for they know not what they say.

Mollie, you do not understand why I was not on that boat. I will tell you. I left Saint Louis on her but on the way down, Mr. Brown, the pilot that was killed by the explosion (poor fellow), quarreled with Henry without cause, while I was steering. Henry started out of the pilot house. Brown jumped up and collared him—turned him half away around and *struck him in the face!*—and him nearly six feet high—struck my little brother. I was wild from that moment. I left the boat to steer herself and avenged the insult. And the Captain said I was right, that he would discharge Brown in N. Orleans if he could get another pilot, and would do it in St. Louis, anyhow. Of course both of us could not return to St. Louis on the same boat. No pilot could be found, and the Captain sent me to the *A. T. Lacey* with orders to her Captain to bring me to Saint Louis. Had another pilot been found, poor Brown would have been the "lucky" man.

I was on the *Pennsylvania* five minutes before she left N. Orleans, and I must tell you the truth, Mollie—*three hundred* human beings perished by that fearful disaster. Henry was asleep—was blown up—then fell back on the hot boilers, and I suppose that rubbish fell on him, for he is injured internally. He got into the water and swam to shore, and got into the flatboat with the other survivors.* He had nothing on but his wet shirt and he lay there burning up with a southern sun and freezing in the wind till the *Kate Frisbee* came along. His wounds were not dressed till he got to Memphis 15 hours after the explosion. He was senseless and motionless for 12 hours after that.

But may God bless Memphis, the noblest city on the face of the earth. She has done her duty by these poor afflicted creatures, especially Henry, for he has had five—aye, ten, fifteen, *twenty* times the

* Henry had returned once to the *Pennsylvania* to render assistance to the passengers. Later he had somehow made his way to the flatboat.—A.B.P.

care and attention that anyone else has had. Dr. Peyton, the best physician in Memphis (he is exactly like the portraits of Webster), sat by him for 36 hours. There are 32 scalded men in that room, and you would know Dr. Peyton better than I can describe him if you could follow him around and hear each man murmur as he passed, "May the God of Heaven bless you, Doctor!" The ladies have done well too. Our second Mate, a handsome, noble-hearted young fellow, will die. Yesterday a beautiful girl of 15 stooped timidly down by his side and handed him a pretty bouquet. The poor suffering boy's eyes kindled, his lips quivered out a gentle, "God bless you, Miss," and he burst into tears. He made them write her name on a card for him, that he might not forget it.

Pray for me, Mollie, and pray for my poor sinless brother.

Your unfortunate Brother,
Saml. L. Clemens

P. S. I got here two days after Henry.

The *Pennsylvania's* boilers had exploded early on a mid-June morning while the ship was being loaded with wood some sixty miles below Memphis. Henry was just about a month short of twenty when he was killed. Clemens was in his twenty-third year at the time.

To Orion Clemens, written in St. Louis, 1859

. . . I am not talking nonsense, now. I am in earnest. I want you to keep your troubles and your plans out of the reach of meddlers, until the latter are consummated, so that in case you fail, no one will know it but yourself.

Above all things (between you and me) never tell Ma any of your troubles. She never slept a wink the night your last letter came, and she looks distressed yet. Write only cheerful news to her. You know that she will not be satisfied so long as she thinks anything is going on that she is ignorant of, and she makes a little fuss about it when her suspicions are awakened. But that makes no difference. *I* know that it is better that she be kept in the dark concerning all things of an unpleasant nature. She upbraids me occasionally for giving her only the bright side of my affairs (but unfortunately for her she has to put up with it, for I know that troubles that I curse awhile and forget would disturb her slumbers for some time.) (Parenthesis No. 2—Possibly because she is deprived of the soothing consolation of swearing.) Tell her the good news and me the bad.

Putting all things together, I begin to think I am rather lucky than otherwise, a notion which I was slow to take up. The other night I was about to round to for a storm, but concluded that I could find a smoother bank somewhere. I landed 5 miles below. The storm came, passed away and did not injure us. Coming up, day before yesterday, I looked at the spot I first chose, and half the trees on the bank were torn to shreds. We couldn't have lived 5 minutes in such a tornado. And I am also lucky in having a berth while all the young pilots are idle. This is the luckiest circumstance that ever befell me. Not on account of the wages, for that is a secondary consideration, but from the fact that the *City of Memphis* is the largest boat in the trade and the hardest to pilot, and consequently I can get a reputation on her, which is a thing I never could accomplish on a transient boat. I can "bank" in the neighborhood of $100 a month on her, and that will satisfy me for the present (principally because the other youngsters are *sucking their fingers.*) Bless me! what a pleasure there is in revenge! and what vast respect Prosperity commands! Why, six months ago I could enter the "Rooms" and receive only a customary fraternal greeting, but now they say, "Why, how *are* you, old fellow—when did you get in?"

And the young pilots who used to tell me patronizingly that I could never learn the river cannot keep from showing a little of their chagrin at seeing me so far ahead of them. Permit me to "blow my horn," for I derive a *living* pleasure from these things, and I must confess that when I go to pay my dues I rather like to let the damned rascals get a glimpse of a hundred dollar bill peeping out from amongst notes of smaller dimensions, whose face I do *not* exhibit! You will despise this egotism but I tell you there is a "stern joy" in it. . . .

The clairvoyant of the following was Madame Caprell, famous in her day.

To Orion, Keokuk, Iowa

New Orleans, *February 6, 1861*

... She's a very pleasant little lady, rather pretty, about 28, say 5 feet 2 and one quarter, would weigh 116, has black eyes and hair, is polite and intelligent, used good language, and talks much faster than I do.

She invited me into the little back parlor, closed the door and we were alone. We sat down facing each other. Then she asked my age. Then she put her hands before her eyes a moment and commenced talking as if she had a good deal to say and not much time to say it in. Something after this style:

Madame. Yours is a watery planet. You gain your livelihood on the water. But you should have been a lawyer. There is where your talents lie. You might have distinguished yourself as an orator or as an editor. You have written a great deal. You write well but you are rather out of practice. No matter, you will be *in* practice some day. You have a superb constitution and as excellent health as any man in the world. You have great powers of endurance. In your profession your strength holds out against the longest sieges without flagging. Still, the upper part of your lungs, the top of them, is slightly affected—you must take care of yourself. You do not drink but you use *entirely* too much tobacco, and you must stop it. Mind, not moderate, but *stop* the use of it totally. Then I can almost promise you 86 when you will surely die. Otherwise look out for 28, 31, 34, 47 and 65. Be careful, for you are not of a long-lived race. That is on your *father's* side. You are the only healthy member of your family and the only one in it who has anything like the certainty of attaining to a great age. So stop using tobacco and be careful of yourself. . . . In some respects you take after your father but you are much *more* like your mother, who belongs to the long-lived, energetic side of the house. . . . You never brought all your energies to bear upon any subject but what you accomplished it. For instance, you are self-made, self-educated.

S.L.C. Which proves nothing.

Madame. Don't interrupt. When you sought your present occupation you found a thousand obstacles in the way, obstacles unknown, not even suspected by any save you and me, since you keep such matters to yourself, but you fought your way and hid the long struggle under a mask of cheerfulness, which saved your friends anxiety on your account. To do all this requires all the qualities I have named.

S.L.C. You flatter well, Madame.

Madame. Don't interrupt. Up to within a short time you had always lived from hand to mouth. Now you are in easy circumstances, for which you need give credit to no one but yourself. The turning point in your life occurred in 1840-7-8.

S.L.C. Which was?

Madame. A death perhaps, and this threw you upon the world and made you what you are. It was always intended that you should make yourself. Therefore, it was well that this calamity occurred as early as it did. You will never die of water although your career upon it in the future seems well sprinkled with misfortune. You will continue upon the water for some time yet. You will not retire finally until ten years from now. . . . What is your brother's age? 35—and a lawyer? and in pursuit of an office? Well, he stands a better chance than the other two, and he may get it. He is too visionary, is always flying off on a new hobby. This will never do. Tell him I said so. He is a good lawyer, a *very* good lawyer, and a fine speaker, is very popular and much respected, and makes many friends. But although he retains their friendship, he loses their confidence by displaying his instability of character. . . . The land he has now will be very valuable after a while.

S.L.C. Say 250 years hence or thereabouts. Madame—

Madame. No—less time—but never mind the land, that is a secondary consideration. Let him drop that for the present and devote himself to his business and politics with all his might, for he must hold offices under the Government. . . .

After a while you will possess a good deal of property, retire at the end of ten years, after which your pursuits will be literary. Try the law. You will certainly succeed. I am done now. If you have any questions to ask, ask them freely, and if it be in my power I will answer without reserve, without reserve.

I asked a few questions of minor importance, paid her $2 and left, under the decided impression that going to the fortune teller's was just as good as going to the opera, and the cost scarcely a trifle more.

Ergo, I will disguise myself and go again one of these days when other amusements fail. Now isn't she the devil? That is to say, isn't she a right smart little woman?

When you want money let Ma know and she will send it. She and Pamela are always fussing about change, so I sent them a hundred and twenty quarters yesterday—fiddler's change enough to last till I get back, I reckon.

Sam

TWO

[[1861–62]]

Carson City, Nevada Territory — "As to churches, I believe
they have got a Catholic one here, but like that one the
New York fireman spoke of, I believe 'they don't run her now'" —
excursion to Lake Bigler (Tahoe) — mining fever — "I have been
a slave several times in my life but I'll never be one again"

The Civil War began some two months after the previous letter was written. According to Paine, "Young Clemens went to Hannibal, and enlisting in a private company, composed mainly of old schoolmates, went soldiering for two rainy, inglorious weeks, by the end of which he had had enough of war, and furthermore had discovered that he was more of a Union abolitionist than a slave-holding secessionist, as he had at first supposed."

Or as Clemens himself put it in his autobiography, "I was in New Orleans when Louisiana went out of the Union, January 26, 1861, and I started North the next day. Every day on the trip a blockade was closed by the boat, and the batteries at Jefferson Barracks (below St. Louis) fired two shots through the chimneys the last night of the voyage. In June I joined the Confederates in Ralls County, Missouri, as a second lieutenant under General Tom Harris and came near having the distinction of being captured by Colonel Ulysses S. Grant. I resigned after two weeks' service in the field, explaining that I was 'incapacitated by fatigue' through persistent retreating."

Orion was a Unionist. His friend Edward Bates, a member of Lincoln's first cabinet, obtained for him the position of Secretary of the new Territory of Nevada, and, as Clemens later wrote, "Orion and I cleared for that country in the overland stagecoach, I paying the fares, which were pretty heavy, and carrying with me what money I had been able to save—this was eight hundred dollars, I should say—and it was all in silver coin and a good deal of a nuisance because of its weight. And we had another nuisance, which was an Unabridged Dictionary. It weighed about a thousand pounds and was a ruinous expense, because the stagecoach company charged for extra baggage by the ounce. We could have kept a family for a time on what that dictionary cost in the way of extra

29

freight—and it wasn't a good dictionary, anyway—didn't have any modern words in it—only had obsolete ones that they used to use when Noah Webster was a child."

The Clemens brothers arrived in the territory August 14, 1861. Sam Clemens was in his twenty-sixth year.

To Jane Clemens, St. Louis

[Date not given, but *Sept.* or *Oct. 1861*]

My Dear Mother,

I hope you *will* all come out here someday. But I shan't consent to invite you until we can receive you in *style.* But I guess we shall be able to do that one of these days. I intend that Pamela shall live on Lake Bigler [Tahoe] until she can knock a bull down with her fist— say, about three months.

"Tell everything as it is—no better, and no worse." Well, "Gold Hill" sells at $5,000 per foot, cash down. "Wild Cat" isn't worth ten cents. The country is fabulously rich in gold, silver, copper, lead, coal, iron, quicksilver, marble, granite, chalk, plaster of Paris (gypsum), thieves, murderers, desperadoes, ladies, children, lawyers, Christians, Indians, Chinamen, Spaniards, gamblers, sharpers, coyotes (pronounced Ki-yo-ties), poets, preachers and jackass rabbits. I overheard a gentleman say the other day that it was "the damndest country under the sun." And that comprehensive conception I fully subscribe to.

It never rains here, and the dew never falls. No flowers grow here, and no green thing gladdens the eye. The birds that fly over the land carry their provisions with them. Only the crow and the raven tarry with us. Our city lies in the midst of a desert of the purest, most unadulterated and compromising *sand,* in which infernal soil nothing but that fag-end of vegetable creation, "sage-brush," ventures to grow. If you will take a lilliputian cedar tree for a model and build a dozen imitations of it with the stiffest article of telegraph wire, set them one foot apart and then try to walk through them, you'll understand (provided the floor is covered 12 inches deep with sand) what it is to wander through a sage-brush desert. When crushed, sage brush emits an odor which isn't exactly magnolia and equally isn't exactly polecat, but is a sort of compromise between the two. It looks a good deal like grease-wood and is the ugliest plant that was ever conceived of. It is gray in color. On the plains, sage-brush and grease-wood grow about twice as large as the common geranium, and in my opinion they are a very good substitute for that useless vegetable. Grease-wood is a perfect—*most* perfect—imitation in miniature of a live oak tree, barring the color of it.

As to the *other* fruits and flowers of the country, there ain't any except "Pulu" or "Tuler," or whatever they call it, a species of unpoetical willow that grows on the banks of the Carson, a *river*, 20 yards wide, knee-deep, and so villainously rapid and crooked that it looks like it had wandered into the country without intending it and had run about in a bewildered way and got lost in its hurry to get out again before some thirsty man came along and drank it up.

I said we are situated in a flat, sandy desert. True. And surrounded on all sides by such prodigious mountains that when you gaze at them awhile and begin to conceive of their grandeur and next to feel their vastness expanding your soul, and ultimately find yourself growing and swelling and spreading into a giant—I say when this point is reached, you look disdainfully down upon the insignificant village of Carson, and in that instant you are seized with a burning desire to stretch forth your hand, put the city in your pocket and walk off with it.

As to churches, I believe they *have* got a Catholic one here, but like that one the New York fireman spoke of, I believe "they don't *run* her now." Now, although we are *surrounded* by sand, the greatest part of the town is built upon what was once a very pretty grassy spot, and the streams of pure water that used to poke about it in rural sloth and solitude now pass through on dusty streets and gladden the hearts of men by reminding them that there is at least something here that hath its prototype among the homes they left behind them. And up "King's Canon," (please pronounce can-yon, after the manner of the natives) there are "ranches," or farms, where they say hay grows, and grass, and beets and onions, and turnips, and other "truck" which is suitable for cows—yes, and even Irish potatoes. Also cabbages, peas and beans.

The houses are mostly frame, unplastered, but "papered" inside with flour sacks sewed together, and the handsomer the "brand" upon the sacks is, the neater the house looks. Occasionally you stumble on a stone house. On account of the dryness of the country the shingles on the houses warp till they look like short joints of stove pipe split lengthwise. . . .

To his mother and sister, St. Louis

. . . The level ranks of flame were relieved at intervals by the standard bearers, as we called the tall dead trees, wrapped in fire and waving their blazing banners a hundred feet in the air. Then we could turn from this scene to the lake and see every branch and leaf and cataract of flame upon its bank perfectly reflected as in a gleaming, fiery mirror. The mighty roaring of the conflagration, together with our solitary and somewhat unsafe position (for there was no one within six miles of us) rendered the scene very impressive.

Occasionally one of us would remove his pipe from his mouth and say, *"Superb! Magnificent! Beautiful!* But by the Lord God Almighty, if we attempt to sleep in this little patch tonight we'll never live till morning! For if we don't burn up we'll certainly suffocate."

But he was persuaded to sit up until we felt pretty safe as far as the *fire* was concerned, and then we turned in with many misgivings. When we got up in the morning we found that the fire had burned small pieces of driftwood within six feet of our boat and had made its way to within 4 or 5 steps of us on the south side. We looked like *lava* men, covered as we were with ashes, and begrimed with smoke. We were very black in the face but we soon washed ourselves white again.

John D. Kinney, a Cincinnati boy, and a first-rate fellow, too, who came out with Judge Turner, was my comrade. We staid at the lake four days. I had plenty of fun, for John constantly reminded me of Sam Bowen when we were on our campaign in Missouri. But first and foremost, for *Annie's,* Mollie's and Pamela's comfort, be it known that I have never been guilty of profane language since I have been in this Territory, and Kinney hardly ever swears. But *sometimes* human nature gets the better of him.

On the second day we started to go by land to the lower camp, a distance of three miles over the mountains, each carrying an axe. I don't think we got *lost* exactly but we wandered four hours over the steepest, rockiest and most dangerous piece of country in the world. I couldn't keep from laughing at Kinney's distress, so I kept behind so that he could not see me. After he would get over a dangerous place with infinite labor and constant apprehension, he would stop, lean on his axe and look around, then behind, then ahead, and then drop his head and ruminate awhile.

Then he would draw a long sigh and say: "Well, could any billy-goat have scaled that place without breaking his ——— neck?"

And I would reply, "No, I don't think he could."

"No, you don't think he could," mimicking me. "Why don't you *curse* the infernal place. You know you *want* to. I do, and *will* curse the ——— thieving country as long as I live."

Then we would toil on in silence for awhile.

Finally I told him, "Well, John, what if we *don't* find our way out of this today. We'll know all about the country when we *do* get out."

"Oh stuff. I know enough, and *too much,* about the damned villainous locality already."

Finally we reached the camp. But as we brought no provisions with us, the first subject that presented itself to us was, how to get back. John swore he wouldn't *walk* back, so we rolled a drift log apiece into the lake and set about making paddles, intending to straddle the logs and paddle ourselves back home sometime or other. But the lake objected, got stormy, and we had to give it up. So we set out for the only house on this side of the lake—three miles from there, down the shore. We found the way without any trouble, reached there before sundown, played three games of cribbage, borrowed a dug-out and pulled back six miles to the upper camp. As we had eaten nothing since sunrise we did not waste time in cooking our supper or in eating it either. After supper we got out our pipes, built a rousing camp fire in the open air, established a faro bank (an institution of this country) on our huge flat granite dining table and bet white beans till one o'clock, when John went to bed.

We were up before the sun the next morning, went out on the lake and caught a fine trout for breakfast. But unfortunately I spoilt part of the breakfast. We had coffee and tea boiling on the fire in coffee pots, and fearing they might not be strong enough, I added more ground coffee and more tea, but you know mistakes will happen. I put the tea in the coffee pot and the coffee in the teapot, and if you imagine that they were not villainous mixtures, just try the effect once.

And so Bella is to be married on the 1st of Oct. Well, I send her and her husband my very best wishes, and—I may not be here—but wherever I am on that night, we'll have a rousing campfire and a jollification in honor of the event.

In a day or two we shall probably go to the lake and build another cabin and fence, and get everything into satisfactory trim before our trip to Esmeralda about the first of November.

What has become of Sam Bowen? I would give my last shirt to have him out here. I will make no promises but I believe if John would give him a thousand dollars and send him out here he would not regret it. He might possibly do very well here but he could do little without capital.

Remember me to all my St. Louis and Keokuk friends, and tell Challie and Hallie Renson that I heard a military band play, "What Are the Wild Waves Saying?" the other night, and it reminded me very forcibly of them. It brought Ella Creel and Belle across the desert too in an instant, for they sang the song in Orion's yard the first time I ever heard it. It was like meeting an old friend. I tell you I could have swallowed that whole band, trombone and all, if such a compliment would have been any gratification to them.

Love to the young folks,
Sam

To Pamela Moffett, St. Louis

Carson City, Oct. 25, 1861

My Dear Sister,

I have just finished reading your letter and Ma's of Sept. 8th. How in the world could they have been so long coming? You ask me if I have forgotten my promise to lay a claim for Mr. Moffett. By no means. I have already laid a timber claim on the borders of a lake (Bigler) which throws Como in the shade, and if we succeed in getting one Mr. Jones to move his sawmill up there, Mr. Moffett can just consider that claim better than bank stock. Jones says he will move his mill up next spring. In that claim I took up about two miles in length by one in width, and the names in it are as follows: "Sam. L. Clemens, Wm. A. Moffett, Thos. Nye" and three others. It is situated on "Sam Clemens Bay"—so named by Capt. Nye—and it goes by that name among the inhabitants of that region.

I had better stop about "the lake," though—for whenever I think of it I want to go there and *die,* the place is so beautiful. I'll build a country seat there one of these days that will make the Devil's mouth water if he ever visits the earth. Jim Lampton will never know whether I laid a claim there for him or not until he comes here *himself.* We have now got about 1,650 feet of mining ground, and if it proves *good,* Mr. Moffett's name will go in. If not, I can get "feet" for him in the Spring which *will* be good.

You see, Pamela, the trouble does not consist in getting mining ground, for that is plenty enough, but the money to work it with after you get it is the mischief. When I was in Esmeralda a young fellow gave me fifty feet in the "Black Warrior," an unprospected claim. The other day he wrote me that he had gone down eight feet on the ledge and found it eight feet thick, and pretty good rock, too. He said he could take out rock *now* if there were a mill to crush it. But the mills are all engaged (there are only four of them) so, if I were willing, he would suspend work until Spring. I wrote him to let it alone at present because, you see, in the Spring I can go down myself and help him look after it. There will then be twenty mills there.

Orion and I have confidence enough in this country to think that if the war will let us alone we can make Mr. Moffett rich without its ever costing him a cent of money or particle of trouble. We shall lay plenty of claims for him but if they never *pay* him anything they will never cost him anything. Orion and I are not financiers. Therefore, you *must* persuade Uncle Jim to come out here and help us in that line. I have written to him twice to come. I wrote him today. In both letters I told him not to let you or Ma know that we dealt in such romantic nonsense as "brilliant prospects" because I always did hate for anyone to know what my plans or hopes or prospects were—for, if I kept people in ignorance in these matters, no one could be disappointed but myself if they were not realized. You know I never told you that I went on the river under a promise to pay Bixby $500, until I had paid the money and cleared my skirts of the possibility of having my judgment criticised. I would not say anything about our prospects now if we were nearer home. But I suppose at this distance you are more anxious than you would be if you saw us every month, and therefore it is hardly fair to keep you in the dark. However, keep these matters to yourselves, and then if we fail we'll keep the laugh in the family.

What we want now is something that will commence paying immediately. We have got a chance to get into a claim where they say a tunnel has been run 150 feet and the ledge struck. I got a horse yesterday and went out with the Attorney General and the claim owner, and we tried to go to the claim by a new route and got lost in the mountains. Sunset overtook us before we found the claim. My horse got too lame to carry me, and I got down and drove him ahead of me till within four miles of town. Then we sent Rice on ahead. Bunker, whose horse was in good condition, undertook to lead mine and I followed after him. Darkness shut him out from my view in less than a minute, and within the next minute I lost the road and got to wandering in the sage brush. I would find the road occasionally and then lose it again in a minute or so. I got to Carson about nine o'clock at night but not by the road I traveled when I left it. The General says my horse did very well for awhile but soon refused to lead. Then he dismounted and had a jolly time driving both horses ahead of him and chasing them here and there through the sage brush (it does my *soul* good when I think of it) until he got to town, when both animals deserted him, and he cursed them handsomely and came home alone. Of course the horses went to their stables.

Tell Sammy I will lay a claim for him and he must come out and attend to it. He must get rid of that propensity for tumbling down, though, for when we get fairly started here I don't think we shall have time to pick up those who fall. . . .

That is Stoughter's house, I expect, that Cousin Jim has moved into. This is just the country for Cousin Jim to live in. I don't believe it would take him six months to make $100,000 here if he had 3,000 dollars to commence with. I suppose he can't leave his family, though.

Tell Mrs. Benson I never intend to be a lawyer. I have been a slave several times in my life, but I'll never be one again. I always intend to be so situated (*unless* I marry) that I can "pull up stakes" and clear out whenever I feel like it.

We are very thankful to you, Pamela, for the papers you send. We have received half a dozen or more, and, next to letters, they are the most welcome visitors we have.

Write *oftener*, Pamela.

Yr Brother
Sam

To Jane Clemens and Pamela Moffett, St. Louis

Carson City, *Feb. 8, 1862*

My dear Mother and Sister,

By George, Pamela, I begin to fear that I have invoked a spirit of some kind or other which I will find some difficulty in laying. I wasn't much terrified by your growing *inclinations* but when you begin to call *presentiments* to your aid I confess that I "weaken." Mr. Moffett is right, as I said before, and I am not much afraid of his going wrong. Men are easily dealt with but when you get the women started you are in for it, you know. But I have decided on two things, viz: Any of you, or all of you, may live in California, for that is the Garden of Eden reproduced, but you shall never live in Nevada. And secondly, none of you, save Mr. Moffett, shall ever cross the Plains. If you were only going to Pike's Peak, a little matter of 700 miles from St. Jo, you might take the coach and I wouldn't say a word. But I consider it over 2,000 miles from St. Jo to Carson, and the first 6 or 800 miles is mere Fourth of July compared to the balance of the route. But Lord bless you, a *man* enjoys every foot of it. If you ever come here or to California it must be by sea. Mr. Moffett must come by overland *coach*, though, by all means. He would consider it the jolliest little trip he ever took in his life. Either June, July or August are the proper months to make the journey in. He could not suffer from heat, and three or four heavy army blankets would make the cold nights comfortable. If the coach were full of passengers, two good blankets would probably be sufficient. If he comes and brings plenty of money and fails to invest it to his entire satisfaction I will prophesy no more.

But I will tell you a few things which you wouldn't have found out if I hadn't got myself into this scrape. I expect to return to St. Louis in July—per steamer. I don't say that I *will* return then or that I shall *be able* to do it, but I *expect to*—you bet. I came down here from Humboldt in order to look after our Esmeralda interests, and my sore-backed horse and the bad roads have prevented me from making the journey. Yesterday one of my old Esmeralda friends, Bob Howland, arrived here, and I have had a talk with him. He owns with me in the "Horatio and Derby" ledge. He says our tunnel is in 52 feet, and a small stream of water has been struck, which bids fair to become a "big thing" by the time the ledge is reached— sufficient to supply a mill. Now, if you knew anything of the value of water here, you would perceive at a glance that if the water should amount to 50 or 100 inches *we* wouldn't care whether school kept or not. If the ledge should prove to be worthless we'd *sell the water* for money enough to give us quite a lift. But you see, the ledge *will not* prove to be worthless. We have located near by a fine site for a mill, and when we strike the ledge, you know, we'll have a mill site, water power and pay-rock, all handy. *Then* we shan't care whether we have capital or not. Mill folks will build us a mill and wait for their pay. If nothing goes wrong we'll strike the ledge in June, and if we do I'll be home in July, you know.

Pamela, don't you know that undemonstrated human calculations won't do to bet on? Don't you know that I have only *talked* as yet, but proved nothing? Don't you know that I have expended money in this country but have made none myself? Don't you know that I have never held in my hands a gold or silver bar that belonged to me? Don't you know that it's all talk and no cider so far? Don't you know that people who always feel jolly, no matter where they are or what happens to them, who have the organ of hope preposterously developed, who are endowed with an uncongealable sanguine temperament, who never feel concerned about the price of corn and who cannot, by any possibility, discover any but the *bright* side of a picture, are very apt to go to extremes and exaggerate with 40-horse microscopic power?

Of course I never tried to raise these suspicions in your mind, but then your knowledge of the fact that some people's poor frail human nature is a sort of crazy institution anyhow ought to have suggested them to you. Now, if I hadn't thoughtlessly got you into the notion of coming out here and thereby got myself into a scrape, I wouldn't have given you that highly colored paragraph about the mill, etc., because, you know, if that pretty little picture should fail and wash out and go the Devil generally, it wouldn't cost me the loss of an hour's sleep, but you fellows would be so much distressed on my account as I could possibly be if "circumstances beyond my control" were to prevent my being present at my own funeral. But—but—

> "In the bright lexicon of youth,
> There's no such word as Fail—"
> and I'll prove it!

And look here. I came near forgetting it. Don't you say a word to me about "trains" across the plains. Because I am down on that arrangement. That sort of thing is "played out," you know. The Overland Coach or the Mail Steamer is the thing.

You want to know something about the route between California and Nevada Territory? Suppose you take my word for it that it is exceedingly jolly. Or take, for a winter view, J. Ross Brown's picture in *Harper's Monthly* of pack mules tumbling fifteen hundred feet down the side of a mountain. Why bless you, there's *scenery* on that route. You can stand on some of those noble peaks and see Jerusalem and the Holy Land. And you can start a boulder and send it tearing up the earth and crashing over trees—down—down—down—to the very devil, Madam. And you would probably stand up there and look and stare and wonder at the magnificence spread out before you till you starved to death, if let alone. But you should take someone along to keep you moving.

Since you want to know, I will inform you that an eight-stamp water mill, put up and ready for business, would cost about $10,000 to $12,000. Then, the water to run it with would cost from $1,000 to $30,000—and even more, according to the location. What I mean by that is that water powers in *this* vicinity are immensely valuable. So also in Esmeralda. But Humboldt is a *new* country, and things don't cost so much there yet. I saw a good water power sold there for $750.00.

But here is the way the thing is managed. A man with a good water power on Carson river will lean his axe up against a tree (provided you find him chopping cord-wood at $4 a day) and taking his chalk pipe out of his mouth to afford him an opportunity to answer your questions, will look you coolly in the face and tell you his little property is worth forty or fifty thousand dollars! But you can easily fix *him*. You tell him that you'll build a quartz mill on his property and make him a fourth or a third or half owner in said mill in consideration of the privilege of using said property, and that will bring him to his milk in a jiffy. So he spits on his hands and goes in again with his axe until the mill is finished, when lo! out pops the quondam wood chopper, arrayed in purple and fine linen and prepared to deal in bank stock or bet on the races or take government loans, with an air, as to the *amount*, of the most don't care-a-d-dest unconcern that you can conceive of.

By George, if I *just* had a thousand dollars I'd be all right! Now there's the "Horatio," for instance. There are five or six shareholders in it, and I *know* I could buy half of their interests at, say $20 per foot, now that flour is worth $50 per barrel and they are pressed for money. But I am hard up myself and can't buy, and in June they'll strike the ledge and then "good-bye canary." I can't get it for love or money. Twenty dollars a foot! Think of it. For ground that is *proven* to be rich. Twenty dollars, Madam—and we wouldn't part with a foot of our 75 for five times the sum. So it will be in Humboldt next summer. The boys will get pushed and sell ground for a song that is worth a fortune.

But I am at the helm now. I have convinced Orion that he hasn't business talent enough to carry on a peanut stand, and he has solemnly promised me that he will meddle no more with mining or other matters not connected with the Secretary's office. So, you see, if mines are to be bought or sold or tunnels run or shafts sunk, parties have to come to me, and me only. I'm the "firm," you know.

"How long does it take one of those infernal trains to go through?" Well, anywhere between three and five months.

Tell Margaret that if you ever come to live in California that you can promise her a home for a hundred years, and a bully one, but she wouldn't like the country. Some people are malicious enough to think that if the devil were set at liberty and told to confine himself to Nevada Territory that he would come here and look sadly around awhile and then get homesick and go back to hell again. But I hardly believe it, you know. I am saying, mind you, that *Margaret* wouldn't like the country, perhaps—nor the devil either, for that matter or any other man—but *I* like it. When it rains here it never lets up till it has done all the raining it has got to do, and after that there's a dry spell, you bet. Why, I have had my whiskers and moustaches so full of alkali dust that you'd have thought I worked in a starch factory and boarded in a flour barrel.

Since we have been here there has not been a fire although the houses are built of wood. They "holler" fire sometimes, though, but I am always too late to see the smoke before the fire is out, if they ever have any. Now they raised a yell here in front of the office a moment ago. I put away my papers and locked up everything of value and changed my boots and pulled off my coat and went and got a bucket of water and came back to see what the matter was, remarking to myself, "I guess I'll be on hand *this* time, anyway." But I met a friend on the pavement and he said, "Where you been? Fire's out half an hour ago."

Ma says Axtele was above "suspition," but I have searched through Webster's Unabridged and can't find the word. However, it's of no consequence. I hope he got down safely. I knew Axtele and his wife as well as I know Dan Haines. Mrs. A. once tried to embarrass me in the presence of company by asking me to name her baby, when she was well aware that I didn't know the sex of that phenomenon. But I told her to call it Frances and spell it to suit herself. That was about nine years ago, and Axtele had no property and could hardly support his family by his earnings. He was a pious cuss, though. Member of Margaret Sexton's Church.

And Ma says "It looks like a man can't hold public office and be honest." Why, certainly not, Madam. A man *can't* hold public office and be honest. Lord bless you, it is a common practice with Orion to go about town stealing little things that happen to be lying around loose. And I don't remember having heard him speak the truth since we have been in Nevada. He even tries to prevail upon *me* to do these things. Ma, but I wasn't brought up in that way, you know. You showed the public what *you* could do in that line when you raised me, Madam. But then you ought to have raised me first, so that Orion could have had the benefit of my example. Do you know that he stole all the stamps out of an 8-stamp quartz mill one night and brought them home under his overcoat and hid them in the back room?

Yrs etc.
Sam

To Jane Clemens, St. Louis

Carson City, April 2, 1862

My Dear Mother,

Yours of March 2nd has just been received. I see I am in for it again with Annie. But she ought to know that I was always stupid. She used to try to teach me lessons from the Bible but I never could understand them. Doesn't she remember telling me the story of Moses one Sunday last Spring, and how hard she tried to explain it and simplify it so that I could understand it—but I *couldn't?* And how she said it was strange that while her ma and her grandma and her uncle Orion could understand anything in the world, I was so dull that I couldn't understand the "ea-siest thing?" And doesn't she remember that finally a light broke in upon me and I said it was all right, that I knew old Moses himself, and that he kept a clothing store in Market Street? And then she went to her ma and said she didn't know what would become of her uncle Sam, he was too dull to learn anything ever! And I'm just as dull yet. Now I have no doubt her letter was spelled right and was correct in all particulars, but then I had to read it according to my lights, and they being inferior, she ought to overlook the mistakes I make, especially as it is not *my* fault that I wasn't born with good sense. I am sure she will detect an encouraging ray of intelligence in that last argument. . . .

I am waiting here, trying to rent a better office for Orion. I have got the refusal after next week of a room 16 × 50 on first floor of a fire-proof brick—rent: eighteen hundred dollars a year. Don't know yet whether we can get it or not. If it is not rented before the week is up, we can.

I was sorry to hear that Dick was killed. I gave him his first lesson in the musket drill. We had half a dozen muskets in our office when it was over Isbell's Music Rooms.

I hope I am wearing the last white shirt that will embellish my person for many a day, for I do hope that I shall be out of Carson long before this reaches you.

> Love to all.
>
> Very Respectfully
>
> Sam

Annie was Pamela's daughter, who would some day marry Charles L. Webster, Clemens's partner in the book publishing business. Dick was Dick Hingham, of Orion's Keokuk printing shop. He was killed while charging the fortifications at Fort Donelson. In the following, Beack Jolly was a pilot. Bixby was Horace Bixby.

To Pamela Moffett, St. Louis

Esmeralda, Cal., *Aug. 15, 1862*

My Dear Sister,

I mailed a letter to you and Ma this morning, but since then I have received yours to Orion and me. Therefore I must answer right away, else I may leave town without doing it at all. What in thunder are pilot's wages to me? Which question, I beg humbly to observe, is of a *general* nature and not discharged particularly at you. But it is singular, isn't it, that such a matter should interest Orion when it is of no earthly consequence to me? I never have *once* thought of returning home to go on the river again, and I never expect to do any more piloting at any price. My livelihood must be made in this country, and if I have to wait longer than I expected, let it be so, I have no fear of failure. You know I have extravagant hopes, for Orion tells you everything which he ought to keep to himself, but it's his nature to do that sort of thing, and I let him alone. I did think for awhile of going home this fall but when I found that that was and had been the cherished intention and the darling aspiration every year of these old careworn Californians for twelve weary years, I felt a little uncomfortable, but I stole a march on Disappointment and said I would *not* go home this fall. I will spend the winter in San Francisco if possible. Do not tell anyone that I had any idea of piloting again at present, for it is all a mistake. This country suits me, and—it *shall* suit me, whether or no. . . .

Dan Twing and I and Dan's dog "cabin" together, and will continue to do so for awhile until I leave for—

The mansion is 10 × 12, with a "domestic" roof. Yesterday it rained, the first shower for five months. "Domestic," it appears to me, is not waterproof. We went outside to keep from getting wet. Dan makes the bed when it is his turn to do it, and when it is my turn I don't, you know. The dog is not a good hunter and he isn't worth shucks to watch but he scratches up the dirt floor of the cabin and catches flies and makes himself generally useful in the way of washing dishes. Dan gets up first in the morning and makes a fire, and I get up last and sit by it while he cooks breakfast. We have a cold lunch at noon and I cook supper—very much against my will. However, one must have *one* good meal a day, and if I were to live on Dan's abominable cookery I should lose my appetite, you know.

Dan attended Dr. Chorpenning's funeral yesterday and he felt as though he ought to wear a white shirt and we had a jolly good time finding such an article. We turned over all our traps and he found one at last but I shall always think it was suffering from yellow fever. He also found an old black coat, greasy and wrinkled to that degree that it appeared to have been quilted at some time or other. In this gorgeous costume he attended the funeral. And when he returned, his own dog drove him away from the cabin, not recognizing him. This is true.

You would not like to live in a country where flour was $40 a barrel? Very well then, I suppose you would not like to live here, where flour was $100 a barrel when I first came here. And shortly afterwards it couldn't be had at any price, and for one month the people lived on barley, beans and beef and nothing beside. Oh no, we didn't luxuriate then! Perhaps not. But we said wise and severe things about the vanity and wickedness of high living. We preached our doctrine and practised it. Which course I respectfully recommend to the clergymen of St. Louis.

Where is Beack Jolly? And Bixby?

Your Brother
Sam

THREE

[1863-67]

Virginia City, Nevada Territory — "I have just heard five pistol shots down the street" — San Francisco — "We fag ourselves completely out every day and go to sleep without rocking every night" — Hawaii — the lecturer — the Quaker City *excursion*

By the end of the summer of 1862 Clemens abandoned his efforts as a miner and accepted a job as reporter on the Virginia City *Territorial Enterprise* at a salary of $25 a week. It was early in February 1863 that he adopted his pseudonym. In the following, Virginia is Virginia City and Carson is Carson City. The Unreliable, Clement T. Price, was a rival reporter and a friend of Clemens. The two often joshed each other in print.

To Jane Clemens and Pamela Moffett, St. Louis

Virginia, *April 11, 1863*

My dear Mother and Sister,

It is very late at night and I am writing in my room, which is not quite as large or as nice as the one I had at home. My board, washing and lodging cost me seventy-five dollars a month.

I have just received your letter, Ma, from Carson, the one in which you doubt my veracity about the statements I made in a letter to you. That's right. I don't recollect what the statements were but I suppose they were mining statistics. I have just finished writing up my report for the morning paper and giving the Unreliable a column of advice about how to conduct himself in church, and now I will tell you a few more lies while my hand is in. For instance, some of the boys made me a present of fifty feet in the East India G. and S. M. Company ten days ago. I was offered ninety-five dollars a foot for it, yesterday, in gold. *I refused it,* not because I think the claim is worth a cent for I *don't,* but because I had a curiosity to see how high it would go before people find out how worthless it is. Besides, what if one mining claim *does* fool me? I have got plenty more. I am not in a particular hurry to get rich. I suppose I couldn't well help getting rich here some time or other, whether I wanted to or not. You folks do not believe in Nevada and I am glad you don't. Just keep on thinking so.

I was at the Gould and Curry mine the other day and they had two or three tons of choice rock piled up, which was valued at $20,000 a ton. I gathered up a hatfull of chunks on account of their beauty as specimens. They don't let everybody supply themselves so liberally. I send Mr. Moffett a little specimen of it for his cabinet. If you don't know what the white stuff on it is I must inform you that it is purer silver than the minted coin. There is about as much gold in it as there is silver but it is not visible. I will explain to you some day how to detect it.

Pamela, you wouldn't do for a local reporter because you don't appreciate the interest that attaches to *names.* An item is of no use unless it speaks of some *person,* and not then unless that person's *name* is distinctly mentioned. The most interesting letter one can write to an absent friend is one that treats of *persons* he has been acquainted with rather than the public events of the day. Now you speak of a young lady who wrote to Hollie Benson that she had seen me, and you didn't mention her *name.* It was just a mere chance that I ever guessed who she was—but I did, finally, though I don't remember her name now. I was introduced to her in San Francisco by Hon. A. B. Paul and saw her afterwards in Gold Hill. They were a very pleasant lot of girls, she and her sisters.

P. S. I have just heard five pistol shots down street—as such things are in my line, I will go and see about it.

P. S. No 2. 5 A.M. The pistol did its work well. One man, a Jackson County Missourian, shot two of my friends (police officers) through the heart. Both died within three minutes. Murderer's name is John Campbell.

To Jane Clemens and Pamela Moffett, St. Louis

Lick House, S. F., *June 1, '63*

My dear Mother and Sister,

The Unreliable and myself are still here and still enjoying ourselves. I suppose I know at least a thousand people here, a great many of them citizens of San Francisco but the majority belonging in Washoe,° and when I go down Montgomery Street, shaking hands with Tom, Dick and Harry, it is just like being in Main Street in Hannibal and meeting the old familiar faces. I *do hate* to go back to Washoe. We fag ourselves completely out every day and go to sleep without rocking every night. We dine out and we lunch out and we eat, drink and are happy, as it were. After breakfast I don't often see the hotel again until midnight, or after. I am going to the Dickens mighty fast. I know a regular village of families here in the house but I never have time to call on them. Thunder! we'll know a little more about this town before we leave than some of the people who live in it.

We take trips across the Bay to Oakland, and down to San Leandro, and Alameda, and those places, and we go out to the Willows and Hayes Park and Fort Point and up to Benicia, and yesterday we were invited out on a yachting excursion and had a sail in the fastest yacht on the Pacific Coast.

Rice says: "Oh no, *we* are not having any fun, Mark. Oh no, I reckon not. It's somebody else. It's probably the 'gentleman in the wagon'!" (popular slang phrase)

When I invite Rice to the Lick House to dinner, the proprietors send us champagne and claret, and then we *do* put on the most disgusting airs. Rice says our calibre is too light, we can't stand it to be noticed!

I rode down with a gentleman to the Ocean House the other day to see the sea horses and also to listen to the roar of the surf and watch the ships drifting about here and there and far away at sea. When I stood on the beach and let the surf wet my feet I recollected doing the same thing on the shores of the Atlantic, and then I had a

° Washoe: Nevada Territory; also Washoe City, Nevada.

proper appreciation of the vastness of this country, for I had traveled from ocean to ocean across it. . . .

To Jane Clemens and Pamela Moffett, St. Louis

Steamboat Springs [Nevada], *August 19, '63*

My dear Mother and Sister,

Ma, you have given my vanity a deadly thrust. Behold, I am prone to boast of having the widest reputation as a local editor of any man on the Pacific coast, and you gravely come forward and tell me "if I work hard and attend closely to my business I may aspire to a place on a big San Francisco daily some day." There's a comment on human vanity for you! Why, blast it, I was under the impression that I could get such a situation as that any time I asked for it. But I don't want it. No paper in the United States can afford to pay me what my place on the "Enterprise" is worth. If I were not naturally a lazy, idle, good-for-nothing vagabond I could make it pay me $20,000 a year. But I don't suppose I shall ever be any account. I lead an easy life, though, and I don't care a cent whether school keeps or not. Everybody knows me, and I fare like a prince wherever I go, be it on this side of the mountains or the other. And I am proud to say I am the most conceited ass in the Territory.

You think that picture looks old? Well, I can't help it. In reality I am not as old as I was when I was eighteen.

I took a desperate cold more than a week ago and I seduced Wilson (a Missouri boy, reporter of the *Daily Union*) from his labors and we went over to Lake Bigler. But I failed to cure my cold. I found the "Lake House" crowded with the wealth and fashion of Virginia, and I could not resist the temptation to take a hand in all the fun going. Those Virginians, men and women both, are a stirring set and I found if I went with them on all their eternal excursions I should bring the consumption home with me, so I left day before yesterday and came back into the Territory again. A lot of them had purchased a site for a town on the Lake shore, and they gave me a lot. When you come out I'll build you a house on it. The Lake seems more supernaturally beautiful now, than ever. It is the masterpiece of the Creation.

The hotel here at the Springs is not so much crowded as usual and I am having a very comfortable time of it. The hot, white steam puffs up out of fissures in the earth like the jets that come from a steamboat's 'scape pipes, and it makes a boiling, surging noise like a steamboat, too—hence the name. We put eggs in a handkerchief and dip them in the springs. They "soft boil" in 2 minutes and boil as hard as a rock in 4 minutes. These fissures extend more than a quarter of a mile, and the long line of steam columns looks very pretty. A large bath house is built over one of the springs and we go in it and steam ourselves as long as we can stand it and then come out and take a cold shower bath. You get baths, board and lodging all for $25 a week, cheaper than living in Virginia without baths. . . .

Yrs aft
Mark

To Jane Clemens and Pamela Moffett, St. Louis

[San Francisco], *Sept. 25, 1864*

My dear Mother and Sister,

You can see by my picture that this superb climate agrees with me. And it ought, after living where I was never out of sight of snow peaks twenty-four hours during three years. Here we have neither snow nor cold weather, fires are never lighted and yet summer clothes are never worn, you wear spring clothing the year round.

Steve Gillis, who has been my comrade for two years and who came down here with me, is to be married in a week or two to a very pretty girl worth $130,000 in her own right, and then I shall be alone again until they build a house, which they will do shortly.

We have been here only four months, yet we have changed our lodgings five times, and our hotel twice. We are very comfortably fixed where we are now and have no fault to find with the rooms or with the people. We are the only lodgers in a well-to-do private family, with one grown daughter and a piano in the parlor adjoining our room. But I need a change and must move again. I have taken rooms further down the street. I shall stay in this little quiet street because it is full of gardens and shrubbery, and there are none but dwelling houses in it.

I am taking life easy now and I mean to keep it up for awhile. I don't work at night any more. I told the *Call* folks to pay me $25 a week and let me work only in daylight. So I get up at ten every morning and quit work at five or six in the afternoon. You ask if I work for greenbacks? Hardly. What do you suppose I could do with greenbacks here?

I have engaged to write for the new literary paper, the *Californian.* Same pay I used to receive on the *Golden Era.* One article a week, fifty dollars a month. I quit the *Era* long ago. It wasn't high-toned enough. The *Californian* circulates among the highest class of the community and is the best weekly literary paper in the United States. And I suppose I ought to know.

I work as I always did, by fits and starts. I wrote two articles last night for the *Californian,* so that lets me out for two weeks. That would be about seventy-five dollars in greenbacks, wouldn't it?

Been down to San Jose (generally pronounced Sanno*zay,* emphasis on last syllable) today fifty miles from here, by railroad. Town of 6,000 inhabitants, buried in flowers and shrubbery. The climate is finer than ours here because it is not so close to the ocean and is protected from the winds by the coast range.

I had an invitation today to go down on an excursion to San Luis Obispo and from thence to the city of Mexico, to be gone six or eight weeks or possibly longer, but I could not accept on account of my contract to act as chief mourner or groomsman at Steve's wedding.

I have triumphed. They refused me and other reporters some information at a branch of the Coroner's office—Massey's undertaker establishment—a few weeks ago. I published the wickedest article on them I ever wrote in my life, and you can rest assured we got all the information we wanted after that.

By the new census San Francisco has a population of 130,000. They don't count the hordes of Chinamen.

Yrs affly

Sam

I send a picture for Annie and one for Aunt Ella. That is, if she will have it.

To Jane Clemens and Pamela Moffett, St. Louis

San Francisco, *Jan. 20, 1866*

My dear Mother and Sister,

I do not know what to write, my life is so uneventful. I wish I was back there piloting up and down the river again. Verily all is vanity and little worth—save piloting.

To think that after writing many an article a man might be excused for thinking tolerably good, those New York people should single out a villainous backwoods sketch to compliment me on!—"Jim Smiley and His Jumping Frog"—a squib which would never have been written but to please Artemus Ward, and then it reached New York too late to appear in his book.

But no matter. His book was a wretchedly poor one, generally speaking, and it could be no credit to either of us to appear between its covers.

This paragraph is from the New York correspondence of the San Francisco *Alta:*

[*Clipping pasted in*]

"Mark Twain's story in the *Saturday Press* of November 18th, called 'Jim Smiley and His Jumping Frog,' has set all New York in a roar, and he may be said to have made his mark. I have been asked fifty times about it and its author, and the papers are copying it far and near. It is voted the best thing of the day. Cannot the *Californian* afford to keep Mark all to itself? It should not let him scintillate so widely without first being filtered through the California press."

The New York publishing house of Carleton & Co. gave the sketch to the *Saturday Press* when they found it was too late for the book.

Though I am generally placed at the head of my breed of scribblers in this part of the country, the place properly belongs to Bret Harte, I think, though he denies it, along with the rest. He wants me to club a lot of old sketches together with a lot of his and publish a book. I wouldn't do it, only he agrees to take all the trouble. But I want to know whether we are going to make anything out of it, first. However, he has written to a New York publisher, and if we are offered a bargain that will pay for a month's labor we will go to work and prepare the volume for the press.

Yours affy,
Sam

On March 5th Clemens, now thirty, decided to accept an offer by the *Sacramento Union* to write twenty or thirty letters about a trip to the Sandwich (Hawaiian) Islands, "for which they pay me as much money as I would get if I staid at home," he wrote to his mother and sister. "My friends seem determined that I shall not lack acquaintances . . . and they have already sent me letters of introduction to everybody down there worth knowing. I am to remain there a month and ransack the islands, the great cataracts and the volcanoes completely. . . ." Actually, he remained in the islands five months.

To Jane Clemens and Pamela Moffett, St. Louis

Honolulu, Sandwich Islands, *April 3, 1866*

My dear Mother and Sister,

I have been here two or three weeks, and like the beautiful tropical climate better and better. I have ridden on horseback all over this island (Oahu) in the meantime and have visited all the ancient battlefields and other places of interest. I have got a lot of human bones which I took from one of these battlefields. I guess I will bring you some of them. I went with the American Minister and took dinner this evening with the King's Grand Chamberlain, who is related to the royal family, and although darker than a mulatto he has an excellent English education and in manners is an accomplished gentleman. The dinner was as ceremonious as any I ever attended in California—five regular courses and five kinds of wine and one of brandy. He is to call for me in the morning with his carriage and we will visit the King at the palace. Both are good Masons.

The King is a Royal Arch Mason. After dinner tonight they called in the "singing girls" and we had some beautiful music, sung in the native tongue.

The steamer I came here in sails tomorrow, and as soon as she is gone I shall sail for the other islands of the group and visit the great volcano, the grand wonder of the world. Be gone two months.

Yrs.

Sam

To Jane Clemens and Pamela Moffett, St. Louis

Wailuku Sugar Plantation,
Island of Maui, S. I., *May 4, 1866*

My dear Mother and Sister,

11 o'clock at night. This is the infernalist darkest country when the moon don't shine. I stumbled and fell over my horse's lariat a minute ago and hurt my leg, so I must stay here tonight.

I got the same leg hurt last week. I said I hadn't got hold of a spirited horse since I had been on the island, and one of the proprietors loaned me a big vicious colt. He was altogether too spirited. I went to tighten the cinch before mounting him, when he let out with his left leg and kicked me across a ten-acre lot. A native rubbed and doctored me so well that I was able to stand on my feet in half an hour. It was then half after four and I had an appointment to go seven miles and get a girl and take her to a card party at five.

I have been clattering around among the plantations for three weeks now, and next week I am going to visit the extinct crater of Mount Haleakala, the largest in the world. It is ten miles to the foot of the mountain. It rises 10,000 feet above the valley. The crater is 29 miles in circumference and 1,000 feet deep. Seen from the summit, the city of St. Louis would look like a picture in the bottom of it.

As soon as I get back from Haleakala (pronounced Hally-ekka-lah) I will sail for Honolulu again and thence to the Island of Hawaii (pronounced Hah-wy-ye) to see the greatest *active* volcano in the world, that of Kilauea (pronounced Kee-low-way-ah), and from thence back to San Francisco, and then, doubtless, to the States. I have been on this trip two months and it will probably be two more before I get back to California.

Yrs affy

Sam

When Clemens returned to San Francisco on August 13 he wrote in his notebook, "Home again. No—not home again—in prison again, and all the wild sense of freedom gone. City seems so cramped and so dreary with toil and care and business anxieties. God help me, I wish I were at sea again."

Soon he embarked on his first lecture tour—of California and Nevada. It was a great success both critically and financially. He went to New York and was present for the publication of his first book, which contained a number of his sketches and the jumping frog story. He was about to join the *Quaker City* Holy Land excursion, newspaper letters for which would become the basis of *The Innocents Abroad*.

To Bret Harte, San Francisco

Westminster Hotel, *May 1, 1867*

Dear Bret,

I take my pen in hand to inform you that I am well and hope these few lines will find you enjoying the same God's blessing.

The book is out and is handsome. It is full of damnable errors of grammar and deadly inconsistencies of spelling in the Frog sketch because I was away and did not read the proofs, but be a friend and say nothing about these things. When my hurry is over I will send you an autograph copy to pisen the children with.

I am to lecture in Cooper Institute next Monday night. Pray for me.

We sail for the Holy Land June 8. Try to write me (to this hotel) and it will be forwarded to Paris, where we remain 10 or 15 days.

Regards and best wishes to Mrs. Bret and the family.

Truly Yr Friend
Mark

To Jane Clemens and family, St. Louis

Westminster Hotel, New York, *June 1, 1867*

Dear Folks,

I know I ought to write oftener (just got your last) and more fully but I cannot overcome my repugnance to telling what I am doing or what I expect to do or propose to do. Then what have I left to write about? Manifestly nothing.

It isn't any use for me to talk about the voyage, because I can have no faith in that voyage till the ship is under way. How do I know she will ever sail? My passage is paid, and if the ship sails I sail in her, but I make no calculations, have bought no cigars, no sea-going clothing, have made no preparation whatever. Shall not pack my trunk till the morning we sail. Yet my hands are full of what I am going to do the day *before* we sail, and what isn't done that day will go undone.

All I do know or feel is that I am wild with impatience to move—move—*move!* Half a dozen times I have wished I had sailed long ago in some ship that wasn't going to keep me chained here to chafe for lagging ages while she got ready to go. Curse the endless delays! They always kill me. They make me neglect every duty and then I have a conscience that tears me like a wild beast. I wish I never had to stop anywhere a month. I do more mean things the moment I get a chance to fold my hands and sit down than ever I can get forgiveness for.

Yes, we are to meet at Mr. Beach's next Thursday night, and I suppose we shall have to be gotten up, regardless of expense, in swallow-tails, white kids and everything *en régle.*

I am resigned to Rev. Mr. Hutchinson's or anybody else's supervision. I don't mind it. I am fixed. I have got a splendid, immoral, tobacco-smoking, wine-drinking, godless roommate who is as good and true and right-minded a man as ever lived, a man whose blameless conduct and example will always be an eloquent sermon to all who shall come within their influence. But send on the professional preachers. There are none I like better to converse with. If they're not narrow-minded and bigoted they make good companions.

I asked them to send the *N. Y. Weekly* to you—no charge. I am not going to write for it. Like all other papers that pay one splendidly, it circulates among stupid people and the *canaille.* I have made no arrangement with any New York paper. I will see about that Monday or Tuesday.

Love to all
Goodbye,
Yrs affy
Sam

The "immoral" roommate was Dan Slote, the Dan of *Innocents Abroad*. Zeb and John Leavenworth, mentioned in the next letter, were river pilots whom Clemens had known on the Mississippi. Orion had lost his Nevada job and was trying to practice law. Bill Stewart was U.S. Senator Stewart of Nevada.

To Jane Clemens and family, St. Louis

New York, *June 7th, 1867*

Dear Folks,

I suppose we shall be many a league at sea tomorrow night, and goodness knows I shall be unspeakably glad of it.

I haven't got *any*thing to write, else I *would* write it. I have just written myself clear out in letters to the *Alta*, and I think they are the stupidest letters that were ever written from New York. Corresponding has been a perfect drag ever since I got to the states. If it continues abroad I don't know what the *Tribune* and *Alta* folks will think.

I have withdrawn the Sandwich Island book. It would be useless to publish it in these dull publishing times. As for the Frog book, I don't believe that will ever pay anything worth a cent. I published it simply to advertise myself, not with the hope of making anything out of it.

Well, I haven't anything to write except that I am tired of staying in one place, that I am in a fever to get away. Read my *Alta* letters. They contain everything I could possibly write to you. Tell Zeb and John Leavenworth to write me. They can get plenty of gossip from the pilots.

An importing house sent two cases of exquisite champagne aboard the ship for me today—Veuve Clicquot and Lac d'Or. I and my roommate have set apart every Saturday as a solemn fast day, wherein we will entertain no light matters of frivolous conversation but only get drunk. (That is a joke.) His mother and sisters are the best and most homelike people I have yet found in a brownstone front. There is no style about them except in house and furniture.

I wish Orion were going on this voyage, for I believe he could not help but be cheerful and jolly. I often wonder if his law business is going satisfactorily to him, but knowing that the dull season is setting in now (it looked like it had already set in before) I have felt as if I could almost answer the question myself, which is to say in plain words, I was afraid to ask. I wish I had gone to Washington in the winter instead of going West. I could have gouged an office out of Bill Stewart for him and that would atone for the loss of my home visit. But I am so worthless that it seems to me I never do anything or accomplish anything that lingers in my mind as a pleasant memory. My mind is stored full of unworthy conduct toward Orion and towards you all, and an accusing conscience gives me peace only in excitement and restless moving from place to place. If I could say I had done one thing for any of you that entitled me to your good opinion (I say nothing of your love, for I am sure of *that,* no matter how unworthy of it I may make myself, from Orion down you have always given me that, all the days of my life, when God Almighty knows I seldom deserve it), I believe I could go home and stay there and I *know* I would care little for the world's praise or blame. There is no satisfaction in the world's praise anyhow, and it has no worth to me save in the way of business. I tried to gather up its compliments to send to you but the work was distasteful and I dropped it.

You observe that under a cheerful exterior I have got a spirit that is angry with me and gives me freely its contempt. I can get away from that at sea and be tranquil and satisfied. And so, with my parting love and benediction for Orion and all of you, I say goodbye and God bless you all, and welcome the wind that wafts a weary soul to the sunny lands of the Mediterranean!

Yrs Forever,
Sam

To Jane Clemens and family, St. Louis

Yalta, Russia, *Aug. 25, 1867*

Dear Folks,

We have been representing the United States all we knew how today. We went to Sebastopol, after we got tired of Constantinople (got your letter there, and one at Naples), and there the Commandant and the whole town came aboard and were as jolly and sociable as old friends. They said the Emperor of Russia was at Yalta, 30 miles or 40 away, and urged us to go there with the ship and visit him—promised us a cordial welcome. They insisted on sending a telegram to the Emperor, and also a courier overland to announce our coming. But we knew that a great English Excursion party, and also the Viceroy of Egypt in his splendid yacht, had been refused an audience within the last fortnight, so we thought it not safe to try it. They said, no difference—the Emperor would hardly visit our ship, because that would be a most extraordinary favor, and one which he uniformly refuses to accord under any circumstances, but he would certainly receive us at his palace. We still declined. But we had to go to Odessa, 250 miles away, and there the Governor General urged us, and sent a telegram to the Emperor, which we hardly expected to be answered, but it was, and promptly. So we sailed back to Yalta.

We all went to the palace at noon today (3 miles) in carriages and on horses sent by the Emperor, and we had a jolly time. Instead of the usual formal audience of 15 minutes, we staid 4 hours and were made a good deal more at home than we could have been in a New York drawing-room. The whole tribe turned out to receive our party—Emperor, Empress, the oldest daughter (Grand Duchess Marie, a pretty girl of 14), a little Grand Duke, her brother, and a platoon of Admirals, Princes, Peers of the Empire, etc., and in a little while an aid-de-camp arrived with a request from the Grand Duke Michael, the Emperor's brother, that we would visit his palace and breakfast with him. The Emperor also invited us, on behalf of his absent eldest son and heir (aged 22) to visit *his* palace and consider it a visit to him. They all talk English and they were all very neatly but very plainly dressed. You all dress a good deal finer than they were dressed. The Emperor and his family threw off all reserve and showed us all over the palace themselves. It is very rich and very elegant but in no way gaudy.

I had been appointed chairman of a committee to draught an address to the Emperor in behalf of the passengers, and as I fully expected, and as they fully intended, I had to write the address myself. I didn't mind it, because I have no modesty and would as soon write to an Emperor as to anybody else, but considering that there were 5 on the committee, I thought they might have contributed *one* paragraph among them, anyway. They wanted me to *read* it to him, too, but I declined that honor, not because I hadn't cheek enough (and some to spare) but because our Consul at Odessa was along, and also the Secretary of our Legation at St. Petersburgh, and of course one of those *ought* to read it. The Emperor accepted the address—it was his business to do it—and so many others have praised it warmly that I begin to imagine it must be a wonderful sort of document and herewith send you the original draught of it to be put into alcohol and preserved forever like a curious reptile.

They live right well at the Grand Duke Michael's. Their breakfasts are not gorgeous but very excellent. And if Mike were to say the word I would go there and breakfast with him tomorrow.

Ys aff

Sam

P. S. They had told us it would be polite to invite the Emperor to visit the ship, though he would not be likely to do it. But he didn't give us a chance. He has requested permission to come on board with his family and all his relations tomorrow and take a sail, in case it is calm weather. I can entertain them. My hand is in, now, and if you want any more Emperors fêted in style, trot them out.

FOUR

⟦1867–71⟧

Washington — "It was the unholiest gang that ever cavorted through Palestine" — courting Livy Langdon — The Innocents Abroad — Elmira, N. Y. — Buffalo — "I own millions and millions of feet of affluent silver leads in Nevada" — marriage to Livy

Clemens returned to New York on the *Quaker City* November 19, 1867, a trifle more than a fortnight before his thirty-second birthday. His travel letters to the *San Francisco Alta California*, the *New York Tribune* and the *New York Herald* had made him well known across the country. Two days later Elisha Bliss, Jr., of the American Publishing Company of Hartford, Connecticut, a subscription publisher, wrote to him, expressing strong interest in issuing a book by him, perhaps one based on the travel letters. Clemens was in Washington, trying to scout out a government job for Orion.

To Elisha Bliss, Jr., Hartford

Washington, *Dec. 2, 1867*

E. Bliss, Jr. Esq.
Sec'y American Publishing Co.
Dear Sir,

I only received your favor of Nov. 21st last night at the rooms of the *Tribune* Bureau here. It was forwarded from the *Tribune* office, New York, where it had lain eight or ten days. This will be a sufficient apology for the seeming discourtesy of my silence.

I wrote fifty-two [three] letters for the *San Francisco Alta California* during the Quaker City excursion, about half of which number have been printed thus far. The *Alta* has few exchanges in the East, and I suppose scarcely any of these letters have been copied on this side of the Rocky Mountains. I could weed them of their chief faults of construction and inelegancies of expression and make a volume that would be more acceptable in many respects than any I could now write. When those letters were written my impressions were fresh but now they have lost that freshness. They were warm then, they are cold now. I could strike out certain letters and write new ones wherewith to supply their places. If you think such a book would suit your purpose please drop me a line specifying the size and general style of the volume, when the matter ought to be ready, whether it should have pictures in it or not, and particularly what your terms with me would be and what amount of money I might possibly make out of it. The latter clause has a degree of importance for me which is almost beyond my own comprehension. But you understand that, of course.

I have other propositions for a book but have doubted the propriety of interfering with good newspaper engagements, except my way as an author could be demonstrated to be plain before me. But I know Richardson and learned from him some months ago something of an idea of the subscription plan of publishing. If that is your plan invariably, it looks safe.

I am on the *N.Y. Tribune* staff here as an "occasional," among other things, and a note from you addressed to

Very truly &c.

Sam L. Clemens

New York Tribune Bureau, Washington, will find me without fail.

Richardson was A. D. Richardson, author of *Field, Dungeon and Escape* and *Beyond the Mississippi.*

To Jane Clemens and Pamela Moffett, St. Louis

224 F. Street, Wash, *Jan. 8, 1868*

My dear Mother and Sister,

And so the old Major has been there, has he? I would like mighty well to see him. I was a sort of benefactor to him once. I helped to snatch him out when he was about to ride into a Mohammedan mosque in that queer old Moorish town of Tangier in Africa. If he had got in, the Moors would have knocked his venerable old head off for his temerity.

I have just arrived from New York. Been there ever since Christmas, staying at the house of Dan Slote, my *Quaker City* roommate, and having a splendid time. Charley Langdon, Jack Van Nostrand, Dan and I (all *Quaker City* nighthawks) had a blowout at Dan's house and a lively talk over old times. We went through the Holy Land together, and I just laughed till my sides ached, at some of our reminiscences. It was the unholiest gang that ever cavorted through Palestine, but those are the best boys in the world. We needed Moulton badly.

I started to make calls New Year's Day but I anchored for the day at the first house I came to. Charlie Langdon's sister was there (beautiful girl) and Miss Alice Hooker, another beautiful girl, a niece of Henry Ward Beecher's. We sent the old folks home early with instructions not to send the carriage till midnight, and then I just staid there and worried the life out of those girls. I am going to spend a few days with the Langdons in Elmira, New York, as soon as I get time, and a few days at Mrs. Hooker's in Hartford, Conn., shortly.

Henry Ward Beecher sent for me last Sunday to come over and dine (he lives in Brooklyn, you know) and I went. Harriet Beecher Stowe was there, and Mrs. and Miss Beecher, Mrs. Hooker and my old *Quaker City* favorite, Emma Beach.

We had a very gay time, if it was Sunday. I expect I told more lies than I have told before in a month.

I went back by invitation after the evening service and finished the blowout and then staid all night at Mr. Beach's. Henry Ward is a brick.

I found out at 10 o'clock last night that I was to lecture tomorrow evening and so you must be aware that I have been working like sin all night to get a lecture written. I have finished it. I call it "Frozen Truth." It is a little top-heavy, though, because there is more truth in the title than there is in the lecture.

But thunder, I mustn't sit here writing all day, with so much business before me.

Goodby, and kind regards to all.

Yrs affy
Sam L. Clemens

Jack Van Nostrand was the "Jack" of *The Innocents Abroad.* "Charlie Langdon's sister" was Olivia Langdon, whom Clemens was destined to marry.

To Jane Clemens and family, St. Louis

Lockport, N. Y. *Feb. 27, 1869*

Dear Folks,

I enclose $20 for Ma. I thought I was getting ahead of her little assessments of $35 a month but find I am falling behind with her instead and have let her go without money. Well, I did not mean to do it. But you see when people have been getting ready for months in a quiet way to get married, they are bound to grow stingy and go to saving up money against that awful day when it is sure to be needed.

I am particularly anxious to place myself in a position where I can carry on my married life in good shape on *my own hook,* because I have paddled my own canoe so long that I could not be satisfied now to let anybody help me, and my proposed father-in-law is naturally so liberal that it would be just like him to want to give us a start in life. But I don't want it that way. I can start myself. I don't want any help. I can run this institution without any outside assistance, and I shall have a wife who will stand by me like a soldier through thick and thin and never complain.

She is only a little body but she hasn't her peer in Christendom. I gave her only a plain gold engagement ring, when fashion impera- tively demands a two-hundred-dollar diamond one, and told her it was typical of her future lot—namely, that she would have to flour- ish on substantials rather than luxuries. (But you see I know the girl—she don't care anything about luxuries.) She is a splendid girl. She spends no money but her usual year's allowance, and she spends nearly every cent of that on other people. She will be a good sensible little wife, without any airs about her. I don't make intercession for her beforehand and ask you to love her, for there isn't any use in that, you couldn't help it if you were to try.

I warn you that whoever comes within the fatal influence of her beautiful nature is her willing slave for evermore. I take my affida- vit on that statement. Her father and mother and brother embrace and pet her constantly, precisely as if she were a *sweetheart* instead of a blood relation. She has unlimited power over her father and yet she never uses it except to make him help people who stand in need of help. . . .

But if I get fairly started on the subject of my bride I never shall get through, and so I will quit right here. I went to Elmira a little over a week ago and staid four days and then had to go to New York on business.

To Jane Clemens and family, St. Louis

Elmira [New York], *June 4, [1869]*

Dear Folks,

Livy sends you her love and loving good wishes, and I send you mine. The last 3 chapters of the book came tonight. We shall read it in the morning and then, thank goodness, we are *done.*

In twelve months (or rather I believe it is fourteen) I have earned just *eighty dollars* by my pen. Two little magazine squibs and one newspaper letter. Altogether the idlest, laziest 14 months I ever spent in my life. And in that time my *absolute* and *necessary* expenses have been scorchingly heavy, for I have now less than three thousand six hundred dollars in bank out of the eight or nine thousand I have made during those months, lecturing.

My expenses were something frightful during the winter. I feel ashamed of my idleness and yet I have had really *no* inclination to do anything but court Livy. I haven't any other inclination *yet.* I have determined not to work as hard traveling any more as I did last winter, and so I have resolved not to lecture outside of the 6 New England States next winter. My Western course would easily amount to $10,000 but I would rather make 2 or 3 thousand in New England than submit again to so much wearing travel. (I *have* promised to talk ten nights for a thousand dollars in the State of New York, provided the places are close together.) But after all if I get located in a newspaper in a way to suit me, in the meantime, I don't want to lecture *at all* next winter, and probably shan't.

I most cordially hate the lecture field. And after all, I shudder to think that I may never get out of it. In all conversations with Gough, and Anna Dickinson, Nasby, Oliver Wendell Holmes, Wendell Phillips and the other old stagers, I could not observe that *they* ever expected or hoped to get out of the business. *I* don't want to get wedded to it as they are. Livy thinks we can live on a very moderate sum and that we'll not need to lecture. I know very well that she can live on a small allowance but I am not so sure about myself. I can't scare her by reminding her that her father's family expenses are forty thousand dollars a year, because she produces the documents at once to show that precious little of this outlay is on *her* account. But I must not commence writing about Livy, else I shall never stop. There isn't such another little piece of perfection in the world as she is.

My time is become so short now that I doubt if I'll get to California this summer. If I manage to buy into a paper, I think I will visit you a while and not go to Cal. at all. I shall know something about it after my next trip to Hartford. We all go there on the 10th, the whole family, to attend a wedding on the 17th. I am offered an interest in a Cleveland paper which would pay me $2,300 to $2,500 a year, and a salary added of $3,000. The salary is fair enough but the interest is not large enough, and so I must look a little further. The Cleveland folks say they *can* be induced to do a little better by me, and urge me to come out and talk business. But it don't strike me, I feel little or no inclination to go.

I believe I haven't anything else to write, and it is bed-time. I want to write to Orion but I keep putting it off. I keep putting *every*thing off. Day after day Livy and I are together all day long and until 10 at night, and then I feel dreadfully sleepy. If Orion will bear with me and forgive me I will square up with him yet. I will even let him kiss Livy.

My love to Mollie and Annie and Sammie and all. Goodbye.

Affectionately,
Sam

"The last three chapters of the book." This was *The Innocents Abroad*.
The next letter was written in response to an invitation for Clemens to attend a banquet in New York.

To the New York Society of California Pioneers,
New York City

Elmira, *October 11, 1869*

Gentlemen,

Circumstances render it out of my power to take advantage of the
invitation extended to me through Mr. Simonton and be present at
your dinner at New York. I regret this very much, for there are
several among you whom I would have a right to join hands with on
the score of old friendship, and I suppose I would have a sublime
general right to shake hands with the rest of you on the score of
kinship in California ups and downs in search of fortune.

If I were to tell some of my experience you would recognize California blood in me. I fancy the old, old story would sound familiar,
no doubt. I have the usual stock of reminiscences. For instance: I
went to Esmeralda early. I purchased largely in the "Wide West,"
"Winnemucca" and other fine claims and was very wealthy. I fared
sumptuously on bread when flour was $200 a barrel and had beans
for dinner every Sunday, when none but bloated aristocrats could
afford such grandeur. But I finished by feeding batteries in a quartz
mill at $15 a week and wishing I was a battery myself and had
somebody to feed me. My claims in Esmeralda are there yet. I suppose I could be persuaded to sell.

I went to Humboldt District when it was new. I became largely
interested in the "Alba Nueva" and other claims with gorgeous
names and was rich again—in prospect. I owned a vast mining property there. I would not have sold out for less than $400,000 at that
time. But I will now. Finally I walked home—200 miles—partly for
exercise and partly because stage fare was expensive. Next I entered
upon an affluent career in Virginia City, and by a judicious investment of labor and the capital of friends became the owner of about
all the worthless wild cat mines there were in that part of the country. Assessments did the business for me there. There were a hundred and seventeen assessments to one dividend, and the proportion
of income to outlay was a little against me. My financial barometer
went down to 32 Fahrenheit, and the subscriber was frozen out.

I took up extensions on the main lead, extensions that reached to
British America in one direction and to the Isthmus of Panama in

the other, and I verily believe I would have been a rich man if I had ever found those infernal extensions. But I didn't. I ran tunnels till I tapped the Arctic Ocean, and I sunk shafts till I broke through the roof of perdition, but those extensions turned up missing every time. I am willing to sell all that property and throw in the improvements.

Perhaps you remember that celebrated "North Ophir?" I bought that mine. It was very rich in pure silver. You could take it out in lumps as large as a filbert. But when it was discovered that those lumps were melted half dollars, and hardly melted at that, a painful case of "salting" was apparent and the undersigned adjourned to the poorhouse again.

I paid assessments on "Hale and Norcross" until they sold me out and I had to take in washing for a living, and the next month that infamous stock went up to $7,000 a foot.

I own millions and millions of feet of affluent silver leads in Nevada, in fact the entire undercrust of that country nearly, and if Congress would move that State off my property so that I could get at it I would be wealthy yet. But no, there she squats and here am I. Failing health persuades me to sell. If you know of any one desiring a permanent investment, I can furnish one that will have the virtue of being eternal.

I have been through the California mill, with all its "dips, spurs and angles, variations and sinuosities." I have worked there at all the different trades and professions known to the catalogues. I have been everything from a newspaper editor down to a cow-catcher on a locomotive, and I am encouraged to believe that if there had been a few more occupations to experiment on I might have made a dazzling success at last and found out what mysterious designs Providence had in creating me.

But you perceive that although I am not a Pioneer, I have had a sufficiently variegated time of it to enable me to talk Pioneer like a native, and feel like a Forty-Niner. Therefore, I cordially welcome you to your old-remembered homes and your long-deserted firesides, and close this screed with the sincere hope that your visit here will be a happy one and not embittered by the sorrowful surprises that absence and lapse of years are wont to prepare for wanderers; surprises which come in the form of old friends missed from their places; silence where familiar voices should be; the young grown old;

change and decay everywhere; home a delusion and a disappointment; strangers at hearthstone; sorrow where gladness was; tears for
laughter; the melancholy pomp of death where the grace of life has
been!

With all good wishes for the Returned Prodigals, and regrets that
I cannot partake of a small piece of the fatted calf (rare and no
gravy)

I am yours, cordially,
Mark Twain

To James Gillis in his cabin on Jackass Hill, Tuolumne Co., California

Elmira, N. Y. Jan. 26, '70

Dear Jim,

I remember that old night just as well! And somewhere among my
relics I have your remembrance stored away. It makes my heart
ache yet to call to mind some of those days. Still, it shouldn't, for
right in the depths of their poverty and their pocket-hunting vaga-
bondage lay the germ of my coming good fortune. You remember
the one gleam of jollity that shot across our dismal sojourn in the rain
and mud of Angels' Camp. I mean that day we sat around the tav-
ern stove and heard that chap tell about the frog and how they filled
him with shot. And you remember how we quoted from the yarn
and laughed over it out there on the hillside while you and dear old
Stoker panned and washed. I jotted the story down in my notebook
that day and would have been glad to get ten or fifteen dollars for it.
I was just that blind. But then we were so hard up! I published that
story and it became widely known in America, India, China, England, and the reputation it made for me has paid me thousands and
thousands of dollars since. Four or five months ago I bought into the
Express (I have ordered it sent to you as long as you live, and if the
bookkeeper sends you any bills, you let me hear of it). I went heavily
in debt, never could have dared to do that, Jim, if we hadn't heard
the Jumping Frog story that day.

And wouldn't I love to take old Stoker by the hand, and wouldn't
I love to see him in his great specialty, his wonderful rendition of

"Rinalds" in the "Burning Shame!" Where is Dick and what is he doing? Give him my fervent love and warm old remembrances.

A week from today I shall be married—to a girl even better and lovelier than the peerless "Chapparal Quails." You can't come so far Jim, but still I cordially *invite* you to come anyhow, and I invite Dick too. And if you two boys *were* to land here on that pleasant occasion, we would make you right royally welcome.

Truly your friend,
Saml L. Clemens

P. S.—"California plums are good, Jim—particularly when they are stewed."

Stoker was Dick Stoker. "Chapparal Quails": some girls who had lived with their parents on a small ranch and who were locally famous for their beauty and for having many suitors. "California plums": according to Paine, "The mention of 'California plums' refers to some inedible fruit which Gillis once, out of pure goodness of heart, bought of a poor wandering squaw and then, to conceal his motive, declared that they were something rare and fine and persisted in eating them though even when stewed they nearly choked him."

The Innocents Abroad was published in July 1869. By the end of January 1870 more than 30,000 copies had been sold.

To Elisha Bliss, Hartford

Elmira, *Jan. 28 '70*

Friend Bliss,

... Yes, I *am* satisfied with the way you are running the book. You are running it in staving, tip-top, first-class style. I never wander into any corner of the country but I find that an agent has been there before me, and many of that community have read the book. And on an average about ten people a day come and hunt me up to thank me and tell me I'm a benefactor! I guess this is part of the program we didn't expect in the first place.

I think you are rushing this book in a manner to be proud of, and you will make the finest success of it that has ever been made with a subscription book, I believe. What with advertising, establishing agencies, &c, you have got an enormous lot of machinery under way and hard at work in a wonderfully short space of time. It is easy to see, when one travels around, that one must be endowed with a deal of genuine generalship in order to maneuver a publication whose line of battle stretches from end to end of a great continent, and whose foragers and skirmishers invest every hamlet and besiege every village hidden away in all the vast space between.

I'll back you against any publisher in America, Bliss, or elsewhere.

Yrs as ever
Clemens

Clemens and Olivia Langdon were married in Elmira the evening of February 2, 1870. He was in his thirty-fifth year. She was a decade his junior. They made their home in Buffalo.

To Orion, St. Louis

Elmira, *July 15, 1870*

My Dear Bro.,

Per contract I must have another 600-page book ready for my publisher Jan. 1, and I only began it today. The subject of it is a secret because I may possibly change it. But as it stands I propose to do up Nevada and Cal., beginning with the trip across the country in the stage. Have you a memorandum of the route we took, or the names of any of the Stations we stopped at? Do you remember any of the scenes, names, incidents or adventures of the coach trip?—for I remember next to *nothing* about the matter. Jot down a foolscap page of items for me. I wish I could have two days' talk with you.

I suppose I am to get the biggest copyright, this time, ever paid on a subscription book in this country.

Give our love to Mollie. Mr. Langdon is very low.

Yr Bro
Sam

The new book was to be *Roughing It*. The "biggest copyright" was a royalty of 7½ percent of the retail price. Mr. Langdon was Livy's father, who died early in August.

To Orion, St. Louis

Buf., *1870*

Dear Bro.,

I find that your little memorandum book is going to be ever so much use to me and will enable me to make quite a coherent narrative of the Plains journey instead of slurring it over and jumping 2,000 miles at a stride. The book I am writing will sell. In return for the use of the little memorandum book I shall take the greatest pleasure in forwarding to you the third $1,000 which the publisher of the forthcoming work sends me—or the *first* $1,000, I am not particular—they will both be in the first quarterly statement of account from the publisher.

In great haste,

Yr Obliged Bro.

Sam

Love to Mollie. We are all getting along tolerably well.

To Orion, St. Louis

Buf. *Sept. 9th, 1870*

My Dear Bro,

O here! I don't want to be consulted at all about Tenn. I don't want it even mentioned to me. When I make a suggestion it is for you to act upon it or throw it aside, but I beseech you never to ask my advice, opinion or consent about that hated property. If it was because I felt the slightest personal interest in the infernal land that I *ever* made a suggestion, the suggestion would never be made.

Do exactly as you please with the land. Always remember this: that so trivial a percentage as ten per cent will never sell it.

It is only a bid for a somnambulist.

I have no time to turn round. A young lady visitor (schoolmate of Livy's) is dying in the house of typhoid fever (parents are in South Carolina) and the premises are full of nurses and doctors and we are all fagged out.

Yrs.

Sam

Clemens, having grown tired of Buffalo, planned to move temporarily to Elmira and permanently to Hartford.

To Elisha Bliss, Hartford

Elmira, *Monday, May 15th 1871*

Friend Bliss,

Yrs rec'd enclosing check for $703.35. The old *Innocents* holds out handsomely.

I have MS enough on hand now to make (allowing for engravings) about 400 pages of the book, consequently am two-thirds done. I intended to run up to Hartford about the middle of the week and take it along, because it has chapters in it that ought by all means to be in the prospectus, but I find myself so thoroughly interested in my work now (a thing I have not experienced for months) that I can't bear to lose a single moment of the inspiration. So I will stay here and peg away as long as it lasts. My present idea is to write as much more as I have already written and then cull from the mass the very best chapters and discard the rest. I am not half as well satisfied with the first part of the book as I am with what I am writing now. When I get it done I want to see the man who will begin to read it and not finish it. If it falls short of the *Innocents* in any respect I shall lose my guess.

When I was writing the *Innocents* my daily stint was 30 pages of MS and I hardly ever got beyond it, but I have gone over that nearly every day for the last ten. That shows that I am writing with a red-hot interest. Nothing grieves me now, nothing troubles me, nothing bothers me or gets my attention. I don't think of anything but the book, and I don't have an hour's unhappiness about anything and don't care two cents whether school keeps or not. It will be a bully book. If I keep up my present lick three weeks more I shall be able and willing to scratch out half of the chapters of the Overland narrative, and shall do it.

You do not mention having received my second batch of MS, sent a week or two ago—about 100 pages.

If you want to issue a prospectus and go right to canvassing, say the word and I will forward some more MS or send it by hand, special messenger. Whatever chapters you think are unquestionably good we will retain, of course, so they can go into a prospectus as well one time as another. The book will be done soon, now. I have· 1200 pages of MS already written and am now writing 200 a week— more than that, in fact. During the past week wrote 23 one day, then 30, 33, 35, 52 and 65. How's that?

It will be a starchy book and should be full of snappy pictures, especially pictures worked in with the letterpress. The dedication will be worth the price of the volume. Thus:

To the Late Cain
This Book is Dedicated

Not on account of respect for his memory, for it merits little respect; not on account of sympathy with him, for his bloody deed placed him without the pale of sympathy, strictly speaking: but out of a mere human commiseration for him that it was his misfortune to live in a dark age that knew not the beneficent Insanity Plea.

I think it will do.

Yrs.
Clemens

P. S.—The reaction is beginning and my stock is looking up. I am getting the bulliest offers for books and almanacs, am flooded with lecture invitations, and one periodical offers me $6,000 cash for 12 articles of any length and on any subject, treated humorously or otherwise.

The Redpath of the following was Clemens's lecture agent. Nasby was Petroleum Vesuvius Nasby, the pseudonym of David R. Locke, a fellow humorist.

To James Redpath, Boston

Hartford, *Tuesday Aug. 8, 1871*

Dear Red,

I am different from other women. My mind changes oftener. People who have no mind can easily be steadfast and firm, but when a man is loaded down to the guards with it, as I am, every heavy sea of foreboding or inclination, maybe of indolence, shifts the cargo. See? Therefore, if you will notice, one week I am likely to give rigid instructions to confine me to New England. Next week send me to Arizona. The next week withdraw my name. The next week give you full untrammelled swing. And the week following modify it. You must try to keep the run of my mind, Redpath, it is your business, being the agent, and it always was too many for me. It appears to me to be one of the finest pieces of mechanism I have ever met with. Now about the West, this week I am willing that you shall retain all the Western engagements. But what I shall want *next* week is still with God.

Let us not profane the mysteries with soiled hands and prying eyes of sin.

Yours,
Mark

P. S. Shall be here 2 weeks. Will run up there when Nasby comes.

FIVE

[1872-76]

Hartford — *"62,000 copies of* Roughing It *sold and delivered in 4 months"* — *London* — The Gilded Age — *Elmira, N. Y.* — *"Susie Crane has built the loveliest study for me you ever saw"* — *Brother Orion Clemens* — Tom Sawyer

The Innocents Abroad was reviewed favorably in the *Atlantic Monthly* by William Dean Howells, then the magazine's assistant editor. Toward the end of 1869 Clemens met Howells, who was to become a very important friend and literary adviser of his.

To William Dean Howells, Boston

Hartford, *June 15, 1872*

Friend Howells,

Could you tell me how I could get a copy of your portrait as published in *Hearth and Home?* I hear so much talk about it as being among the finest works of art which have yet appeared in that journal that I feel a strong desire to see it. Is it suitable for framing? I have written the publishers of H & H time and again but they say that the demand for the portrait immediately exhausted the edition and now a copy cannot be had even for the European demand, which has now begun. Bret Harte has been here and says his family would not be without that portrait for any consideration. He says his children get up in the night and yell for it. I would give anything for a copy of that portrait to put up in my parlor. I have Oliver Wendell Holmes's and Bret Harte's as published in *Every Saturday,* and of all the swarms that come every day to gaze upon them none go away that are not softened and humbled and made more resigned to the will of God. If I had yours to put up alongside of them I believe the combination would bring more souls to earnest reflection and ultimate conviction of their lost condition than any other kind of warning would.

Where in the nation can I get that portrait? Here are heaps of people that want it, that *need* it. There is my uncle. *He* wants a copy. He is lying at the point of death. He has *been* lying at the point of death for two years. He wants a copy, and I want him to *have* a copy. And I want you to send a copy to the man that shot my dog. I want to see if he is dead to every human instinct.

Now you send me that portrait. I am sending you mine in this letter, and am glad to do it, for it has been greatly admired. People who are judges of art find in the execution a grandeur which has not been equalled in this country, and an expression which has not been approached in *any*.

Yrs truly,
S. L. Clemens

P. S. 62,000 copies of *Roughing It* sold and delivered in 4 months.

Clemens decided to go to England to collect materials for a new travel book. He was received so handsomely in England that he lost himself in socializing. Writing to his sister-in-law, Susan Crane, whose husband was named Theodore, he remarked, "If you and Theodore will come over in the Spring with Livy and me and spend the summer you will see a country that is so beautiful that you will be obliged to believe in Fairyland . . . and Theodore can browse with me among dusty old dens that look now as they looked five hundred years ago; and puzzle over books in the British Museum that were made before Christ was born; and in the customs of their public dinners, and the ceremonies of every official act, and the dresses of a thousand dignitaries, trace the speech and manners of all the centuries that have dragged their lagging decades over England since the Heptarchy fell asunder. I would a good deal rather live here if I could get the rest of you over."

To Jane Clemens and Pamela Moffett

London, *Nov. 6, 1872*

My dear Mother and Sister,

I have been so everlasting busy that I *couldn't* write, and moreover I have been so unceasingly lazy that I couldn't have written anyhow. I came here to take notes for a book but I haven't done much but attend dinners and make speeches. But have had a jolly good time and I do hate to go away from these English folks. They make a stranger feel entirely at home and they laugh so easily that it is a comfort to make after-dinner speeches here. I have made hundreds of friends, and last night in the crush of the opening of the New Guild-hall Library and Museum I was surprised to meet a familiar face every few steps. Nearly 4,000 people of both sexes came and went during the evening, so I had a good opportunity to make a great many new acquaintances.

Livy is willing to come here with me next April and stay several months, so I am going home next Tuesday. I would sail on Saturday but that is the day of the Lord Mayor's annual grand state dinner, when they say 900 of the great men of the city sit down to table, a great many of them in their fine official and court paraphernalia, so I must not miss it. However, I may yet change my mind and sail Saturday. I am looking at a fine Magic lantern which will cost a deal of money, and if I buy it Sammy may come and learn to make the gas and work the machinery and paint pictures for it on glass. I mean to give exhibitions for charitable purposes in Hartford and charge a dollar a head.

> In a hurry, Ys affly
> Sam

Clemens sailed for New York on November 12th. That winter he began building the Hartford house on Farmington Avenue. By the spring he planned to sail for England with Livy, his daughter Susy and a girlhood friend of Livy's, Clara Spaulding of Elmira. Hearing of the proposed journey, the *New York Daily Graphic* requested a word of farewell.

To the Editor of *The Daily Graphic*, New York City

> Hartford, *Apl. 17, 1873*

Ed. *Graphic,*

Your note is received. If the following two lines which I have cut from it are your natural handwriting, then I understand you to ask me "for a farewell letter in the name of the American people." Bless you, the joy of the American people is just a little premature. I haven't gone yet. And what is more, I am not going to *stay* when I *do* go.

Yes, it is true. I am only going to remain beyond the sea six months, that is all. I love stir and excitement, and so the moment the spring birds begin to sing and the lagging weariness of summer to threaten I grow restless, I get the fidgets, I want to pack off somewhere where there's something going on. But you know how that is, you must have felt that way. This very day I saw the signs in the air of the coming dullness and I said to myself, "How glad I am that I have already chartered a steamship!" There was absolutely nothing in the morning papers. You can see for yourself what the telegraphic headings were:

BY TELEGRAPH
————

A Father Killed by His Son

————

A Bloody Fight in Kentucky

————

An Eight-year-old Murderer

————

A Town in a State of
General Riot

————

A Court House Fired, and
Negroes Therein Shot
while Escaping

————

A Louisiana Massacre

————

Two to Three Hundred Men
Roasted Alive!

————

A Lively Skirmish in Indiana

————

(and thirty other similar headings)

The items under those headings all bear date of yesterday, Apl. 16 (refer to your own paper), and I give you my word of honor that that string of commonplace stuff was everything there was in the telegraphic columns that a body could call news. Well, said I to myself, this is getting pretty dull, this is getting pretty dry, there don't appear to be anything going on anywhere. Has this progressive nation gone to sleep? Have I got to stand another month of this torpidity before I can begin to browse among the lively capitals of Europe?

But never mind—things may revive while I am away.

During the last two months my next-door neighbor, Chas. Dudley Warner, has dropped his *Back-Log Studies* and he and I have written a bulky novel in partnership. He has worked up the fiction and I have hurled in the facts. I consider it one of the most astonishing novels that ever was written. Night after night I sit up reading it over and over again and crying. It will be published early in the Fall, with plenty of pictures. Do you consider this an advertisement? And if so, do you charge for such things when a man is your friend?

Yours truly,

Saml. L. Clemens,

"Mark Twain"

The "bulky novel in partnership" was *The Gilded Age.*

Early in his life in Hartford, Clemens met the Reverend Joseph Hopkins Twichell, who was to become his closest personal friend. Twichell's wife's name was Harmony. In the following, the new baby is Clara Clemens. Modoc is Susy Clemens. The "loveliest study" was at Quarry Farm outside of Elmira.

To Rev. and Mrs. Twichell, Hartford

Elmira, *June 11,* '74

My dear old Joe and Harmony,

The baby is here and is the great American Giantess, weighing 7¾ pounds. We had to wait a good long time for her but she was full compensation when she *did* come.

The Modoc was delighted with it and gave it her doll at once. There is nothing selfish about the Modoc. She is fascinated with the new baby. The Modoc rips and tears around outdoors most of the time and consequently is as hard as a pine knot and as brown as an Indian. She is bosom friend to all the ducks, chickens, turkeys and guinea hens on the place. Yesterday as she marched along the winding path that leads up the hill through the red clover beds to the summer house there was a long procession of these fowls stringing contentedly after her, led by a stately rooster who can look over the Modoc's head. The devotion of these vassals has been purchased with daily largess of Indian meal, and so the Modoc, attended by her bodyguard, moves in state wherever she goes.

Susie Crane has built the loveliest study for me you ever saw. It is octagonal, with a peaked roof, each octagon filled with a spacious window, and it sits perched in complete isolation on top of an elevation that commands leagues of valley and city and retreating ranges of distant blue hills. It is a cosy nest, with just room in it for a sofa and a table and three or four chairs, and when the storms sweep down the remote valley and the lightning flashes above the hills beyond and the rain beats upon the roof over my head, imagine the luxury of it! It stands 500 feet above the valley and 2½ miles from it.

However, one must not write all day. We send continents of love to you and yours.

Affectionately

Mark

Clemens's mother and sister were now living in Fredonia, New York.

To Jane Clemens and Pamela Moffett, Fredonia, N. Y.

Elmira, *Aug. 15*

My dear Mother and Sister,

I came away from Fredonia ashamed of myself, almost too much humiliated to hold up my head and say goodbye. For I began to comprehend how much harm my conduct might do you socially in your village. I would have gone to that detestable oyster-brained bore and apologized for my inexcusable rudeness to him but that I was satisfied he was of too small a calibre to know how to receive an apology with magnanimity.

Pamela appalled me by saying people had hinted that they wished to visit Livy when she came but that she had given them no encouragement. I feared that those people would merely comprehend that their courtesies were not wanted and yet not know exactly *why* they were not wanted.

I came away feeling that in return for your constant and tireless efforts to secure our bodily comfort and make our visit enjoyable, I had basely repaid you by making you sad and sore-hearted and leaving you so. And the natural result has fallen to me likewise, for a guilty conscience has harassed me ever since and I have not had one short quarter of an hour of peace to this moment.

You spoke of Middletown. Why not go there and live? Mr. Crane says it is only about a hundred miles this side of New York on the Erie road. The fact that one or two of you might prefer to live somewhere else is not a valid objection. There are no 4 people who would all choose the same place. So it will be in vain to wait for the day when your tastes shall be a unit. I seriously fear that our visit has damaged you in Fredonia, and so I wish you were out of it.

The baby is fat and strong and Susie the same. Susie was charmed with the donkey and the doll.

Ys affectionately
Saml

P. S. Dear Ma and Pamela. I am mainly grieved because I have been rude to a man who has been kind to you, and if you ever feel a desire to apologize to him for me you may be sure that I will endorse the apology, no matter how strong it may be. I went to his bank to apologize to him but my conviction was strong that he was not man enough to know how to take an apology and so I did not make it.

It is not known now what Clemens's "inexcusable rudeness" was. The Doctor John Brown of the next letter was the author of *Rab and His Friend*, whom Clemens had met in Edinburgh.

To Dr. John Brown, Edinburgh, Scotland

Quarry Farm, Near Elmira, N. Y. *Sept. 4, 1874*

Dear Friend,

I have been writing fifty pages of manuscript a day, on an average, for some time now, on a book (a story) and consequently have been so wrapped up in it and so dead to anything else that I have fallen mighty short in letter writing. But night before last I discovered that that day's chapter was a failure in conception, moral truth to nature and execution—enough blemish to impair the excellence of almost any chapter—and so I must burn up the day's work and do it all over again. It was plain that I had worked myself out, pumped myself dry. So I knocked off and went to playing billiards for a change. I haven't had an idea or a fancy for two days now—an excellent time to write to friends who have plenty of ideas and fancies of their own and so will prefer the offerings of the heart before those of the head. Day after tomorrow I go to a neighboring city to see a five-act drama of mine brought out and suggest amendments in it, and would about as soon spend a night in the Spanish Inquisition as sit there and be tortured with all the adverse criticisms I can contrive to imagine the audience is indulging in. But whether the play be successful or not, I hope I shall never feel obliged to see it performed a second time. My interest in my work dies a sudden and violent death when the work is done.

I have invented and patented a pretty good sort of scrapbook (I think) but I have backed down from letting it be known as mine just at present, for I can't stand being under discussion on a play and a scrapbook at the same time!

I shall be away two days and then return to take our tribe to New York, where we shall remain five days buying furniture for the new house and then go to Hartford and settle solidly down for the winter. After all that fallow time I ought to be able to go to work again on the book. We shall reach Hartford about the middle of September, I judge.

We have spent the past four months up here on top of a breezy hill six hundred feet high some few miles from Elmira, N.Y. and overlooking that town. (Elmira is my wife's birthplace and that of Susie and the new baby.) This little summer house on the hilltop (named Quarry Farm because there's a quarry on it) belongs to my wife's sister, Mrs. Crane.

A photographer came up the other day and wanted to make some views, and I shall send you the result per this mail.

My study is a snug little octagonal den with a coal-grate, 6 big windows, one little one, and a wide doorway (the latter opening upon the distant town). On hot days I spread the study wide open, anchor my papers down with brickbats, and write in the midst of the hurricanes, clothed in the same thin linen we make shirts of. The study is nearly on the peak of the hill. It is right in front of the little perpendicular wall of rock left where they used to quarry stones. *On* the peak of the hill is an old arbor roofed with bark and covered with the vine you call the "American Creeper"—its green is almost bloodied with red. The Study is 30 yards below the old arbor and 100 yards above the dwelling house—it is remote from *all* noises. . . .

Now isn't the whole thing pleasantly situated?

In the picture of me in the study you glimpse (through the left-hand window) the little rock bluff that rises behind the pond, and the bases of the little trees on top of it. The small square window is over the fireplace. The chimney divides to make room for it. Without the stereoscope it looks like a framed picture. All the study windows have Venetian blinds. They long ago went out of fashion in America but they have not been replaced with anything half as good yet.

The study is built on top of a tumbled rock heap that has morning glories climbing about it and a stone stairway leading down through and dividing it.

There now, if you have not time to read all this, turn it over to "Jock" and drag in the judge to help.

Mrs. Clemens must put in a late picture of Susie, a picture which she maintains is good but which I think is slander on the child.

We revisit the Rutland Street home many a time in fancy, for we hold every individual in it in happy and grateful memory.

> Goodbye,
> Your friend,
> Saml. L. Clemens

P. S. I gave the P. O. Department a blast in the papers about sending misdirected letters of mine back to the writers for reshipment, and got a blast in return, through a New York daily, from the New York postmaster. But I notice that misdirected letters *find* me now without any unnecessary fooling around.

> S.L.C.

Clemens was working on *Tom Sawyer*. The play mentioned below was based on *The Gilded Age*.

To W. D. Howells, Boston

Farmington Avenue, Hartford, *Sept. 20, 1874*

My dear Howells,

All right, my boy, send proof sheets *here*. I amend dialect stuff by talking and talking and *talking* it till it sounds right, and I had difficulty with this negro talk because a negro sometimes (rarely) says "goin'" and sometimes "gwyne," and they make just such discrepancies in other words, and when you come to reproduce them on paper they look as if the variation resulted from the writer's carelessness. But I want to work at the proofs and get the dialect as nearly right as possible.

We are in part of the new house. Goodness knows when we'll get in the rest of it—full of workmen yet.

I worked a month at my play and launched it in New York last Wednesday. I believe it will go. The newspapers have been complimentary. It is simply a *setting* for the one character, Col. Sellers. As a *play* I guess it will not bear a critical assault in force.

The Warners are as charming as ever. They go shortly to the devil for a year, which is but a poetical way of saying they are going to afflict themselves with the unsurpassable (bad word) of *travel* for a spell. I believe they mean to go and see you first, so they mean to start from heaven to the other place, not from earth. How is that? I think that is no slouch of a compliment—kind of a dim religious light about it. I enjoy that sort of thing.

Yrs ever
Mark

Soon Clemens was writing about the Mississippi—articles that appeared in the *Atlantic* as *Old Times on the Mississippi* and were incorporated in his book, *Life on the Mississippi.*

To Jane Clemens and Pamela Moffett, Fredonia, N. Y.

Hartford, *Sunday, 1874*

My dear Mother and Sister,

I saw Gov. Jewell today and he said he was still moving in the matter of Sammy's appointment° and would stick to it till he got a result of a positive nature one way or the other, but thus far he did not know whether to expect success or defeat.

Ma, whenever you need money I hope you won't be backward about saying so—you can always have it. We stint ourselves in some ways but we have no desire to stint you. And we don't intend to, either.

I *can't* "encourage" Orion. Nobody can do that conscientiously, for the reason that before one's letter has time to reach him he is off on some new wild-goose chase. Would you encourage in literature a man who the older he grows the worse he writes? Would you encourage Orion in the glaring insanity of studying law? If he were packed and crammed full of law it would be worthless lumber to him, for his is such a capricious and ill-regulated mind that he would apply the principles of the law with no more judgment than a child of ten years. I know what I am saying. I laid one of the plainest and simplest of legal questions before Orion once, and the helpless and hopeless mess he made of it was absolutely astonishing. Nothing aggravates me so much as to have Orion mention law or literature to me.

Well, I cannot encourage him to try the ministry, because he would change his religion so fast that he would have to keep a traveling agent under wages to go ahead of him to engage pulpits and board for him.

I cannot conscientiously encourage him to do *anything* but potter around his little farm and put in his odd hours contriving new and impossible projects at the rate of 365 a year, which is his customary average. He says he did well in Hannibal! Now there is a man who ought to be entirely satisfied with the grandeurs, emoluments and activities of a hen farm.

If you ask me to pity Orion I can do that. I can do it every day and all day long. But one can't "encourage" quicksilver, because the instant you put your finger on it it isn't there. No, I am saying too much—he *does* stick to his literary and legal aspirations, and he naturally *would* select the very two things which he is wholly and preposterously unfitted for. If I ever become able, I mean to put Orion on a regular pension without revealing the fact that it is a

°As a West Point cadet.

pension. That is best for him. Let him consider it a periodical loan, and pay interest out of the principal. Within a year's time he would be looking upon himself as a benefactor of mine, in the way of furnishing me a good permanent investment for money, and that would make him happy and satisfied with himself. If he had money he would share with me in a moment, and I have no disposition to be stingy with *him*.

Affly
Sam

Livy sends love.

The "story" mentioned in the following was *Tom Sawyer*. Osgood was James R. Osgood, the publisher of some of Clemens's works, among them *Life on the Mississippi*.

To W. D. Howells, Boston

Hartford, *July 5th, 1875*

My dear Howells,

I have finished the story and didn't take the chap beyond boyhood. I believe it would be fatal to do it in any shape but autobiographically, like Gil Blas. I perhaps made a mistake in not writing it in the first person. If I went on now and took him into manhood he would just lie like all the one-horse men in literature and the reader would conceive a hearty contempt for him. It is *not* a boy's book at all. It will only be read by adults. It is only written for adults.

Moreover the book is plenty long enough as it stands. It is about 900 pages of MS, and may be 1000 when I shall have finished "working up" vague places, so it would make from 130 to 150 pages of the *Atlantic*, about what the *Foregone Conclusion* made, isn't it?

I would dearly like to see it in the *Atlantic*, but I doubt if it would pay the publishers to buy the privilege or me to sell it. Bret Harte has sold his novel (same size as mine, I should say) to *Scribner's Monthly* for $6,500 (publication to begin in September, I think) and he gets a royalty of 7½ per cent from Bliss in book form afterwards.

He gets a royalty of ten per cent on it in England (issued in serial numbers) and the same royalty on it in book form afterwards, and is to receive an advance payment of five hundred pounds the day the first No. of the serial appears. If I could do as well, here, and there, with mine it might possibly pay me but I seriously doubt it, though it is likely I could do better in England than Bret, who is not widely known there.

You see I take a vile, mercenary view of things, but then my household expenses are something almost ghastly.

By and by I shall take a boy of twelve and run him on through life (in the first person), but not Tom Sawyer, he would not be a good character for it.

I wish you would promise to read the MS of *Tom Sawyer* some time and see if you don't really decide that I am right in closing with him as a boy, and point out the most glaring defects for me. It is a tremendous favor to ask and I expect you to refuse and would be ashamed to expect you to do otherwise. But the thing has been so many months in my mind that it seems a relief to snake it out. I don't know any other person whose judgment I could venture to take fully and entirely. Don't hesitate about saying no, for I know how your time is taxed, and I would have honest need to blush if you said yes.

Osgood and I are "going for" the puppy G _____ on infringement of trademark. To win one or two suits of this kind will set literary folks on a firmer bottom. I wish Osgood would sue for stealing Holmes's poem. Wouldn't it be gorgeous to sue R _____ for *petty larceny?* I will promise to go into court and swear I think him capable of stealing peanuts from a blind pedlar.

Yrs ever,
Clemens

Howells read *Tom Sawyer* in manuscript and greatly admired it. He wrote to Clemens, "Give me a hint when it's to be out and I'll start the sheep to jumping in the right places," meaning that he would write and publish an early review of the novel in the *Atlantic* and thereby influence reviewers for less prestigious publications. Later he urged that Bliss "hurry out" *Tom Sawyer,* remarking, "That boy is going to make a prodigious hit."

To Howells, Boston

Hartford, *Jan. 18, '76*

My dear Howells,

Thanks, and ever so many, for the good opinion of *Tom Sawyer*. Williams has made about 300 rattling pictures for it, some of them very dainty. Poor devil, what a genius he has and how he does murder it with rum. He takes a book of mine and without suggestion from anybody builds no end of pictures just from his reading of it.

There was never a man in the world so grateful to another as I was to you day before yesterday when I sat down (in still rather wretched health) to set myself to the dreary and hateful task of making final revision of *Tom Sawyer* and discovered, upon opening the package of MS, that your pencil marks were scattered all along. This was splendid, and swept away all labor. Instead of *reading* the MS I simply hunted out the pencil marks and made the emendations which they suggested. I reduced the boy battle to a curt paragraph. I finally concluded to cut the Sunday school speech down to the first two sentences, leaving no suggestion of satire, since the book is to be for boys and girls. I tamed the various obscenities until I judged that they no longer carried offense. So, at a single sitting I began and finished a revision which I had supposed would occupy 3 or 4 days and leave me mentally and physically fagged out at the end. I was careful not to inflict the MS upon you until I had thoroughly and painstakingly revised it. Therefore, the only faults left were those that would discover themselves to others, not me, and these you had pointed out.

There was one expression which perhaps you overlooked. When Huck is complaining to Tom of the rigorous system in vogue at the widow's, he says the servants harass him with all manner of compulsory decencies, and he winds up by saying; "and they comb me all to hell." (No exclamation point.) Long ago, when I read that to Mrs. Clemens, she made no comment. Another time I created occasion to read that chapter to her aunt and her mother (both sensitive and loyal subjects of the kingdom of heaven, so to speak) and *they* let it pass. I was glad, for it was the most natural remark in the world for that boy to make, and he had been allowed few privileges of speech in the book. When I saw that you too had let it go without protest I was glad, and afraid too, afraid you hadn't observed it. Did you? And did you question the propriety of it? Since the book is now professedly and confessedly a boy's and girl's book, that darn word bothers me some nights but it never did until I had ceased to regard the volume as being for adults.

Don't bother to answer *now* (for you've writing enough to do without allowing me to add to the burden) but tell me when you see me again.

Which we do hope will be next Saturday or Sunday or Monday. Couldn't you come now and mull over the alterations which you are going to make in your MS, and make them after you go back? Wouldn't it assist the work if you dropped out of harness and routine for a day or two and have that sort of revivification which comes of a holiday—forgetfulness of the workshop? I can always work after I've been to your house, and if you will come to mine now and hear the club toot their various horns over the exasperating metaphysical question which I mean to lay before them in the disguise of a literary extravaganza, it would just brace you up like a cordial.

(I feel sort of mean trying to persuade a man to put down a critical piece of work at a critical time, but yet I am honest in thinking it would not hurt the work nor impair your interest in it to come under the circumstances.) Mrs. Clemens says, "Maybe the Howellses could come *Monday* if they cannot come Saturday. Ask them. It is worth trying." Well, how's that? *Could* you? It would be splendid if you could. Drop me a postal card—I should have a twinge of conscience if I forced you to write a letter (I am honest about that)—and if you find you can't make out to come, tell me that you bodies will come the *next* Saturday if the thing is possible, and stay over Sunday.

Yrs ever
Mark

Howells advised that Clemens delete "that swearing." "I suppose I didn't notice it because the locution was so familiar to my Western sense and so exactly the thing that Huck would say." Clemens changed "they comb me all to hell" to "they comb me all to thunder."

To Howells, Boston

Elmira, *Aug. 9, 1876*

My dear Howells,

I was just about to write you when your letter came—and not one of those obscene postal cards, either, but reverently, upon paper.

I shall read that biography though the letter of acceptance was amply sufficient to corral my vote without any further knowledge of the man. Which reminds me that a campaign club in Jersey City wrote a few days ago and invited me to be present at the raising of a Tilden and Hendricks flag there and to take the stand and give them some "counsel." Well, I could not go, but gave them counsel and advice by letter and in the kindliest terms as to the raising of the flag—advised them "not to raise it."

Get your book out quick, for this is a momentous time. If Tilden is elected I think the entire country will go pretty straight to Mrs. Howells's bad place.

I am infringing on your patent. I started a record of our children's sayings last night. Which reminds me that last week I sent down and got Susie a vast pair of shoes of a most villainous pattern, for I discovered that her feet were being twisted and cramped out of shape by a smaller and prettier article. She did not complain, but looked degraded and injured. At night her mamma gave her the usual admonition when she was about to say her prayers—to wit:

"Now, Susie, think about God."

"Mamma, I can't with those shoes."

The farm is perfectly delightful this season. It is as quiet and peaceful as a South Sea island. Some of the sunsets which we have witnessed from this commanding eminence were marvelous. One evening a rainbow spanned an entire range of hills with its mighty arch, and from a black hub resting upon the hilltop in the exact center, *black* rays diverged upward in perfect regularity to the rainbow's arch and created a very strongly defined and altogether the most majestic, magnificent and startling half-sunk wagon wheel you can imagine. After that a world of tumbling and prodigious clouds came drifting up out of the West and took to themselves a wonderfully rich and brilliant *green* color, the decided green of new spring foliage. Close by them we saw the intense blue of the skies through rents in the cloud-rack, and away off in another quarter were drifting clouds of a delicate pink color. In one place hung a pall of dense black clouds, like compacted pitch smoke. And the stupendous wagon wheel was still in the supremacy of its unspeakable grandeur. So you see, the colors present in the sky at one and the same time were blue, green, pink, black and the varicolored splendors of the rainbow. All strong and decided colors, too. I don't know whether this weird and astounding spectacle most suggested heaven or hell. The wonder, with its constant, stately and always surprising changes, lasted upwards of two hours, and we all stood on the top of the hill by my study till the final miracle was complete and the greatest day ended that we ever saw.

Our farmer, who is a grave man, watched that spectacle to the end and then observed that it was "damn funny."

The double-barreled novel lies torpid. I found I could not go on with it. The chapters I had written were still too new and familiar to me. I may take it up next winter but cannot tell yet. I waited and waited to see if my interest in it would not revive, but gave it up a month ago and began another boys' book—more to be at work than anything else. I have written 400 pages on it, therefore it is very nearly half done. It is Huck Finn's Autobiography. I like it only tolerably well, as far as I have got, and may possibly pigeonhole or burn the MS when it is done.

So the comedy is done, and with a "fair degree of satisfaction." That rejoices me and makes me mad too, for I can't plan a comedy, and what have you done that God should be so good to you? I have racked myself bald-headed trying to plan a comedy harness for some promising characters of mine to work in, and had to give it up. It is a noble lot of blooded stock and worth no end of money but they must stand in the stable and be profitless. I want to be present when the comedy is produced and help enjoy the success.

Warner's book is mighty readable, I think.

> Love to yez.
> Yrs ever
> Mark

"That biography" in the second paragraph of the preceding letter referred to one about Rutherford B. Hayes which Howells was writing as part of his involvement in the Hayes-Tilden presidential campaign. At this time Clemens still occasionally spelled his daughter Susy's name as Susie. "Huck Finn's Autobiography" would become *Huckleberry Finn*.

In the following, Burrough was an old friend who had roomed with Clemens when the latter had worked in the composing room of the *St. Louis Evening News*.

To Frank E. Burrough, St. Louis

Hartford, *Nov. 1 '76*

My dear Burrough,

As you describe me I can picture myself as I was 22 years ago. The portrait is correct. You think I have grown some. Upon my word there was room for it. You have described a callow fool, a self-sufficient ass, a mere human tumble-bug imagining that he is re-modeling the world and is entirely capable of doing it right. Ignorance, intolerance, egotism, self-assertion, opaque perception, dense and pitiful chuckle-headedness—and an almost pathetic unconsciousness of it all. That is what I was at 19 and 20 and that is what the average Southerner is at 60 today. Northerners too of a certain grade. It is of children like this that voters are made. And such is the primal source of our government! A man hardly knows whether to swear or cry over it.

I think I comprehend the position there—perfect freedom to vote just as you choose, provided you choose to vote as *other* people think—social ostracism otherwise. The same thing exists here among the Irish. An Irish Republican is a pariah among his people. Yet that race find fault with the same spirit in Know-Nothingism.

Fortunately a good deal of experience of men enabled me to choose my residence wisely. I live in the freest corner of the country. There are no social disabilities between me and my Democratic personal friends. We break the bread and eat the salt of hospitality freely together and never dream of such a thing as offering impertinent interference in each other's political opinions.

Don't you ever come to New York again and not run up here to see me. I suppose we were away for the summer when you were East, but no matter, you could have telegraphed and found out. We were at Elmira, N.Y. and right on your road and could have given you a good time if you had allowed us the chance.

Yes, Will Bowen and I have exchanged letters now and then for several years, but I suspect that I made him mad with my last— shortly after you saw him in St. Louis, I judge. There is one thing which I can't stand and *won't* stand, from many people. That is sham sentimentality, the kind a schoolgirl puts into her graduating composition, the sort that makes up the Original Poetry column of a country newspaper, the rot that deals in the "happy days of yore," the "sweet yet melancholy past," with its "blighted hopes" and its "vanished dreams"—and all that sort of drivel.

Will's were always of this stamp. I stood it for years. When I get a letter like that from a grown man and he a widower with a family, it gives me the stomach ache. And I just told Will Bowen so last summer. I told him to stop being 16 at 40, told him to stop drooling about the sweet yet melancholy past, and take a pill. I said there was but one solitary thing about the past worth remembering, and that was the fact that it *is* the past—can't be restored. Well, I exaggerated some of these truths a little, but only a little, but my idea was to kill his sham sentimentality once and forever and so make a good fellow of him again. I went to the unheard-of trouble of rewriting the letter and saying the same harsh things softly so as to sugarcoat the anguish and make it a little more endurable, and I asked him to write and thank me honestly for doing him the best and kindliest favor that any friend ever *had* done him—but he hasn't done it yet. Maybe he will sometime. I am grateful to God that I got that letter off before he was married (I get that news from you), else he would just have slobbered all over me and drowned me when that event happened.

I enclose a photograph for the young ladies. I will remark that I do not wear sealskin for grandeur but because I found, when I used to lecture in the winter, that nothing else was able to keep a man warm sometimes in these high latitudes. I wish you had sent pictures of yourself and family. I'll trade picture for picture with you straight through if you are commercially inclined.

Your old friend,
Saml L. Clemens

SIX

[1877-79]

A runaway horse — "Life has come to be a very serious matter with me" — on learning one's trade — Heidelberg — "I hate travel and I hate hotels and I hate the opera and I hate the Old Masters"

To W. D. Howells and wife, Boston

Elmira, *Aug. 25 '77*

My dear Howellses,

I thought I ought to make a sort of record of it for further reference. The pleasantest way to do that would be to write it to somebody. *But* that somebody would let it leak into print and that we wish to avoid. The Howellses would be safe, so let us tell the Howellses about it.

Day before yesterday was a fine summer day away up here on the summit. Aunt Marsh and Cousin May Marsh were here visiting Susie Crane and Livy at our farmhouse. By and by mother Langdon came up the hill in the "high carriage" with Nora the nurse and little Jervis (Charley Langdon's little boy), Timothy the coachman driving. Behind these came Charley's wife and little girl in the buggy, with the new, young, spry, gray horse, a high stepper. Theodore Crane arrived a little latter.

The Bay and Susy were on hand with their nurse, Rosa. I was on hand too. Susy Crane's trio of colored servants ditto, these being Josie, housemaid; Aunty Cord, cook, aged 62, turbaned, very tall, very broad, very fine every way (see her portrait in "A True Story Just as I Heard It" in my *Sketches*); Chocklate (the laundress) (as the Bay calls her—she can't say Charlotte) still taller, still more majestic of proportions, turbaned, very black, straight as an Indian—age 24. Then there was the farmer's wife (colored) and her little girl, Susy.

Wasn't it a good audience to get up an excitement before? Good excitable. inflammable material?

Lewis was still downtown, three miles away, with his two-horse wagon to get a load of manure. Lewis is the farmer (colored). He is of mighty frame and muscle, stocky, stooping, ungainly, has a good manly face and a clear eye. Age about 45—and the most picturesque of men when he sits in his fluttering work-day rags, humped forward into a bunch, with his aged slouch hat mashed down over his ears and neck. It is a spectacle to make the broken-hearted smile. Lewis has worked mighty hard and remained mighty poor. At the end of each whole year's toil he can't show a gain of fifty dollars. He had borrowed money of the Cranes till he owed them $700—and he being conscientious and honest, imagine what it was to him to have to carry this stubborn, helpless load year in and year out.

Well, sunset came, and Ida the young and comely (Charley Langdon's wife) and her little Julia and the nurse Nora drove out at the gate behind the new gray horse and started down the long hill, the high carriage receiving its load under the porte cochère. Ida was seen to turn her face toward us across the fence and intervening lawn. Theodore waved good-bye to her, for he did not know that her sign was a speechless appeal for help.

The next moment Livy said, "Ida's driving too fast down hill!" She followed it with a sort of scream, "Her horse is running away!"

We could see two hundred yards down that descent. The buggy seemed to fly. It would strike obstructions and apparently spring the height of a man from the ground.

Theodore and I left the shrieking crowd behind and ran down the hill bare-headed and shouting. A neighbor appeared at his gate—a tenth of a second too late!—the buggy vanished past him like a thought. My last glimpse showed it for one instant far down the descent, springing high in the air out of a cloud of dust, and then it disappeared. As I flew down the road my impulse was to shut my eyes as I turned them to the right or left, and so delay for a moment the ghastly spectacle of mutilation and death I was expecting.

I ran on and on, still spared this spectacle, but saying to myself: "I shall see it at the turn of the road. They never can pass that turn alive." When I came in sight of that turn I saw two wagons there bunched together, one of them full of people. I said, "Just so—they are staring petrified at the remains."

But when I got amongst that bunch, there sat Ida in her buggy and nobody hurt, not even the horse or the vehicle. Ida was pale but serene. As I came tearing down, she smiled back over her shoulder at me and said, "Well, we're *alive* yet, *aren't* we?" A miracle had been performed—nothing else.

You see, Lewis, the prodigious, humped upon his front seat, had been toiling up on his load of manure. He saw the frantic horse plunging down the hill toward him on a full gallop, throwing his heels as high as a man's head at every jump. So Lewis turned his team diagonally across the road just at the "turn," thus making a V with the fence. The running horse could not escape that, but must enter it. Then Lewis sprang to the ground and stood in this V. He gathered his vast strength, and with a perfect Creedmoor aim he seized the gray horse's bit as he plunged by and fetched him up standing!

It was down hill, mind you. Ten feet *further* down hill neither Lewis nor any other man could have saved them, for they would have been on the abrupt "turn" then. But how this miracle was ever accomplished at all by human strength, generalship and accuracy is clean beyond my comprehension and grows more so the more I go and examine the ground and try to believe it was actually done. I know one thing well. If Lewis had missed his aim he would have been killed on the spot in the trap he had made for himself, and we should have found the rest of the remains away down at the bottom of the steep ravine.

Ten minutes later Theodore and I arrived opposite the house, with the servants straggling after us, and shouted to the distracted group on the porch, "Everybody safe!"

Believe it? Why how *could* they? They knew the road perfectly. We might as well have said it to people who had seen their friends go over Niagara.

However, we convinced them. And then, instead of saying something or going on crying, they grew very still—words could not express it, I suppose.

Nobody could do anything that night, or sleep either, but there was a deal of moving talk, with long pauses between—pictures of that flying carriage, these pauses represented—this picture intruded itself all the time and disjointed the talk.

But yesterday evening late, when Lewis arrived from downtown he found his supper spread and some presents of books there, with very complimentary writings on the fly-leaves, and certain very complimentary letters, and more or less greenbacks of dignified denomination pinned to these letters and fly-leaves, and one said, among other things (signed by the Cranes), "We cancel $400 of your indebtedness to us," &c. &c.

(The end thereof is not yet, of course, for Charley Langdon is west and will arrive ignorant of all these things today.)

The supper room had been kept locked and imposingly secret and mysterious until Lewis should arrive, but around that part of the house were gathered Lewis's wife and child, Chocklate, Josie, Aunty Cord and our Rosa, canvassing things and waiting impatiently. They were all on hand when the curtain rose.

Now, Aunty Cord is a violent Methodist and Lewis an implacable Dunker-Baptist. Those two are inveterate religious disputants. The revealments having been made, Aunty Cord said with effusion,

"Now let folks go on saying there ain't no God! Lewis, the Lord sent you there to stop that horse."

Says Lewis,

"Then who sent the *horse* there in sich a shape?"

But I want to call your attention to one thing. When Lewis arrived the other evening after saving those lives by a feat which I think is the most marvelous of any I can call to mind—when he arrived, hunched up on his manure wagon and as grotesquely picturesque as usual, everybody wanted to go and see how he looked. They came back and said he was beautiful. It was so, too, and yet he would have *photographed* exactly as he would have done any day these past 7 years that he has occupied this farm.

Aug. 27

P. S. Our little romance in real life is happily and satisfactorily completed. Charley has come, listened, acted—and now John T. Lewis has ceased to consider himself as belonging to that class called "the poor."

It has been known during some years that it was Lewis's purpose to buy a thirty-dollar silver watch some day if he ever got where he could afford it. Today Ida has given him a new, sumptuous gold Swiss stem-winding stopwatch, and if any scoffer shall say, "Behold this thing is out of character," there is an inscription within which will silence him, for it will teach him that this wearer aggrandizes the watch, not the watch the wearer.

I was asked beforehand if this would be a wise gift, and I said, "Yes, the very wisest of all. I know the colored race, and I know that in Lewis's eyes this fine toy will throw the other more valuable testimonials far away into the shade. If he lived in England the Humane Society would give him a gold medal as costly as this watch, and nobody would say, "It is out of character." If Lewis chose to wear a town clock, who would become it better?

Lewis has sound common sense and is not going to be spoiled. The instant he found himself possessed of money, he forgot himself in a plan to make his old father comfortable, who is wretchedly poor and lives down in Maryland. His next act, on the spot, was the proffer to the Cranes of the $300 of his remaining indebtedness to them. This was put off by them to the indefinite future, for he is not going to be allowed to pay that at all, though he doesn't know it.

A letter of acknowledgment from Lewis contains a sentence which raises it to the dignity of literature:

"But I beg to say, humbly, that inasmuch as divine providence saw fit to use me as a instrument for the saving of those presshious lives, the honner conferd upon me was greater than the feat performed."

That is well said.

Yrs ever
Mark

Bay was a family nickname for Clara Clemens.

To an Entertainment Committee, Hartford

Nov. 9

E. S. Sykes, Esq:
Dr. Sir,

Mr. Burton's note puts upon me all the blame of the destruction of an enterprise which had for its object the succor of the Hartford poor. That is to say, this enterprise has been dropped because of the "dissatisfaction with Mr. Clemens's stipulations." Therefore I must be allowed to say a word in my defense.

There were two "stipulations"—exactly two. I made one of them. If the other was made at all, it was a joint one, from the choir *and* me.

My individual stipulation was that my name should be kept out of the newspapers. The joint one was that sufficient tickets to insure a good sum should be sold before the date of the performance should be set. (Understand, we wanted a good *sum*. I do not think any of us bothered about a good *house*. It was money we were after.)

Now, you perceive that my concern is simply with my individual stipulation. Did *that* break up the enterprise?

Eugene Burton said he would sell $300 worth of the tickets himself. Mr. Smith said he would sell $200 or $300 worth himself. My plan for Asylum Hill Church would have ensured $150 from that quarter. All this in the face of my "Stipulation." It was proposed to raise $1000. Did my stipulation render the raising of $400 or $500 in a dozen churches impossible?

My stipulation is easily defensible. When a mere reader or lecturer has appeared 3 or 4 times in a town of Hartford's size he is a good deal more than likely to get a very unpleasant snub if he shoves himself forward about once or twice more. Therefore I long ago made up my mind that whenever I again appeared here it should be only in a *minor* capacity and not as a chief attraction.

Now, I placed that harmless and very justifiable stipulation before the committee the other day. They carried it to headquarters and it was accepted there. I am not informed that any objection was made to it or that it was regarded as an offense. It seems late in the day now, after a good deal of trouble has been taken and a good deal of thankless work done by the committees, to suddenly tear up the contract and then turn and bowl *me* down from long range as being the destroyer of it.

If the enterprise has failed because of my individual stipulation, here you have my proper and reasonable reasons for making that stipulation.

If it has failed because of the *joint* stipulation, put the blame *there* and let us share it collectively.

I think our plan was a good one. I do not doubt that Mr. Burton still approves of it too. I believe the objections come from other quarters and not from him. Mr. Twichell used the following words in last Sunday's sermon (if I remember correctly):

"My hearers, the prophet Deuteronomy says this wise thing: 'Though ye plan a goodly house for the poor and plan it with wisdom and do take off your coats and set to to build it with high courage, yet shall the croaker presently come and lift up his voice (having his coat on) and say, Verily this plan is not well planned— and he will go his way. And the obstructionist will come and lift up his voice (having his coat on) and say, Behold, this is but a sick plan—and he will go his way. And the man that *knows* it all will come and lift up his voice (having his coat on) and say, Lo, call they *this* a plan?—then will he go *his* way. And the places which knew him once shall know him no more forever, because he was not, for God took him. Now therefore I say unto you, Verily that *house will not be builded*. And I say this also: He that waiteth for all men to be satisfied with his plan, let him seek eternal life, for he shall *need* it.' "

This portion of Mr. Twichell's sermon made a great impression upon me, and I was grieved that someone had not wakened me earlier so that I might have heard what went before.

Yrs truly
S. L. Clemens

Clemens had begun to feel the need to write another travel book. Having a trip to Germany in mind, he and his family began a diligent study of German. His mother was now living with Orion and Mollie in Iowa.

To Jane Clemens, Keokuk, Iowa

Hartford, *Feb. 17, 1878*

My dear Mother,

I suppose I am the worst correspondent in the whole world and yet I grow worse and worse all the time. My conscience blisters me for not writing you but it has ceased to abuse me for not writing other folks.

Life has come to be a very serious matter with me. I have a bad-gered, harassed feeling a good part of my time. It comes mainly of business responsibilities and annoyances, and the persecution of kindly letters from well meaning strangers to whom I must be rude-ly silent or else put in the biggest half of my time bothering over answers. There are other things also that help to consume my time and defeat my projects. Well, the consequence is I cannot write a book at home. This cuts my income down. Therefore I have about made up my mind to take my tribe and fly to some little corner of Europe and budge no more until I shall have completed one of the half-dozen books that lie begun, upstairs. Please say nothing about this at present.

We propose to sail the 11th of April. I shall go to Fredonia to meet you but it will not be well for Livy to make that trip, I am afraid. However, we shall see. I will hope she can go.

Mr. Twichell has just come in, so I must go to him. We are all well and send love to you all.

Affly
Sam

Orion, seized by a literary idea which he was exploring, sent his broth-er the manuscript for the latter's opinion. The "Journey in Heaven" men-tioned in the next letter was a story published many years later as "Cap-tain Stormfield's Visit to Heaven." The real-life model for Stormfield as well as for Captain Ned Blakeley of *Roughing It* and Captain Hurricane Jones of "Rambling Notes of an Idle Excursion" was a Captain Ned Wakeman of one of the Pacific steamships, whom Clemens encountered in 1868 on his trip to San Francisco.

To Orion Clemens, Keokuk

Hartford, *Mch. 23, 1878*

My dear Bro.,

Every man must *learn* his trade—not pick it up. God requires that he learn it by slow and painful processes. The apprentice hand in blacksmithing, in medicine, in literature, in everything, is a thing that can't be hidden. It always shows.

But happily there is a market for apprentice work, else the "Innocents Abroad" would have had no sale. Happily too there's a wider market for some sorts of apprentice literature than there is for the very best of journey-work. This work of yours is exceedingly crude but I am free to say it is less crude than I expected it to be and considerably better work than I believed you could do. It is too crude to offer to any prominent periodical, so I shall speak to the *N. Y. Weekly* people. To publish it there will be to bury it. Why could not some good genius have sent me to the *N. Y. Weekly* with my apprentice sketches?

You should not publish it in book form at all—for this reason: it is only an imitation of Verne—it is not a burlesque. But I think it may be regarded as proof that Verne cannot *be* burlesqued.

In accompanying notes I have suggested that you vastly modify the first visit to hell and leave out the second visit altogether. Nobody would or ought to print those things. You are not advanced enough in literature to venture upon a matter requiring so much practice. Let me show you what a man has got to go through.

Nine years ago I mapped out my "Journey in Heaven." I discussed it with literary friends whom I could trust to keep it to themselves.

I gave it a deal of thought from time to time. After a year or more I wrote it up. It was not a success. Five years ago I wrote it again, altering the plan. That MS is at my elbow now. It was a considerable improvement on the first attempt but still it wouldn't do. Last year and year before I talked frequently with Howells about the subject and he kept urging me to do it again.

So I thought and thought at odd moments, and at last I struck what I considered to be the right plan. Mind, I have never altered the *ideas*, from the first—the plan was the difficulty. When Howells was here last I laid before him the whole story without referring to my MS and he said, "You have got it sure this time. But drop the idea of making mere magazine stuff of it. Don't waste it. Print it by itself. Publish it first in England. Ask Dean Stanley to endorse it, which will draw some of the teeth of the religious press, and then reprint it in America." I doubt my ability to get Dean Stanley to do anything of the sort but I shall do the rest—and this is all a secret which you must not divulge.

Now look here—I have tried all these years to think of some way of "doing" hell too—and have always had to give it up. Hell in my book will not occupy five pages of MS, I judge. It will be only covert hints, I suppose, and quickly dropped. I may end by not even referring to it.

And mind you, in my opinion you will find that you can't write up hell so it will stand printing. Neither Howells nor I believe in hell or the divinity of the Savior but no matter, the Savior is none the less a sacred Personage, and a man should have no desire or disposition to refer to him lightly, profanely or otherwise than with the profoundest reverence.

The only safe thing is not to introduce him, or refer to him at all, I suspect. I have entirely rewritten one book 3 (perhaps 4) times, changing the plan every time—1200 pages of MS wasted and burned—and shall tackle it again one of these years and maybe succeed at last. Therefore you need not expect to get *your* book right the first time. Go to work and revamp or rewrite it. God only exhibits his thunder and lightning at intervals, and so they always command attention. These are God's adjectives. You thunder and lightning too much. The reader ceases to get under the bed, by and by.

Mr. Perkins will send you and Ma your checks when we are gone. But don't write him, ever, except a single line in case he forgets the checks, for the man is driven to death with work.

I see you are half promising yourself a monthly return for your book. In my experience, previously counted chickens never *do* hatch. How many of mine I have counted! and never a one of them but failed! It is much better to hedge disappointment by not counting. Unexpected money is a delight. The same sum is a bitterness when you expected more.

My time in America is growing mighty short. Perhaps we can manage in this way: Imprimis, if the *N. Y. Weekly* people know that you are my brother they will turn that fact into an advertisement, a thing of value to *them* but not to you and me. This must be prevented. I will write them a note to say you have a friend near Keokuk, *Charles S. Miller*, who has a MS for sale which you think is a pretty clever travesty on Verne, and if they want it they might write to him in your care. Then if any correspondence ensues between you and them, let Mollie write for you and sign your name, your own hand writing representing Miller's. Keep yourself out of sight till you make a strike on your own merits. There is no other way to get a fair verdict upon your merits.

Later—I've written the note to Smith, and with nothing in it which he can use as an advertisement. I'm called—Goodbye—love to you both.

We leave here next Wednesday for Elmira. We leave there Apl. 9 or 10, and sail 11th.

Yr Bro.

Sam

The Clemens entourage, which included Clara Spaulding and Rosa, a nurse-maid, sailed on the *Holsatia* on April 11, 1878. Just before departing, Clemens wrote to Howells, "And that reminds me, ungrateful dog that I am, that I owe as much to your training as the rude country job printer owes to the city boss who takes him in hand and teaches him the right way to handle his art. I was talking to Mrs. Clemens about this the other day, and grieving because I never mentioned it to you, thereby seeming to ignore it or to be unaware of it. Nothing that has passed under your eye needs any revision before going into a volume, while all my other stuff does need so *much*."

To Howells, Boston

Frankfort on the Main, *May 4, 1878*

My dear Howells,

I only propose to write a single line to say we are still around. Ah, I have such a deep, grateful, unutterable sense of being "out of it all." I think I foretaste some of the advantages of being dead. Some of the joy of it. I don't read any newspapers or care for them. When people tell me England has declared war, I drop the subject, feeling that it is none of my business. When they tell me Mrs. Tilton has confessed and Mr. B. denied, I say both of them have done that before, therefore let the worn stub of the Plymouth whitewash brush be brought out once more, and let the faithful spit on their hands and get to work again regardless of me, for I am out of it all.

We had 2 almost devilish weeks at sea (and I tell you Bayard

Taylor is a really lovable man, which you already knew), then we staid a week in the beautiful, the *very* beautiful city of Hamburg. And since then we have been fooling along, 4 hours per day by rail, with a courier, spending the other 20 in hotels whose enormous bed-chambers and private parlors are an overpowering marvel to me. Day before yesterday, in Cassel, we had a love of a bedroom 31 feet long, and a parlor with 2 sofas, 12 chairs, a writing desk and 4 tables scattered around here and there in it. Made of red silk, too, by George.

The times and times I wish you were along! *You* could throw some fun into the journey whereas I go on day by day in a smileless state of solemn admiration.

What a paradise this is! What clean clothes, what good faces, what tranquil contentment, what prosperity, what genuine freedom, what superb government. And I am so happy, for I am responsible for none of it. I am only here to enjoy. How charmed I am when I overhear a German word which I understand. With love from us 2 to you 2.

Mark

P. S. We are not taking six days to go from Hamburg to Heidel-berg because we prefer it. Quite on the contrary. Mrs. Clemens picked up a dreadful cold and sore throat on board ship and still keeps them in stock—so she could only travel 4 hours a day. She wanted to drive straight through but I had different notions about the wisdom of it. I found that 4 hours a day was the best she could do. Before I forget it, our permanent address is Care Messrs. Koester & Co., Bankers, Heidelberg. We go there tomorrow.

Poor Susy! From the day we reached German soil we have re-quired Rosa to speak German to the children, which they hate with all their souls. The other morning in Hanover, Susy came to us (from Rosa, in the nursery) and said in halting syllables, "Papa, wie viel uhr ist es?"—then turned with pathos in her big eyes and said, "Mamma, I wish Rosa was made in English."

Mr. B. is Henry Ward Beecher, famous preacher and platform lecturer of the day, brother of Harriet Beecher Stowe and pastor of the Plymouth (Congregational) Church in Brooklyn, New York. In 1874, Theodore Tilton accused Beecher of cuckolding him. This created the scandal referred to by C. Bayard Taylor, who sailed on the *Holsatia* with Clemens. Taylor was a man of letters who, among other achievements, translated Goethe's *Faust* (1870–71). He was appointed Minister to Germany in 1878. He died within months of taking up his duties in Berlin.

To Howells, Boston

Schloss Hotel, Heidelberg, *Sunday, a.m., May 26, 1878*

My dear Howells,

. . . divinely located. From this airy porch among the shining groves we look down upon Heidelberg Castle and upon the swift Neckar and the town and out over the wide green level of the Rhine valley—a marvelous prospect. We are in a cul-de-sac formed of hill ranges and river. We are on the side of a steep mountain. The river at our feet is walled, on its other side (yes, on both sides) by a steep and wooded mountain range which rises abruptly aloft from the water's edge. Portions of these mountains are densely wooded. The plain of the Rhine, seen through the mouth of this pocket, has many and peculiar charms for the eye.

Our bedroom has two great glass bird cages (enclosed balconies), one looking toward the Rhine valley and sunset, the other looking up the Neckar cul-de-sac, and naturally we spend nearly all our time in these. When one is sunny the other is shady. We have tables and chairs in them. We do our reading, writing, studying, smoking and suppering in them.

The view from these bird cages is my despair. The pictures change from one enchanting aspect to another in ceaseless procession, never keeping one form half an hour and never taking on an unlovely one.

And then Heidelberg on a dark night! It is massed, away down there, almost right under us, you know, and stretches off toward the valley. Its curved and interlacing streets are a cobweb beaded thick with lights, a wonderful thing to see. Then the rows of lights on the arched bridges and their glinting reflections in the water. And away at the far end, the Eisenbahnhof, with its twenty solid acres of glittering gas jets, a huge garden, as one may say, whose every plant is a flame.

These balconies are the darlingest things. I have spent all the morning in this north one. Counting big and little, it has 256 panes of glass in it, so one is in effect right out in the free sunshine and yet sheltered from wind and rain—and likewise doored and curtained from whatever may be going on in the bedroom. It must have been a noble genius who devised this hotel. Lord, how blessed is the repose, the tranquility of this place! Only two sounds: the happy clamor of the birds in the groves, and the muffled music of the Neckar, tumbling over the opposing dykes. It is no hardship to lie awake awhile nights, for this subdued roar has exactly the sound of a steady rain beating upon a roof. It is so healing to the spirit, and it bears up the thread of one's imaginings as the accompaniment bears up a song.

While Livy and Miss Spaulding have been writing at this table, I have sat tilted back near by with a pipe and the last *Atlantic* and read Charley Warner's article with prodigious enjoyment. I think it is exquisite. I think it must be the roundest and broadest and completest short essay he has ever written. It is clear and compact and charmingly done.

The hotel grounds join and communicate with the Castle grounds, so we and the children loaf in the winding paths of those leafy vastnesses a great deal, and drink beer and listen to excellent music.

When we first came to this hotel a couple of weeks ago, I pointed to a house across the river and said I meant to rent the center room on the 3d floor for a workroom. Jokingly we got to speaking of it as my office and amused ourselves with watching "my people" daily in their small grounds and trying to make out what we could of their dress, &c., without a glass. Well, I loafed along there one day and found on that house the only sign of the kind on that side of the river: "Moblirte Wohnung zu Vermiethen!" I went in and rented that very room which I had long ago selected. There was only one other room in the whole double house unrented.

(It occurs to me that I made a great mistake in not thinking to deliver a very bad German speech, every other sentence pieced out with English, at the Bayard Taylor banquet in New York. I think I could have made it one of the features of the occasion.)*

* He used this plan at a gathering of the American students in Heidelberg on July 4th with great effect, so his idea was not wasted.—A.B.P.

We left Hartford before the end of March and I have been idle ever since. I have waited for a call to go to work. I knew it would come. Well, it began to come a week ago. My notebook comes out more and more frequently every day since; 3 days ago I concluded to move my manuscript over to my den. *Now* the call is loud and decided at last. So tomorrow I shall begin regular, steady work and stick to it till middle of July or 1st August, when I look for Twichell. We will then walk about Germany 2 or 3 weeks, and then I'll go to work again (perhaps in Munich).

We both send a power of love to the Howellses, and we do wish you were here. Are you in the new house? Tell us about it.

Yrs Ever
Mark

Clemens had invited Twichell to tramp in Europe with him as his guest. His motives were both personal (he greatly enjoyed Twichell's company) and professional (he was certain his European sojourn, which would hopefully result in a book, would be made more rich and vivid by Twichell's presence). Twichell, still in Hartford, wrote to Clemens, "Oh, my! Do you realize, Mark, what a symposium it is to be? I do. To begin with, I am thoroughly tired, and the rest will be worth everything. To walk with you and talk with you for weeks together—why, it's my dream of luxury." Twichell joined Clemens on August 1st and the two promptly set out on their adventure.

Twichell's letters to home contain interesting vignettes of Clemens. "Mark is a queer fellow. There is nothing he so delights in as a swift, strong stream. You can hardly get him to leave one when once he is within the influence of its fascinations." "When I got back to the path, Mark was running downstream after it [a piece of driftwood] as hard as he could go, throwing up his hands and shouting in the wildest ecstasy, and when a piece went over a fall and emerged to view in the foam below, he would jump up and down and yell. He said afterward that he had not been so excited in three months."

"When we are driving, his concern is all about the horse. He can't bear to see the whip used or to see a horse pull hard." "Mark today was immensely absorbed in flowers. He scrambled around and gathered a great variety, and manifested the intensest pleasure in them. He crowded a pocket of his notebook with his specimens, and wanted more room."

The two friends separated in Geneva. Twichell headed for home via England, and Clemens rejoined his family.

To Twichell

[No date]

Dear old Joe,

It is actually all over! I was so low-spirited at the station yesterday, and this morning when I woke I couldn't seem to accept the dismal truth that you were really gone, and the pleasant tramping and talking at an end. Ah, my boy! it has been such a rich holiday to me, and I feel under such deep and honest obligations to you for coming. I am putting out of my mind all memory of the times when I misbehaved toward you and hurt you. I am resolved to consider it forgiven, and to store up and remember only the charming hours of the journeys and the times when I was not unworthy to be with you and share a companionship which to me stands first after Livy's. It is justifiable to do this, for why should I let my small infirmities of disposition live and grovel among my mental pictures of the eternal sublimities of the Alps?

Livy can't accept or endure the fact that you are gone. But you *are,* and we cannot get around it. So take our love with you and bear it also over the sea to Harmony, and God bless you both.

Mark

The Clemens party journeyed from Switzerland to Italy and then to Munich, where they prepared to spend the winter.

To Howells, Boston

Munich, *Jan. 30 1879*

My dear Howells,

. . . I wish I *could* give those sharp satires on European life which you mention, but of course a man can't write successful satire except he be in a calm, judicial good humor, whereas I *hate* travel and I *hate* hotels and I *hate* the opera and I *hate* the Old Masters. In truth I don't ever seem to be in a good enough humor with anything to *satirize* it. No, I want to stand up before it and *curse* it and foam at the mouth, or take a club and pound it to rags and pulp. I have got in two or three chapters about Wagner's operas, and managed to do it without showing temper, but the strain of another such effort would burst me.

SEVEN

[1879–80]

Brother Orion — "You must *put him in a book or a play right away" — the Gen. Grant reunion — "I guess this was the memorable night of my life" — of cats and other domestic matters*

"In one form or another," Paine has written, "Orion is ever present [in Clemens's life] . . . Mark Twain loved him, pitied him—also enjoyed him, especially with Howells." Orion sent his brother his new plan to lecture on behalf of religion.

To Howells, Boston

Munich, *Feb 9. [1879]*

My dear Howells,

I have just received this letter from Orion. Take care of it, for it is worth preserving. I got as far as 9 pages in my answer to it, when Mrs. Clemens shut down on it and said it was cruel and made me send the money and simply wish his lecture success. I said I couldn't lose my 9 pages, so she said send them to you. But I will acknowledge that I thought I was writing a very kind letter.

Now just look at this letter of Orion's. Did you ever see the grotesquely absurd and the heart-breakingly pathetic more closely joined together? Mrs. Clemens said, "Raise his monthly pension." So I wrote to Perkins to raise it a trifle.

Now only think of it! He still has 100 pages to write on his lecture, yet in one inking of his pen he has already swooped around the United States and invested the result!

You *must* put him in a book or a play right away. You are the only man capable of doing it. You might die at any moment, and your very greatest work would be lost to the world. *I* could write

Orion's simple biography, and make it effective, too, by merely stating the bald facts—and this I will do if he dies before I do. But *you* must put him into romance. This was the understanding you and I had the day I sailed.

Observe Orion's career—that is, a *little* of it: (1) He has belonged to as many as five different religious denominations. Last March he withdrew from the deaconship in a Congregational Church and the Superintendency of its Sunday School, in a speech in which he said that for many months (it runs in my mind that he said 13 years) he had been a confirmed *infidel* and so felt it to be his duty to retire from the flock.

2. After being a republican for years, he wanted me to buy him a democratic newspaper. A few days before the Presidential election, he came out in a speech and publicly went over to the democrats. He prudently "hedged" by voting for 6 state republicans also.

The new convert was made one of the secretaries of the democratic meeting and placed in the list of speakers. He wrote me jubilantly of what a ten-strike he was going to make with that speech. All right—but think of his innocent and pathetic candor in writing me something like this, a week later:

"I was more diffident than I had expected to be, and this was increased by the silence with which I was received when I came forward, so I seemed unable to get the fire into my speech which I had calculated upon, and presently they began to get up and go out, and in a few minutes they all rose up and went away."

How *could* a man uncover such a sore as that and show it to another? Not a word of complaint, you see—only a patient, sad surprise.

3. His next project was to write a burlesque upon *Paradise Lost*.

4. Then, learning that the *Times* was paying Harte $100 a column for stories, he concluded to write some for the same price. I read his first one and persuaded him not to write any more.

5. Then he read proof on the *N. Y. Eve. Post* at $10 a week and meekly observed that the foreman swore at him and ordered him around "like a steamboat mate."

6. Being discharged from that post, he wanted to try agriculture—was sure he could make a fortune out of a chicken farm. I gave him $900 and he went to a ten-house village 2 miles above Keokuk on

the river bank. This place was a railway station. He soon asked for money to buy a horse and light wagon, because the trains did not run at church time on Sunday and his wife found it rather far to walk.

For a long time I answered demands for "loans" and by next mail always received his check for the interest due me to date. In the most guileless way he let it leak out that he did not underestimate the value of his custom to me, since it was not likely that any other customer of mine paid his interest *quarterly*, and this enabled me to use my capital twice in 6 months instead of only once. But alas, when the debt at least reached $1800 or $2500 (I have forgotten which) the interest ate too formidably into his borrowings and so he quietly ceased to pay it or speak of it. At the end of two years I found that the chicken farm had long ago been abandoned, and he had moved into Keokuk. Later, in one of his casual moments, he observed that there was no money in fattening a chicken on 65 cents worth of corn and then selling it for 50.

7. Finally, if I would lend him $500 a year for two years (this was 4 or 5 years ago) he *knew* he could make a success as a lawyer, and would prove it. This is the pension which we have just increased to $600. The first year his legal business brought him $5. It also brought him an unremunerative case where some villains were trying to chouse some negro orphans out of $700. He still has this case. He has waggled it around through various courts and made some booming speeches on it. The negro children have grown up and married off, now, I believe, and their litigated town lot has been dug up and carted off by somebody, but Orion still infests the courts with his documents and makes the welkin ring with his venerable case. The second year he didn't make anything. The third he made $6, and I made Bliss put a case in his hands—about half an hour's work. Orion charged $50 for it. Bliss paid him $15. Thus four or five years of lawing has brought him $26, but this will doubtless be increased when he gets done lecturing and buys that "law library." Meantime his office rent has been $60 a year, and he has stuck to that lair day by day as patiently as a spider.

8. Then he by and by conceived the idea of lecturing around America as "Mark Twain's Brother"—that to be on the bills. Subject of proposed lecture, "On the Formation of Character."

9. I protested, and he got on his warpaint, couched his lance, and ran a bold tilt against total abstinence and the Red Ribbon fanatics. It raised a fine row among the virtuous Keokukians.

10. I wrote to encourage him in his good work but I had let a mail intervene, so by the time my letter reached him he was already winning laurels as a Red Ribbon Howler.

11. Afterward he took a rabid part in a prayer meeting epidemic; dropped that to travesty Jules Verne; dropped that in the middle of the last chapter last March to digest the matter of an infidel book which he proposed to write; and now he comes to the surface to rescue our "noble and beautiful religion" from the sacrilegious talons of Bob Ingersoll.

Now come! Don't fool away this treasure which Providence has laid at your feet, but take it up and use it. One can let his imagination run riot in portraying Orion, for there is nothing so extravagant as to be out of character with him.

Well—goodbye, and a short life and a merry one be yours. Poor old Methusaleh, how did he manage to stand it so long?

Yrs ever,
Mark

Perkins was Charles E. Perkins, a lawyer. Bliss was Frank Bliss of the American Publishing Company. Bob Ingersoll was Robert G. Ingersoll, orator, lawyer and "the great agnostic" of his time.

To Orion Clemens
[Unsent and enclosed with the foregoing to Howells]

Munich, *Feb. 9 [1879]*

My dear Bro.,

Yours has just arrived. I enclose a draft on Hartford for $25. You will have abandoned the project you wanted it for by the time it arrives but no matter, apply it to your newer and present project, whatever it is. You see I have an ineradicable faith in your unsteadfastness—but mind you, I didn't invent that faith, you conferred it on me yourself. But fire away, fire away! I don't see why a changeable man shouldn't get as much enjoyment out of his changes and transformations and transfigurations as a steadfast man gets out of standing still and pegging at the same old monotonous thing all the time. That is to say, I don't see why a kaleidoscope shouldn't enjoy itself as much as a telescope, nor a grindstone have as good a time as a whetstone, nor a barometer as good a time as a yardstick.

I don't feel like girding at you any more about fickleness of purpose, because I recognize and realize at last that it is incurable. But before I learned to accept this truth, each new weekly project of yours possessed the power of throwing me into the most exhausting and helpless convulsions of profanity. But fire away now! Your magic has lost its might. I am able to view your inspirations dispassionately and judicially and say, "This one or that one or the other one is not up to your average flight, or is above it or below it."

And so, without passion or prejudice or bias of any kind, I sit in judgment upon your lecture project and say it was up to your average. It was indeed above it, for it had possibilities in it and even *practical* ones. While I was not sorry you abandoned it, I should not be sorry if you had stuck to it and given it a trial. But on the whole you did the wise thing to lay it aside, I think, because a lecture is a most easy thing to fail in, and at your time of life and in your own town such a failure would make a deep and cruel wound in your heart and in your pride.

It was decidedly unwise in you to think for a moment of coming before a community who knew you, with such a course of lectures, because Keokuk is not unaware that you have been a Swedenborgian, a Presbyterian, a Congregationalist and a Methodist (on probation) and that just a year ago you were an infidel. If Keokuk had gone to your lecture course it would have gone to be amused, not instructed, for when a man is known to have no settled convictions of his own he can't convince other people. They would have gone to be amused and that would have been a deep humiliation to you. It could have been safe for you to appear only where you were unknown. Then many of your hearers would think you were in earnest. And they would be right.

You *are* in earnest while your convictions are new. But taking it by and large, you probably did best to discard that project altogether. But I leave you to judge of that, for you are the worst judge I know of.

Clemens returned to the United States on September 3, 1879, after an absence of seventeen months. A reporter for a New York paper noted that he looked older than when he had sailed for Germany and that his hair had become quite gray. Clemens settled down at Quarry Farm to resume work on the new travel book. Not hearing from Howells, he wrote to him, asking if he was dead or only asleep. Howells replied that he had been sleeping "the sleep of a torpid conscience. . . . When and where shall we meet? Have you come home with your pockets full of *Atlantic* papers?"

To Howells, Boston

Elmira, *Sept. 15, 1879*

My dear Howells,

When and where? Here on the farm would be an elegant place to meet but of course you cannot come so far. So we will say Hartford or Belmont about the beginning of November. The date of our return to Hartford is uncertain but will be three or four weeks hence, I judge. I hope to finish my book here before migrating.

I think maybe I've got some *Atlantic* stuff in my head but there's none in MS, I believe.

Say—a friend of mine wants to write a play with me, I to furnish the broad comedy cuss. I don't know anything about his ability but his letter serves to remind me of *our* old projects. If you haven't used Orion or Old Wakeman, don't you think you and I can get together and grind out a play with one of those fellows in it? Orion is a field which grows richer and richer the more he mulches it with each new topdressing of religion or other guano. Drop me an immediate line about this, won't you? I imagine I see Orion on the stage, always gentle, always melancholy, always changing his politics and religion, and trying to reform the world, always inventing something, and losing a limb by a new kind of explosion at the end of each of the four acts. Poor old chap, he is good material. I can imagine his wife or his sweetheart reluctantly adopting each of his new religions in turn, just in time to see him waltz into the next one and leave her isolated once more.

(*Mem.* Orion's wife *has* followed him into the outer darkness after 30 years' rabid membership in the Presbyterian Church.)

Well, with the sincerest and most abounding love to you and yours, from all this family, I am,

Yrs ever
Mark

To Howells, Boston

Elmira, *Oct. 9 '79*

My dear Howells,

Since my return the mail facilities have enabled Orion to keep me informed as to his intentions. Twenty-eight days ago it was his purpose to complete a work aimed at religion, the preface to which he had already written. Afterward he began to sell off his furniture with the idea of hurrying to Leadville and tackling silver mining— threw up his law den and took in his sign. Then he wrote to Chicago and St. Louis newspapers asking for a situation as "paragrapher," enclosing a taste of his quality in the shape of two stanzas of "humorous rhymes." By a later mail on the same day he applied to New York and Hartford insurance companies for copying to do.

However, it would take too long to detail all his projects. They comprise a removal to southwest Missouri; application for a reporter's berth on a Keokuk paper; application for a compositor's berth on a St. Louis paper; a re-hanging of his attorney's sign, "though it only creaks and catches no flies;" but last night's letter informs me that he has retackled the religious question, hired a distant den to write in, applied to my mother for $50 to rebuy his furniture, which has advanced in value since the sale—purposes buying $25 worth of books necessary to his labors which he had previously been borrowing, and his first chapter is already on its way to me for my decision as to whether it has enough ungodliness in it or not. Poor Orion!

Your letter struck me while I was meditating a project to beguile you and John Hay and Joe Twichell into a descent upon Chicago which I dream of making to witness the reunion of the great Commanders of the Western Army Corps on the 9th of next month. My sluggish soul needs a fierce upstirring and if it would not get it when Grant enters the meeting place I must doubtless "lay" for the final resurrection. Can you and Hay go? At the same time, confound it, I doubt if I can go myself, for this book isn't done yet. But I would give a heap to be there. I mean to heave some holiness into the Hartford primaries when I go back, and if there was a solitary office in the land which majestic ignorance and incapacity, coupled with purity of heart, could fill, I would run for it. This naturally reminds me of Bret Harte—but let him pass.

We propose to leave here for New York Oct. 21, reaching Hartford 24th or 25th. If upon reflection you Howellses find you *can* stop over here on your way, I wish you would do it and telegraph me. Getting pretty hungry to see you. I had an idea that this was your shortest way home but like as not my geography is crippled again— it usually is.

Yrs ever
Mark

John Hay was a U.S. author, lawyer and diplomat. The "reunion of the great Commanders" was to be a very special welcome to General Ulysses S. Grant after his triumphal journey around the world.

To Livy Clemens, Hartford

Palmer House, Chicago, *Nov. 11*

Livy darling, I am getting a trifle leg weary. Dr. Jackson called and dragged me out of bed at noon yesterday and then went off. I went down stairs and was introduced to some scores of people, and among them an elderly German gentleman named Raster, who said his wife owed her life to me—hurt in Chicago fire and lay menaced with death a long time, but the *Innocents Abroad* kept her mind in a cheerful attitude and so, with the doctor's help for the body, she pulled through.... They drove me to Dr. Jackson's and I had an hour's visit with Mrs. Jackson. Started to walk down Michigan Avenue, got a few steps on my way and met an erect, soldierly looking young gentleman who offered his hand, said "Mr. Clemens, I believe. I wish to introduce myself. You were pointed out to me yesterday as I was driving down street. My name is Grant."

"Col. Fred Grant?"

"Yes. My house is not ten steps away, and I would like you to come and have a talk and a pipe and let me introduce my wife."

So we turned back and entered the house next to Jackson's and talked something more than an hour and smoked many pipes and had a sociable good time. His wife is very gentle and intelligent and pretty, and they have a cunning little girl nearly as big as Bay but only three years old. They wanted me to come in and spend an evening, after the banquet, with them and Gen. Grant, after this grand pow-wow is over but I said I was going home Friday. Then they asked me to come Friday afternoon, when they and the general will receive a few friends, and I said I would. Col. Grant said he and Gen. Sherman used the *Innocents Abroad* as their guide book when they were on their travels.

I stepped in next door and took Dr. Jackson to the hotel and we played billiards from 7 to 11:30 P.M. and then went to a beermill to meet some twenty Chicago journalists—talked, sang songs and made speeches till 6 o'clock this morning. Nobody got in the least degree "under the influence," and we had a pleasant time. Read awhile in bed, slept till 11, shaved, went to breakfast at noon, and by mistake got into the servants' hall. I remained there and breakfasted with twenty or thirty male and female servants though I had a table to myself.

A temporary structure, clothed and canopied with flags, has been erected at the hotel front and connected with the secondstory windows of a drawing-room. It was for Gen. Grant to stand on and review the procession. Sixteen persons, besides reporters, had tickets for this place, and a seventeenth was issued for me. I was there, looking down on the packed and struggling crowd, when Gen. Grant came forward and was saluted by the cheers of the multitude and the waving of ladies' handkerchiefs—for the windows and roofs of all neighboring buildings were massed full of life. Gen. Grant bowed to the people two or three times, then approached my side of the platform, and the mayor pulled me forward and introduced me. It was dreadfully conspicuous. The General said a word or so. I replied and then said, "But I'll step back, General, I don't want to interrupt your speech."

"But I'm not going to make any. Stay where you are. I'll get you to make it for me."

General Sherman came on the platform wearing the uniform of a full general, and you should have heard the cheers. Gen. Logan was going to introduce me but I didn't want any more conspicuousness.

When the head of the procession passed it was grand to see Sheridan, in his military cloak and his plumed chapeau, sitting as erect and rigid as a statue on his immense black horse—by far the most martial figure I ever saw. And the crowd roared again.

It was chilly, and Gen. Deems lent me his overcoat until night. He came a few minutes ago, 5:45 P.M., and got it but brought Gen. Willard, who lent me his for the rest of my stay and will get another for himself when he goes home to dinner. Mine is much too heavy for this warm weather.

I have a seat on the stage at Haverley's Theatre tonight, where the Army of the Tennessee will receive Gen. Grant and where Gen. Sherman will make a speech. At midnight I am to attend a meeting of the Owl Club.

I love you ever so much, my darling, and am hoping to get a word from you *yet*.

Saml

Dr. Jackson was Dr. A. Reeves Jackson, the guide-teasing "Doctor" of *The Innocents Abroad*. Fred Grant was Ulysses S. Grant's son.

To Livy, Hartford

Chicago, *Nov. 12*, '79

Livy darling, it was a great time. There were perhaps thirty people on the stage of the theatre, and I think I never sat elbow-to-elbow with so many historic names before. Grant, Sherman, Sheridan, Schofield, Pope, Logan, Augur, and so on. What an iron man Grant is! He sat facing the house, with his right leg crossed over his left and his right boot sole tilted up at an angle, and his left hand and arm reposing on the arm of his chair—you note that position?

Well, when glowing references were made to other grandees on the stage, those grandees always showed a trifle of nervous consciousness, and as these references came frequently, the nervous change of position and attitude were also frequent. But Grant!—*he* was under a tremendous and ceaseless bombardment of praise and gratulation, but as true as I'm sitting here he never moved a muscle of his body for a single instant, during 30 minutes! You could have played him on a stranger for an effigy. Perhaps he never *would* have moved, but at last a speaker made such a particularly ripping and blood-stirring remark about him that the audience rose and roared and yelled and stamped and clapped an entire minute— Grant sitting as serene as ever—when Gen. Sherman stepped to him, laid his hand affectionately on his shoulder, bent respectfully down and whispered in his ear.

Gen. Grant got up and bowed, and the storm of applause swelled into a hurricane. He sat down, took about the same position and froze to it till by and by there was another of those deafening and protracted roars, when Sherman made him get up and bow again. He broke up his attitude once more—the extent of something more than a hair's breadth—to indicate me to Sherman when the house was keeping up a determined and persistent call for me, and poor bewildered Sherman (who did not know me), was peering abroad over the packed audience for me, not knowing I was only three feet from him and most conspicuously located. (Gen. Sherman was Chairman.)

One of the most illustrious individuals on that stage was "Ole Abe," the historic war eagle. He stood on his perch, the old savage-eyed rascal, three or four feet behind Gen. Sherman, and as he had been in nearly every battle that was mentioned by the orators his soul was probably stirred pretty often, though he was too proud of let on.

Read Logan's bosh, and try to imagine a burly and magnificent Indian in general's uniform striking a heroic attitude and getting that stuff off in the style of a declaiming schoolboy.

Please put the enclosed scraps in the drawer and I will scrapbook them.

I only staid at the Owl Club till 3 this morning and drank little or nothing. Went to sleep without whisky. Ich liebe dich.

                                                                        Saml

On the same day, Clemens wrote to Howells, "Imagine what it was like to see a bullet-shredded old battle flag reverently unfolded to the gaze of a thousand middle-aged soldiers, most of whom hadn't seen it since they saw it advancing over victorious fields when they were in their prime. And imagine what it was like when Grant, their first commander, stepped into view while they were still going mad over the flag, and then right in the midst of it all somebody struck up, 'When we were marching through Georgia.' Well, you should have heard the thousand voices lift that chorus and seen the tears stream down. If I live a hundred years I shan't ever forget these things, nor be able to talk about them. . . . Grand times, my boy, grand times!"

To Livy, Hartford

Chicago, *Nov. 14 '79*

A little after 5 in the *morning.*

I've just come to my room, Livy darling. I guess this was the memorable night of my life. By George, I never was so stirred since I was born. I heard four speeches which I can never forget. One by Emory Storrs, one by Gen. Vilas (O, wasn't it wonderful!), one by Gen. Logan (mighty stirring), one by somebody whose name escapes me, and one by that splendid old soul, Col. Bob Ingersoll—oh, it was just the supremest combination of English words that was ever put together since the world began. My soul, how handsome he looked as he stood on that table in the midst of those 500 shouting men and poured the molten silver from his lips! Lord, what an organ is human speech when it is played by a master! All these speeches may look dull in print, but how the lightning glared around them when they were uttered, and how the crowd roared in response!

It was a great night, a memorable night. I am so richly repaid for my journey, and how I did wish with all my whole heart that you were there to be lifted into the very seventh heaven of enthusiasm, as I was. The army songs, the military music, the crashing applause—Lord bless me, it was unspeakable.

Out of compliment they placed me last in the list—No. 15. I was to "hold the crowd." And bless my life I was in awful terror when No. 14 rose at 2 o'clock this morning and killed *all* the enthusiasm by delivering the flattest, insipidest, silliest of all responses to "Woman" that ever a weary multitude listened to. Then Gen. Sherman (chairman) announced my toast, and the crowd gave me a good round of applause as I mounted on top of the dinner table, but it was only on account of my name, nothing more—they were all tired and wretched. They let my first sentence go in silence, till I paused and added "we stand on common ground." Then they burst forth like a hurricane and I saw that I *had* them! From that time on I stopped at the end of each sentence and let the tornado of applause and laughter sweep around me, and when I closed with, "And if the child is but the prophecy of the man, there are mighty few who will doubt that he succeeded," I say it who oughtn't to say it, the house came down with a crash. For two hours and a half now I've been shaking hands and listening to congratulations. Gen. Sherman said, "Lord bless you, my boy, I don't know how you do it—it's a secret that's beyond me—but it was great—give me your hand again."

And do you know, Gen. Grant sat through fourteen speeches like a graven image but I fetched him! I broke him up utterly! He told me he laughed till the tears came and every bone in his body ached. (And do you know, the biggest part of the success of the speech lay in the fact that the audience *saw* that for once in his life he had been knocked out of his iron serenity.)

Bless your soul, 'twas immense. I never was so proud in my life. Lots and lots of people—hundreds I might say—told me my speech was the triumph of the evening—which was a lie. Ladies, Tom, Dick and Harry—even the policemen—captured me in the halls and shook hands, and scores of army officers said, "We shall always be grateful to you for coming." General Pope came to hunt me up. I was afraid to speak to him on that theatre stage last night, thinking it might be presumptuous to tackle a man so high up in military history. Gen. Schofield and other historic men paid their compliments. Sheridan was ill and could not come but I'm to go with a general of his staff and see him before I go to Col. Grant's. Gen. Augur—well, I've talked with them *all*, received invitations from them all—from people living everywhere—and as I said before, it's a memorable night. I wouldn't have missed it for anything in the world.

But my sakes, you should have heard Ingersoll's speech on that table! Half an hour ago he ran across me in the crowded halls and put his arms about me and said "Mark, if I live a hundred years I'll always be grateful for your speech. Lord, what a supreme thing it was." But I told him it wasn't any use to talk, *he* had walked off with the honors of that occasion by something of a majority. Bully boy is Ingersoll—traveled with him in the cars the other day and you can make up your mind we had a good time.

Of *course* I forgot to go and pay for my hotel car and so secure it but the army officers told me an hour ago to rest easy, they would go at once at this unholy hour of the night and compel the railways to do their duty by me, and said, "You don't need to *request* the Army of the Tennessee to do your desires. You can *command* its services."

Well, I bummed around that banquet hall from 8 in the evening till 2 in the morning, talking with people and listening to speeches, and I never ate a single bite or took a sup of anything but icewater, so if I seem excited now it is the intoxication of supreme enthusiasm. By George, it was a grand night, a historical night.

And now it is a quarter past 6 A.M.—so goodbye and God bless you and the Bays,° my darlings.

Saml

Show it to Joe if you want to. I saw some of his friends here.

A Tramp Abroad, Clemens's new travel book, gave him a great deal more trouble than he had expected. He completed it early in January 1880, when he was in his forty-fifth year. It was around this time that he first began to hint to Orion about a great financial venture, his investment in the Paige typesetting machine, which he expected to make him a multimillionaire, and which in the course of the next ten or twelve years almost ruined him financially.

To Howells, Belmont, Mass.

Thursday, *June 6th, 1880*

My dear Howells,

There you stick, at Belmont, and now I'm going to Washington

° Family word for babies.

for a few days, and of course between you and Providence that visit is going to get mixed and you'll have been here and gone again just about the time I get back. Bother it all, I wanted to astonish you with a chapter or two from Orion's latest book—not the seventeen which he has begun in the last four months but the one which he began last week.

Last night when I went to bed Mrs. Clemens said, "George didn't take the cat down to the cellar. Rosa says he has left it shut up in the conservatory." So I went down to attend to Abner (the cat). About 3 in the morning Mrs. C. woke me and said, "I do believe I hear that cat in the drawing room. What did you do with him?" I answered up with the confidence of a man who has managed to do the right thing for once, and said, "I opened the conservatory doors, took the library off the alarm, and spread everything open so that there wasn't any obstruction between him and the cellar."

Language wasn't capable of conveying this woman's disgust. But the sense of what she said was, "He couldn't have done any harm in the conservatory, so you must go and make the entire house free to him and the burglars, imagining that he will prefer the coalbins to the drawing room. If you had had Mr. Howells to help you I should have admired but not been astonished, because I should know that *together* you would be equal to it, but how you managed to contrive such a stately blunder all by yourself is what I cannot understand."

So, you see, even *she* knows how to appreciate our gifts.

Brisk times here. Saturday, these things happened: Our neighbor Chas. Smith was stricken with heart disease and came near joining the majority. My publisher, Bliss, ditto, ditto. A neighbor's child died. Neighbor Whitmore's sixth child added to his five other cases of measles. Neighbor Niles sent for, and responded. Susie Warner down, abed. Mrs. George Warner threatened with death during several hours. Her son Frank, whilst imitating the marvels in Barnum's circus bills, thrown from his aged horse and brought home insensible. Warner's friend Max Yortzburg shot in the back by a locomotive and broken into 32 distinct pieces and his life threatened. And Mrs. Clemens, after writing all these cheerful things to Clara Spaulding, taken at midnight, and if the doctor had not been pretty prompt, the contemplated Clemens would have called before his apartments were ready.

However, everybody is all right now except Yortzburg, and he is mending—that is, he is *being* mended. I knocked off during these stirring times and don't intend to go to work again till we go away for the summer 3 or 6 weeks hence. So I am writing to you not because I have anything to say but because you don't have to answer and I need something to do this afternoon. . . .

I have a letter from a Congressman this morning and he says Congress couldn't be persuaded to bother about Canadian pirates at a time like this when *all* legislation must have a political and Presidential bearing, else Congress won't look at it. So have changed my mind and my course. I go north to kill a pirate. I must procure repose *some* way, else I cannot get down to work again.

Pray offer my most sincere and respectful approval to the President. Is approval the proper word? I find it is the one I most value here in the household and seldomest get.

With our affection to you both.

Yrs ever
Mark

Paine wrote with reference to the following letter, "It was always dangerous to send strangers with letters of introduction to Mark Twain. They were so apt to arrive at the wrong time or to find him in the wrong mood. Howells was willing to risk it, and that the result was only amusing instead of tragic is the best proof of their friendship."

To Howells, Belmont, Mass.

June 9, '80

Well, old practical joker, the corpse of Mr. X has been here and I have bedded it and fed it and put down my work during 24 hours and tried my level best to make it do something or say something or appreciate something. But no, it was *worse* than Lazarus. A kindhearted, well-meaning corpse was the Boston young man, but lawsy bless me, horribly dull company. Now, old man, unless you have great confidence in Mr. X's judgment you ought to make him submit his article to you before he prints it. For only think how true I was to you: Every hour that he was here I was saying gloatingly, "O God-damn you, when you are in bed and your light out I will fix you" (meaning to kill him) . . . but then the thought would follow, "No, Howells sent him. He shall be spared, he shall be respected, he shall travel hellwards by his own route."

Breakfast is frozen by this time and Mrs. Clemens corresponding-ly hot. Goodbye.

Yrs ever,
Mark

Jean Clemens was about a month old when the next letter was written.

To Twichell, Hartford

Quarry Farm, *Aug. 29 ['80]*

Dear old Joe,

Concerning Jean Clemens, if anybody said he "didn't see no p'ints about that frog that's any better'n any other frog," I should think he was convicting himself of being a pretty poor sort of observer. . . . I will not go into details. It is not necessary. You will soon be in Hart-ford, where I have already hired a hall. The admission fee will be but a trifle.

It is curious to note the change in the stock quotation of the Affec-tion Board brought about by throwing this new security on the mar-ket. Four weeks ago the children still put Mamma at the head of the list right along, where she had always been. But now:

Jean
Mamma
Motley ⎫
          ⎬ cats
Fraulein ⎭
Papa

That is the way it stands now. Mamma is become No. 2. I have dropped from No. 4 and am become No. 5. Some time ago it used to be nip and tuck between me and the cats, but after the cats "devel-oped" I didn't stand any more show.

I've got a swollen ear, so I take advantage of it to lie abed most of the day and read and smoke and scribble and have a good time. Last evening Livy said with deep concern, "O dear, I believe an abscess is forming in your ear."

I responded as the poet would have done if he had had a cold in the head—

> "'Tis said that abscess conquers love,
> But O believe it not."

This made a coolness.

Been reading Daniel Webster's Private Correspondence. Have read a hundred of his diffuse, conceited, "eloquent," bathotic (or bathostic) letters written in that dim (no, vanished) Past when he was a student. And Lord, to think that this boy who is so real to me now, and so booming with fresh young blood and bountiful life, and sappy cynicisms about girls, has since climbed the Alps of fame and stood against the sun one brief tremendous moment with the world's eyes upon him, and then—f-z-t-! where is he? Why the only *long* thing, the only *real* thing about the whole shadowy business is the sense of the lagging dull and hoary lapse of time that has drifted by since then, a vast empty level, it seems, with a formless spectre glimpsed fitfully through the smoke and mist that lie along its remote verge.

Well, we are all getting along here firstrate. Livy gains strength daily and sits up a deal. The baby is five weeks old and—but no more of this, somebody may be reading *this* letter 80 years hence. And so, my friend (you pitying snob, I mean, who are holding this yellow paper in your hand in 1960), save yourself the trouble of looking further. I know how pathetically trivial our small concerns will seem to you, and I will not let your eye profane them. No, I keep my news, you keep your compassion. Suffice it you to know, scoffer and ribald, that the little child is old and blind now, and once more toothless, and the rest of us are shadows, these many, many years. Yes, and *your* time cometh!

Mark

EIGHT

[1881–83]

Helping a young sculptor — on telling a yarn orally — "I wish the summer were seven years long" — paranoia regarding the New York Tribune — Hannibal, Missouri revisited — "I have been clasping hands with the moribund"

To Howells, Boston

Private and Confidential

Hartford, *Feb. 21, 1881*

My dear Howells,

Well, here is our romance.

It happened in this way. One morning a month ago—no, three weeks—Livy and Clara Spaulding and I were at breakfast at 10 A.M. and I was in an irritable mood, for the barber was up stairs waiting and his hot water was getting cold, when the colored George returned from answering the bell and said, "There's a lady in the drawing-room wants to see you."

"A book agent!" says I, with heat. "I won't see her. I will die in my tracks, first."

Then I got up with a soul full of rage and went in there and bent scowling over that person and began a succession of rude and raspy questions, and without even offering to sit down.

Not even the defendant's youth and beauty and (seeming) timidity were able to modify my savagery for a time, and meantime question and answer were going on. She had risen to her feet with the first question and there she stood, with her pretty face bent floorward whilst I inquired, but always with her honest eyes looking me in the face when it came her turn to answer.

And this was her tale and her plea, diffidently stated but straightforwardly, and bravely and most winningly, simply and earnestly. I put it in my own fashion, for I do not remember her words:

Mr. Karl Gerhardt, who works in Pratt & Whitney's machine shops, has made a statue in clay, and would I be so kind as to come and look at it and tell him if there is any promise in it? He has none to go to and he would be so glad.

"O, dear me," I said, "I don't know anything about art. There's nothing *I* could tell him."

But she went on, just as earnestly and as simply as before, with her plea—and so she did after repeated rebuffs. And dull as I am, even *I* began by and by to admire this brave and gentle persistence and to perceive how her heart of hearts was in this thing and how she *couldn't* give it up but *must carry* her point. So at last I wavered, and promised in general terms that I would come down the first day that fell idle, and as I conducted her to the door, I tamed more and more, and said I would come during the very next week.

"We shall be so glad—but—but would you please come early in the week? The statue is just finished and we are *so* anxious—and—and—we did hope you could come this week—and"

Well, I came down another peg and said I would come Monday as sure as death, and before I got to the dining room remorse was doing its work and I was saying to myself, "Damnation, how can a man be such a hound? Why didn't I go with her *now?*"

Yes, and how mean I should have felt if I had known that out of her poverty she had hired a hack and brought it along to convey me. But luckily for what was left of my peace of mind, I didn't know that.

Well, it appears that from here she went to Charley Warner's. There was a better light there and the eloquence of her face had a better chance to do its office. Warner fought, as I had done, and he was in the midst of an article and very busy, but no matter, she won him completely. He laid aside his MS and said, "Come, let us go and see your father's statue. That is—is he your father?"

"No, he is my husband."

So this child was married, you see.

This was a Saturday. Next day Warner came to dinner and said, "*Go!*—go tomorrow—don't fail." He was in love with the girl and with her husband too and said he believed there was merit in the statue. Pretty crude work, maybe, but merit in it.

Patrick and I hunted up the place next day. The girl saw us driving up and flew down the stairs and received me. Her quarters were the second story of a little wooden house—another family on the ground floor. The husband was at the machine shop. The wife kept no servant, she was there alone. She had a little parlor with a chair or two and a sofa, and the artist husband's hand was visible in a couple of plaster busts, one of the wife and another of a neighbor's child; visible also in a couple of water colors of flowers and birds; an ambitious unfinished portrait of his wife in oils; some paint decorations on the pine mantel; and an excellent human ear, done in some plastic material at 16.

Then we went into the kitchen, and the girl flew around with enthusiasm and snatched rag after rag from a tall something in the corner, and presently there stood the clay statue, life size—a graceful girlish creature, nude to the waist and holding up a single garment with one hand, the expression attempted being a modified scare—she was interrupted when about to enter the bath.

Then this young wife posed herself alongside the image and so remained, a thing I didn't understand. But presently I did. Then I said:

"O, it's *you!*"

"Yes," she said, "I was the model. He has no model but me. I have stood for this many and many an hour, and you can't think how it does tire one! But I don't mind it. He works all day at the shop, and then nights and Sundays he works on his statue as long as I can keep up."

She got a big chisel to use as a lever, and between us we managed to twist the pedestal round and round so as to afford a view of the statue from all points. Well sir, it was perfectly charming, this girl's innocence and purity, exhibiting her naked self, as it were, to a stranger and alone and never once dreaming that there was the slightest indelicacy about the matter. And so there wasn't, but it will be many a long day before I run across another woman who can do the like and show no trace of self-consciousness.

Well, then we sat down and I took a smoke and she told me all about her people in Massachusetts. Her father is a physician and it is an old and respectable family. (I am able to believe anything she says.) And she told me how "Karl" is 26 years old and how he has had passionate longings all his life toward art but has always been poor and obliged to struggle for his daily bread, and how he felt sure that if he could only have *one* or *two* lessons in—

"Lessons? Hasn't he had any lessons?"

No. He had never had a lesson.

And presently it was dinner time and "Karl" arrived, a slender young fellow with a marvelous head and a noble eye, and he was as simple and natural and as beautiful in spirit as his wife was. But *she* had to do the talking mainly—there was too much thought behind his cavernous eyes for glib speech.

I went home enchanted. Told Livy and Clara Spaulding all about the paradise down yonder where those two enthusiasts are happy with a yearly expense of $350. Livy and Clara went there next day and came away enchanted. A few nights later the Gerhardts kept their promise and came here for the evening. It was billiard night and I had company and so was not down, but Livy and Clara became more charmed with these children than ever.

Warner and I planned to get somebody to criticise the statue whose judgment would be worth something. So I laid for Champney and after two failures I captured him and took him around, and he said, "This statue is full of faults but it has merits enough in it to make up for them," whereat the young wife danced around as delighted as a child.

When we came away Champney said, "I did not want to say too much there but the truth is it seems to me an extraordinary performance for an untrained hand. You ask if there is promise enough there to justify the Hartford folk in going to an expense of training this young man. *I* should say, *yes*, decidedly. But still, to make everything safe, you had better get the judgment of a sculptor."

Warner was in New York. I wrote him and he said he would fetch up Ward, which he did. Yesterday they went to the Gerhardts and spent two hours, and Ward came away bewitched with those people and marveling at the winning innocence of the young wife, who dropped naturally into model-attitude beside the statue (which is stark naked from head to heel now—G. had removed the drapery, fearing Ward would think he was afraid to try legs and hips) just as she has always done before.

Livy and I had two long talks with Ward yesterday evening. He spoke strongly. He said, "If any stranger had told me that this apprentice did not model that thing from plaster casts, I would not have believed it." He said, "It is full of crudities but it is full of genius too. It is such a statue as the man of average talent would achieve after two years training in the schools. And the *boldness* of the fellow in going straight to *nature!* He is an apprentice. His work shows that all over. But the stuff is in him sure. Hartford must send him to Paris—two years. Then if the promise holds good, keep him there three more, and warn him to study, study, work, work, and keep his name out of the papers, and neither ask for orders nor accept them when offered."

Well, you see, that's all *we* wanted. After Ward was gone Livy came out with the thing that was in her mind. She said, "Go privately and start the Gerhardts off to Paris and say nothing about it to anyone else."

So I tramped down this morning in the snowstorm, and there was a stirring time. They will sail a week or ten days from now.

As I was starting out at the front door, with Gerhardt beside me and the young wife dancing and jubilating behind, this latter cried out impulsively, "Tell Mrs. Clemens I want to hug her. I want to hug you *both!*"

I gave them my old French book and they were going to tackle the language straight off.

Now this letter is a secret—keep it quiet—I don't think Livy would mind my telling you these things but then she might, you know, for she is a queer girl.

Yrs ever,
Mark

Charley Warner was Charles Dudley Warner, Hartford author, neighbor and friend, with whom Clemens collaborated in writing *The Gilded Age*. Champney was J. Wells Champney, a portrait painter. Ward was J. Q. A. Ward, a sculptor.

Joel Chandler Harris's Uncle Remus tales were great favorites of Clemens, who read some of them aloud both at home and in public. Eventually, in appreciation, he wrote to Harris and mentioned "The Golden Arm," a Negro story of his own childhood, which he advised Harris to make use of. In his reply Harris disclaimed originality for the tales, adding, "I understand that my relations toward Uncle Remus are similar to those that exist between an almanac maker and the calendar." Unfamiliar with "The Golden Arm," he asked for an outline of it. He also solicited some advice about publishing.

To Joel Chandler Harris, Atlanta

Elmira, N. Y., *Aug. 10*

My dear Mr. Harris,

You can argue *yourself* into the delusion that the principle of life is in the stories themselves and not in their setting but you will save labor by stopping with that solitary convert, for he is the only intelligent one you will bag. In reality the stories are only alligator pears. One merely eats them for the sake of the salad dressing. Uncle Remus is most deftly drawn and is a lovable and delightful creation. He and the little boy and their relations with each other are high and fine literature and worthy to live for their own sakes, and certainly the stories are not to be credited with *them*. But enough of this. I seem to be proving to the man that made the multiplication table that twice one are two.

I have been thinking yesterday and today (plenty of chance to think, as I am abed with lumbago at our little summering farm among the solitudes of the mountaintops) and I have concluded that I can answer one of your questions with full confidence—thus: Make it a subscription book. Mighty few books that come strictly under the head of *literature* will sell by subscription, but if Uncle Remus won't the gift of prophecy has departed out of me. When a book *will* sell by subscription it will sell two or three times as many copies as it would in the trade, and the profit is bulkier because the retail price is greater. . . .

You didn't ask me for a subscription publisher. If you had I should have recommended Osgood to you. He inaugurates his subscription department with my new book in the fall. . . .

Now the doctor has been here and tried to interrupt my yarn about "The Golden Arm" but I've got through anyway.

Of course I *tell* it in the negro dialect—that is necessary. But I have not written it so, for I can't spell it in your matchless way. It is marvelous the way you and Cable spell the negro and creole dialects.

Two grand features are lost in print: the weird wailing, the rising and falling cadences of the wind, so easily mimicked with one's mouth; and the impressive pauses and eloquent silences and subdued utterances toward the end of the yarn (which chain the attention of the children hand and foot, and they sit with parted lips and breathless, to be wrenched limb from limb with the sudden and appalling "You got it").

Old Uncle Dan'l, a slave of my uncle's aged 60, used to tell us children yarns every night by the kitchen fire (no other light), and the last yarn demanded every night was this one. By this time there was but a ghastly blaze or two flickering about the back log. We would huddle close about the old man and begin to shudder with the first familiar words, and under the spell of his impressive delivery we always fell a prey to that climax at the end when the rigid black shape in the twilight sprang at us with a shout.

When you come to glance at the tale you will recollect it—it is as common and familiar as the Tar Baby. Work up the atmosphere with your customary skill and it will "go" in print.

Lumbago seems to make a body garrulous—but you'll forgive it.

> Truly yours
> S. L. Clemens

Osgood is the Boston publisher identified earlier. Cable is George Washington Cable.

The Sandwich Islands is the former name of the Hawaiian Islands. The "Charlie" of the next letter is Charles Warren Stoddard, a poet and essayist, "one of the old California literary crowd," as Paine has characterized him, "a gentle, irresponsible soul, well loved by all who knew him, and always, by one or another, provided against want." Stoddard, who was partial to the Hawaiian Islands, had decided to try to live on his literary earnings there.

To Charles Warren Stoddard, the Sandwich [Hawaiian] Islands

Hartford, *Oct. 26 '81*

My dear Charlie,

Now what have I ever done to you that you should not only slide off to Heaven before you have earned a right to go, but must add the gratuitous villainy of informing me of it? . . .

The house is full of carpenters and decorators whereas what we really need here is an incendiary. If the house would only burn down we would pack up the cubs and fly to the isles of the blest and shut ourselves up in the healing solitudes of the crater of Haleakala and get a good rest, for the mails do not intrude there, nor yet the telephone and the telegraph. And after resting we would come down the mountain a piece and board with a godly, breech-clouted native and eat poi and dirt and give thanks to whom all thanks belong, for these privileges, and never housekeep any more.

I think my wife would be twice as strong as she is but for this wearing and wearying slavery of housekeeping. However, she thinks she must submit to it for the sake of the children, whereas, I have always had a tenderness for parents too, so for her sake and mine I sigh for the incendiary. When the evening comes and the gas is lit and the wear and tear of life ceases, we want to keep house always. But next morning we wish once more that we were free and irresponsible boarders.

Work? One *can't*, you know, to any purpose. I don't really get anything done worth speaking of except during the three or four months that we are away in the summer. I wish the summer were seven years long. I keep three or four books on the stocks all the time but I seldom add a satisfactory chapter to one of them at home. Yes, and it is all because my time is taken up with answering the letters of strangers. It can't be done through a short hand amanuensis—I've tried that—it wouldn't work—I couldn't learn to dictate. What does possess strangers to write so many letters? I never could find that out. However, I suppose I did it myself when I was a stranger. But I will never do it again.

Maybe you think I am not happy? The very thing that gravels me is that I am. I don't want to be happy when I can't work. I am resolved that hereafter I won't be. What I have always longed for was the privilege of living forever away up on one of those mountains in the Sandwich Islands overlooking the sea.

Yours ever

Mark

Occasionally Clemens went to Canada in an effort to protect his copyright. He made such a trip in November 1881 with Osgood in connection with *The Prince and the Pauper*.

To Livy, Hartford

Montreal, *Sunday, November 27, 1881*

Livy dear, a mouse kept me awake last night till 3 or 4 o'clock, so I am lying abed this morning. I would not give sixpence to be out yonder in the storm, although it is only snow.

[This paragraph was in the form of a rebus. *See below.*]

There—that's for the children—was not sure that they could read writing, especially Jean, who is strangely ignorant in some things.

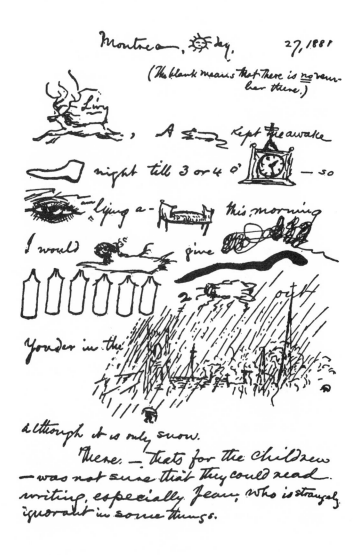

I can not only look out upon the beautiful snowstorm past the vigorous blaze of my fire and upon the snow-veiled buildings which I have sketched, and upon the churchward drifting umbrellas, and upon the buffalo-clad cabmen stamping their feet and thrashing their arms on the corner yonder. But I also look out upon the spot where the first white men stood, in the neighborhood of four hundred years ago, admiring the mighty stretch of leafy solitudes and being admired and marveled at by an eager multitude of naked savages. The discoverer of this region and namer of it, Jacques Cartier, has a square named for him in the city. I wish you were here. You would enjoy your birthday, I think.

I hoped for a letter and thought I had one when the mail was handed in a minute ago but it was only that note from Sylvester Baxter. You must write—do you hear?—or I will be remiss myself.

Give my love and a kiss to the children, and ask them to give you my love and a kiss from

Saml

Sylvester Baxter was a Boston newspaper reporter and author.

To Howells, Boston

Hartford, Jan. 28 '82

My dear Howells,

Nobody knows better than I that there are times when swearing cannot meet the emergency. How sharply I feel that at this moment. Not a single profane word has issued from my lips this morning. I have not even had the *impulse* to swear, so wholly ineffectual would swearing have manifestly been in the circumstances. But I will tell you about it.

About three weeks ago a sensitive friend, approaching his revelation cautiously, intimated that the *N. Y. Tribune* was engaged in a kind of crusade against me. This seemed a higher compliment than I deserved. But no matter, it made me very angry. I asked many questions and gathered, in substance, this: Since Reid's return from Europe, the *Tribune* had been flinging sneers and brutalities at me with such persistent frequency "as to attract general remark." I was an angered—which is just as good an expression, I take it, as an hungered. Next, I learned that Osgood, among the rest of the "general," was worrying over these constant and pitiless attacks. Next came the testimony of another friend, that the attacks were not merely "frequently" but "almost *daily*." Reflect upon that: "Almost *daily*" insults for two months on a stretch. What would *you* have done?

As for me, I did the thing which was the natural thing for me to do, that is, I set about contriving a plan to accomplish one or the other of two things: 1. Force a peace; or 2. Get revenge. When I got my plan finished it pleased me marvelously. It was in six or seven sections, each section to be used in its turn and by itself, the assault to begin at once with No. 1, and the rest to follow one after the other to keep the communication open while I wrote my biography of Reid. I meant to wind up with this latter great work and then dismiss the subject for good.

Well, ever since then I have worked day and night making notes and collecting and classifying material. I've got collectors at work in England. I went to New York and sat three hours taking evidence while a stenographer set it down. As my labors grew, so also grew my fascination. Malice and malignity faded out of me, or maybe I *drove* them out of me, knowing that a malignant book would hurt nobody but the fool who wrote it. I got thoroughly in love with this work, for I saw that I was going to write a book which the very devils and angels themselves would delight to read and which would draw disapproval from nobody but the hero of it (and Mrs. Clemens, who was bitter against the whole thing). One part of my plan was so delicious that I *had* to try my hand on it right away just for the luxury of it. I set about it, and sure enough it panned out to admiration. I wrote that chapter most carefully and I couldn't find a fault with it. (It was not for the biography—no, it belonged to an immediate and deadlier project.)

Well, five days ago this thought came into my mind—(from Mrs. Clemens's): "Wouldn't it be well to make *sure* that the attacks have been 'almost daily'?—and to also make sure that their number and character will justify me in doing what I am supposing to do?"

I at once set a man to work in New York to seek out and copy every unpleasant reference which had been made to me in the *Tri-bune* from Nov. 1st to date. On my own part I began to watch the current numbers, for I had subscribed for the paper.

The result arrived from my New York man this morning. O, what a pitiable wreck of high hopes! The "almost daily" assaults, for two months, consist of—1. adverse criticism of P. & P. from an enraged idiot in the London *Atheneum;* 2. paragraph from some indignant Englishman in the *Pall Mall Gazette* who pays me the vast compli-ment of gravely rebuking some imaginary ass who has set me up in the neighborhood of Rabelais; 3. a remark of the *Tribune's* about the Montreal dinner, touched with an almost invisible satire; 4. a remark of the *Tribune's* about refusal of Canadian copyright, not compli-mentary but not necessarily malicious—and of course adverse criti-cism which is not malicious is a thing which none but fools irritate themselves about.

There—that is the prodigious bugaboo in its entirety! Can you conceive of a man's getting himself into a sweat over so diminutive a provocation? I am sure I can't. What the devil can those friends of mine have been thinking about, to spread those 3 or 4 harmless things out into two months of daily sneers and affronts? The whole offense, boiled down, amounts to just this: one uncourteous remark of the *Tribune* about my *book*—not me—between Nov. 1 and Dec. 20; and a couple of foreign criticisms (of my writings, not me) be-tween Nov. 1 and Jan. 26! If I can't stand that amount of friction, I certainly need reconstruction. Further boiled down, this vast out-pouring of malice amounts to simply this: *One* jest from the *Tribune* (one can make nothing more serious than that out of it). *One jest—* and that is all, for the foreign criticisms do not count, they being matters of news and proper for publication in anybody's newspaper.

And to offset that one jest, the *Tribune* paid me one compliment Dec. 23 by publishing my note declining the New York New En-gland dinner, while merely (in the same breath,) *mentioning* that similar letters were read from General Sherman and other men whom we all know to be persons of *real* consequence.

Well, my mountain has brought forth its mouse, and a sufficiently small mouse it is, God knows. And my three weeks' hard work have got to go into the ignominious pigeon hole. Confound it, I could have earned ten thousand dollars with infinitely less trouble. However, I shouldn't have done it, for I am too lazy now in my sere and yellow leaf to be willing to work for anything but love. . . . I kind of envy you people who are permitted for your righteousness' sake to dwell in a boarding house. Not that I should *always* want to live in one, but I should like the change occasionally from this housekeeping slavery to that wild independence. A life of don't-care-a-damn in a boarding house is what I have asked for in many a secret prayer. I shall come by and by and require of you what you have offered me there.

Yours ever,

Mark

Reid was Whitelaw Reid, editor of the *New York Tribune* in 1882. Later he was Minister to France and Ambassador to Great Britain.

In the spring of 1882 Clemens made his long deferred trip down the Mississippi so he could finish his river book. With him were Osgood and a young male stenographer, a Roswell Phelps of Hartford. They boarded the steamer *Gold Dust* in St. Louis. Clemens, hoping to travel under an assumed name, was recognized both in the city and on the boat. In New Orleans he met Cable, Joel Chandler Harris and Horace Bixby. Bixby, who had taught him the river, was now captain of the *City of Baton Rouge*, a new Anchor Line steamer.

"The Anchor Line steamers were the acme of Mississippi River steamboat building, and they were about the end of it," Paine has written. "They were imposingly magnificent but they were only as gorgeous clouds that marked the sunset of Mississippi steamboat travel."

Clemens returned upriver with Bixby and spent some time in Hannibal.

To Livy, Hartford

Quincy, Ill. *May 17, '82*

Livy darling, I am desperately homesick. But I have promised Osgood, and must stick it out. Otherwise I would take the train at once and break for home.

I have spent three delightful days in Hannibal, loitering around all day long, examining the old localities and talking with the greyheads who were boys and girls with me 30 or 40 years ago. It has been a moving time. I spent my nights with John and Helen Garth, three miles from town, in their spacious and beautiful house. They were children with me and afterwards schoolmates. Now they have a daughter 19 or 20 years old. Spent an hour yesterday with A. W. Lamb, who was not married when I saw him last. He married a young lady whom I knew. And now I have been talking with their grownup sons and daughters. Lieutenant Hickman, the spruce young handsomely uniformed volunteer of 1846, called on me—a grisly elephantine patriarch of 65 now, his grace all vanished.

That world which I knew in its blossoming youth is old and bowed and melancholy now. Its soft cheeks are leathery and wrinkled. The fire is gone out in its eyes and the spring from its step. It will be dust and ashes when I come again. I have been clasping hands with the moribund—and usually they said, "It is for the last time."

Now I am under way again upon this hideous trip to St. Paul with a heart brimming full of thoughts and images of you and Susie and Bay and the peerless Jean. And so good night, my love.

Saml

Toward the end of the summer Clemens was having great trouble in finishing the river book. Howells, in Europe, urged him to come abroad for some fun and to work on their joint literary project, *Orme's Motor,* an American comedy whose chief character would be based on Orion Clemens.

To Howells, Switzerland

Hartford, *Nov. 4th, 1882*

My dear Howells,

Yes, it would be profitable for me to do that, because with your society to help me I should swiftly finish this now apparently interminable book. But I cannot come, because I am not Boss here, and nothing but dynamite can move Mrs. Clemens away from home in the winter season.

I never had such a fight over a book in my life before. And the foolishest part of the whole business is that I started Osgood to editing it before I had finished writing it. As a consequence, large areas of it are condemned here and there and yonder, and I have the burden of these unfilled gaps harassing me and the thought of the broken continuity of the work while I am at the same time trying to build the last quarter of the book. However, at last I have said with sufficient positiveness that I will finish the book at no particular date, that I will not hurry it, that I will not hurry myself, that I will take things easy and comfortably, write when I choose to write, leave it alone when I so prefer. The printers must wait, the artists, the canvassers and all the rest. I have got everything at a dead standstill and that is where it ought to be and that is where it must remain. To follow any other policy would be to make the book worse than it already is. I ought to have finished it before showing to anybody, and then sent it across the ocean to you to be edited, as usual, for you seem to be a great many shades happier than you deserve to be, and if I had thought of this thing earlier I would have acted upon it and taken the tuck somewhat out of your joyousness.

In the same mail with your letter arrived the enclosed from Orme the motor man. You will observe that he has an office. I will explain that this is a law office and I think it probably does him as much good to have a law office without anything to do in it as it would another man to have one with an active business attached. You see, he is on the electric light lay now. Going to light the city and allow me to take all the stock if I want to. And he will manage it free of charge. It never would occur to this simple soul how much less costly it would be to me to hire him on a good salary not to manage it. Do you observe the same old eagerness, the same old hurry, springing from the fear that if he does not move with the utmost swiftness that colossal opportunity will escape him?

Now just fancy this same frantic plunging after vast opportunities going on week after week with this same man during fifty entire years, and he has not yet learned in the slightest degree that there isn't any occasion to hurry, that his vast opportunity will always wait and that whether it waits or flies, he certainly will never catch it. This immortal hopefulness, fortified by its immortal and unteachable misjudgment, is the immortal feature of this character, for a play, and we will write that play We should be fools else. That staccato postscript reads as if some new and mighty business were imminent, for it is slung on the paper telegraphically, all the small words left out. I am afraid something newer and bigger than the electric light is swinging across his orbit. Save this letter for an inspiration. I have got a hundred more.

Cable has been here, creating worshipers on all hands, He is a marvelous talker on a deep subject. I do not see how even Spencer could unwind a thought more smoothly or orderly, and do it in a cleaner, clearer, crisper English. He astounded Twichell with his faculty. You know, when it comes down to moral honesty, limpid innocence and utterly blemishless piety, the Apostles were mere policemen to Cable, so with this in mind you must imagine him at a midnight dinner in Boston the other night, where we gathered around the board of the Summerset Club. Osgood full. Boyle O'Reilly full. Fairchild responsively loaded. And Aldrich and myself possessing the floor and properly fortified. Cable told Mrs. Clemens when he returned here that he seemed to have been entertaining himself with horses, and had a dreamy idea that he must have gone to Boston in a cattle car. It was a very large time. He called it an orgy. And no doubt it was, viewed from his standpoint.

I wish I were in Switzerland, and I wish we could go to Florence, but we have to leave these delights to you. There is no helping it. We all join in love to you and all the family.

Yours as ever

Mark

When Clemens finished the Mississippi book he asked Osgood to publish it for him. He, Clemens, would provide the capital and Osgood would receive a percentage of the profits for his services. A sort of partnership, it was the beginning of Clemens's experiences as a publisher. Meanwhile Howells was writing to Clemens that social life in Florence, Italy, was too much for him, "the most ridiculous time that ever even half-witted people passed."

The Governor Jewell of the following was Marshall Jewell, governor of Connecticut from 1871 to 1873 and later Minister to Russia and Postmaster General of the United States.

To Howells, Florence, Italy

Hartford, *March 1st, 1883*

My dear Howells,

We got ourselves ground up in that same mill, once, in London, and another time in Paris. It is a kind of foretaste of hell. There is no way to avoid it except by the method which you have now chosen. One must live secretly and cut himself utterly off from the human race, or life in Europe becomes an unbearable burden and work an impossibility. I learned something last night and maybe it may reconcile me to go to Europe again sometime. I attended one of the astonishingly popular lectures of a man by the name of Stoddard, who exhibits interesting stereopticon pictures and then knocks the interest all out of them with his comments upon them. But all the world go there to look and listen, and are apparently well satisfied. And they ought to be fully satisfied if the lecturer would only keep still, or die in the first act. But he described how retired tradesmen and farmers in Holland load a lazy scow with the family and the household effects and then loaf along the waterways of the low countries all the summer long, paying no visits, receiving none, and just lazying a heavenly life out in their own private unpestered society, and doing their literary work, if they have any, wholly uninterrupted.

If you had hired such a boat and sent for us we should have a couple of satisfactory books ready for the press now with no marks of interruption, vexatious wearinesses and other hellishnesses visible upon them anywhere. We shall have to do this another time. We have lost an opportunity for the present. Do you forget that Heaven is packed with a multitude of all nations and that these people are all on the most familiar how-the-hell-are-you footing with Talmage swinging around the circle to all eternity hugging the saints and patriarchs and archangels, and forcing you to do the same unless you choose to make yourself an object of remark if you refrain? Then why do you try to get to Heaven? Be warned in time.

We have all read your two opening numbers in the *Century* and consider them almost beyond praise. I hear no dissent from this verdict. I did not know there was an untouched personage in American life but I had forgotten the auctioneer. You have photographed him accurately.

I have been an utterly free person for a month or two and I do not believe I ever so greatly appreciated and enjoyed and realized the absence of the chains of slavery as I do this time. Usually my first waking thought in the morning is, "I have nothing to do to-day, I belong to nobody, I have ceased from being a slave." Of course the highest pleasure to be got out of freedom and having nothing to do is labor. Therefore I labor. But I take my time about it. I work one hour or four as happens to suit my mind, and quit when I please. And so these days are days of entire enjoyment. I told Clark the other day to jog along comfortable and not get in a sweat. I said I believed you would not be able to enjoy editing that library over there, where you have your own legitimate work to do, and be pestered to death by society besides. Therefore I thought if he got it ready for you against your return, that that would be best and pleasantest.

You remember Governor Jewell, and the night he told about Russia, down in the library. He was taken with a cold about three weeks ago, and I stepped over one evening, proposing to beguile an idle hour for him with a yarn or two, but was received at the door with whispers and the information that he was dying. His case had been dangerous during that day only and he died that night, two hours after I left. His taking off was a prodigious surprise, and his death has been most widely and sincerely regretted. Wm. E. Dodge, the father-in-law of one of Jewell's daughters, dropped suddenly dead the day before Jewell died, but Jewell died without knowing that. Jewell's widow went down to New York to Dodge's house the day after Jewell's funeral, and was to return here day before yesterday, and she did—in a coffin. She fell dead of heart disease while her trunks were being packed for her return home. Florence Strong, one of Jewell's daughters, who lives in Detroit, started East on an urgent telegram but missed a connection somewhere and did not arrive here in time to see her father alive. She was his favorite child, and they had always been like lovers together. He always sent her a box of fresh flowers once a week to the day of his death, a custom which he never suspended even when he was in Russia. Mrs. Strong had only just reached her western home again when she was summoned to Hartford to attend her mother's funeral.

I have had the impulse to write you several times. I shall try to remember better henceforth.

With sincerest regards to all of you,

Yours as ever,
Mark

In his study in Elmira during the summer of 1876, Clemens had worked on a tale which he thought of as a continuation of *Tom Sawyer*— *Huckleberry Finn*. By mid-August he had written several hundred manuscript pages of the new novel. But his interest had flagged and he put the manuscript aside for years. In Elmira again, now in the summer of 1883, with the river book behind him and with the trip down the river to inspire him, he picked up *Huck Finn* and it ran away with him. He wrote to Howells on August 22:

"I have written eight or nine hundred manuscript pages in such a brief space of time that I mustn't name the number of days. I shouldn't believe it myself, and of course couldn't expect you to. I used to restrict myself to four and five hours a day and five days in the week but this time I have wrought from breakfast till 5:15 P.M. six days in the week, and once or twice I smouched a Sunday when the boss [Livy] wasn't looking. Nothing is half so good as literature hooked on Sunday on the sly."

NINE

[1884-86]

Presidential politics — Huck Finn *expelled by the Concord, Mass. public library* — *boring authors* — *Gen. Grant's character, including his drinking habit* — *Jane Clemens's secret romance*

By the beginning of 1884 the Paige typesetting machine was costing Clemens several thousand dollars a month, with no end in sight. Clemens had set up his nephew by marriage, Charles L. Webster, in New York as selling agent for *Life on the Mississippi,* and before long he formed his own publishing company, Charles L. Webster & Co., which was to bring out *Huckleberry Finn.*

In the spring he wrote to Howells, "My days are given up to cursings, both loud and deep, for I am reading the *Huck Finn* proofs. They don't make a very great many mistakes but those that do occur are of a nature that make a man swear his teeth loose."

Howells promptly offered to read the proofs for him, and Clemens accepted.

It was the summer of the Cleveland-Blaine presidential campaign. Clemens had mugwumped—that is, had broken ranks with the Republican Party in supporting Cleveland. The latter was to become the first Democratic president since the Civil War. Howells was for Blaine.

Karl Gerhardt had returned to the U. S. after studying sculpture for three years in Paris. St. Gaudens was Augustus Saint-Gaudens, an American sculptor born in Dublin, Ireland.

During that summer Howells was reading the *Huck Finn* proofs.

To Howells, Boston

Elmira, *Aug. 21, '84*

My dear Howells,

This presidential campaign is too delicious for anything. *Isn't* human nature the most consummate sham and lie that was ever invented? Isn't man a creature to be ashamed of in pretty much all his aspects? Man, "know thyself"—and then thou wilt despise thyself to a dead moral certainty. Take three quite good specimens—Hawley, Warner and Charley Clark. Even *I* do not loathe Blaine more than they do, yet Hawley is howling for Blaine; Warner and Clark are eating their daily crow in the paper for him; and all three will vote for him. O Stultification, where is thy sting, O slave where is thy hickory!

I suppose you heard how a marble monument for which St. Gaudens was pecuniarily responsible burned down in Hartford the other day, uninsured—for who in the world would ever think of insuring a marble shaft in a cemetery against a fire?—and left St. Gaudens out of pocket $15,000.

It was a bad day for artists. Gerhardt finished my bust that day and the work was pronounced admirable by all the kin and friends, but in putting it in plaster (or rather taking it *out*) next day it got ruined. It was four or five weeks hard work gone to the dogs. The news flew, and everybody on the farm flocked to the arbor and grouped themselves about the wreck in a profound and moving silence—the farm help, the colored servants, the German nurse, the children, everybody—a silence interrupted at wide intervals by absentminded ejaculations wrung from unconscious breasts as the whole size of the disaster gradually worked its way home to the realization of one spirit after another.

Some burst out with one thing, some another. The German nurse put up her hands and said, "Oh, Schade! Oh, schrecklich!" But Gerhardt said nothing, or almost that. He couldn't word it, I suppose. But he went to work, and by dark had everything thoroughly well under way for a fresh start in the morning, and in three days' time had built a new bust which was a trifle better than the old one, and tomorrow we shall put the finishing touches on it, and it will be about as good a one as nearly anybody can make.

Yrs Ever
Mark

If you run across anybody who wants a bust, be sure and recommend Gerhardt on my sayso.

To Howells, Boston

Elmira, *Sept. 17, '84*

My dear Howells,

Somehow I can't seem to rest quiet under the idea of your voting for Blaine. I believe you said something about the country and the party. Certainly allegiance to these is well, but as certainly a man's *first* duty is to his own conscience and honor. The party of the country come second to that, and never first. I don't ask you to vote *at all*—I only urge you to not soil yourself by voting for Blaine.

When you wrote before, you were able to say the charges against him were not proven. But you know now that they are proven, and it seems to me that that bars you and all other honest and honorable men (who are independently situated) from voting for him.

It is not necessary to vote for Cleveland. The only necessary thing to do, as I understand it, is that a man shall keep *himself* clean (by withholding his vote for an improper man) even though the party and the country go to destruction in consequence. It is not *parties* that make or save countries or that build them to greatness—it is clean men, clean ordinary citizens, rank and file, the masses. Clean masses are not made by individuals standing back till the rest become clean.

As I said before, I think a man's first duty is to his own honor, not to his country and not to his party. Don't be offended. I mean no offence. I am not so concerned about the *rest* of the nation, but— well, goodbye.

Ys Ever
Mark

Huckleberry Finn was officially published in the United States and England in December 1884 but it was not ready for delivery to purchasers until February, by which time some 40,000 copies had been ordered, and 50,000 a few weeks later. The novel, parts of which had appeared in two issues of the *Century* magazine (December 1884 and January 1885), was a success both critically and financially from the beginning.

In November 1884 Clemens had begun a reading and lecture tour with George W. Cable. When the two were in Montreal they were invited by the Tuque Bleue Snow-shoe Club to attend one of the weekly excursions across Mt. Royal. Clemens's letter is to George Iles, author of *Flame, Electricity, and the Camera* "and many other useful works," according to Paine.

To George Iles, for the Tuque Bleue Snow-shoe Club, Montreal

Detroit, *February 12, 1885*
Midnight, P.S.

My dear Iles,

I got your other telegram a while ago and answered it, explaining that I get only a couple of hours in the middle of the day for social life. I know it doesn't seem rational that a man should have to lie abed all day in order to be rested and equipped for talking an hour at night, and yet in my case and Cable's it is so. Unless I get a great deal of rest, a ghastly dullness settles down upon me on the platform and turns my performance into work, and hard work, whereas it ought always to be pastime, recreation, solid enjoyment. Usually it is just this latter, but that is because I take my rest faithfully and prepare myself to do my duty by my audience.

I am the obliged and appreciative servant of my brethren of the Snow-shoe Club, and nothing in the world would delight me more than to come to their house without naming time or terms on my own part—but you see how it is. My cast iron duty is to my audience. It leaves me no liberty and no option.

With kindest regards to the Club and to you, I am

Sincerely yours
S. L. Clemens

To Howells, Boston

Philada. *Feb. 27,* '85

My dear Howells,

Tonight in Baltimore, tomorrow afternoon and night in Washington, and my four months platform campaign is ended at last. It has been a curious experience. It has taught me that Cable's gifts of mind are greater and higher than I had suspected. But—

That "But" is pointed toward his religion. You will never, never know, never divine, guess, imagine, how loathsome a thing the Christian religion can be made until you come to know and study Cable daily and hourly. Mind you, I like him. He is pleasant company. I rage and swear at him sometimes but we do not quarrel. We get along mighty happily together. But in him and his person I have learned to hate all religions. He has taught me to abhor and detest the Sabbath day and hunt up new and troublesome ways to dishonor it. . . .

Ys Ever

Mark

To the Rev. J—, Baltimore

Washington, *Mch. 2*, '85

My dear Sir,

I take my earliest opportunity to answer your favor of Feb. 23.

B. was premature in calling me a "shrewd man." I wasn't one at that time but am one now. That is, I am at least too shrewd to ever again invest in anything put on the market by B. I know nothing whatever about the Bank Note Co. and never did know anything about it. B. sold me about $4,000 or $5,000 worth of the stock at $110 and I own it yet. He sold me $10,000 worth of another rosetinted stock about the same time. I have got that yet, also. I judge that a peculiarity of B.'s stocks is that they are of the staying kind. I think you should have asked somebody else whether I was a shrewd man or not—for two reasons: the stock was advertised in a religious paper, a circumstance which was very suspicious; and the compliment came to you from a man who was interested to make a purchaser of you. I am afraid you deserve your loss. A financial scheme advertised in any religious paper is a thing which any living person ought to know enough to avoid, and when the factor is added that M. runs that religious paper, a dead person ought to know enough to avoid it.

Very Truly Yours

S. L. Clemens

1885 was Clemen's fiftieth year. During it he launched himself fully, although without at first intending to, into the publishing business. *Huckleberry Finn* was selling very well.

To Charles L. Webster, New York

Mch 18, '85

Dear Charley,

The Committee of the Public Library of Concord, Mass. have given us a rattling tiptop puff which will go into every paper in the country. They have expelled Huck from their library as "trash and suitable only for the slums." That will sell 25,000 copies for us sure.

Ys

S.L.C.

Indian Summer of the following was by Howells. *The Bostonians* was by Henry James.

To Howells, Boston

Elmira, *July 21, 1885*

My dear Howells,

You are really my only author. I am restricted to you. I wouldn't give a damn for the rest.

I bored through *Middlemarch* during the past week, with its labored and tedious analyses of feelings and motives, its paltry and tiresome people, its unexciting and uninteresting story, and its frequent blinding flashes of single-sentence poetry, philosophy, wit and what not, and nearly died from the overwork. I wouldn't read another of those books for a farm. I did try to read one other—*Daniel Deronda*. I dragged through three chapters, losing flesh all the time, and then was honest enough to quit, and confess to myself that I haven't any romance literature appetite, as far as I can see, except for your books.

But what I started to say was that I have just read Part II of

Indian Summer, and to my mind there isn't a waste line in it or one that could be improved. I read it yesterday, ending with that opinion, and read it again today, ending with the same opinion emphasized. I haven't read Part I yet because that number must have reached Hartford after we left, but we are going to send downtown for a copy, and when it comes I am to read both parts aloud to the family. It is a beautiful story and makes a body laugh all the time and cry inside and feel so old and so forlorn, and gives him gracious glimpses of his lost youth that fill him with a measureless regret, and build up in him a cloudy sense of his having been a prince, once, in some enchanted far-off land, and of being an exile now and desolate—and Lord, no chance ever to get back there again! That is the thing that hurts.

Well, you have done it with marvelous facility and you make all the motives and feelings perfectly clear without analyzing the guts out of them, the way George Eliot does. I can't stand George Eliot and Hawthorne and those people. I see what they are at a hundred years before they get to it and they just tire me to death. And as for *The Bostonians*, I would rather be damned to John Bunyan's heaven than read that.

Yrs Ever

Mark

Meanwhile General Ulysses S. Grant, although dying, was working steadily on his *Memoirs*, which Clemens's company would publish. "Clemens visited him at Mt. McGregor and brought the dying soldier the comforting news that enough of his books were already sold [by subscription] to provide generously for his family, and that the sales would aggregate at least twice as much by the end of the year," Paine has written. Grant died July 23rd.

To Henry Ward Beecher, Brooklyn

Elmira, N. Y. *Sept. 11, '85*

My dear Mr. Beecher,

My nephew Webster is in Europe making contracts for the *Mem-*

oirs. Before he sailed he came to me with a writing, directed to the printers and binders, to this effect:

"Honor no order for a sight or copy of the *Memoirs* while I am absent, even though it be signed by Mr. Clemens himself."

I gave my permission. There were weighty reasons why I should not only give my permission but hold it a matter of honor to not dissolve the order or modify it at any time. So I did all of that—said the order should stand undisturbed to the end. If a principal could dissolve his promise as innocently as he can dissolve his written order unguarded by his promise, I would send you a copy of the *Memoirs* instantly. I did not foresee *you*, or I would have made an exception.

My idea gained from army men is that the drunkenness (and sometimes pretty reckless spreeing, nights,) ceased before he came East to be Lt. General. (Refer especially to Gen. Wm. B. Franklin.°) It was while Grant was still in the West that Mr. Lincoln said he wished he could find out what brand of whisky that fellow used, so he could furnish it to some of the other generals. Franklin *saw* Grant tumble from his horse drunk, while reviewing troops in New Orleans. The fall gave him a good deal of a hurt. He was then on the point of leaving for the Chattanooga region. I naturally put "that and that together" when I read Gen. O. O. Howards's article in the *Christian Union* three or four weeks ago, where he mentions that the new general arrived lame from a recent accident. (See that article.) And why not write Howard?

Franklin spoke positively of the frequent spreeing. In camp—in time of war.

Captain Grant was frequently threatened by the commandant of his Oregon post with a report to the War Department of his conduct unless he modified his intemperance. The report would mean dismissal from the service. At last the report *had* to be made out, and then, so greatly was the captain beloved, that he was privately informed and was thus enabled to rush his resignation to Washington ahead of the report. Did the report *go*, nevertheless? I don't know. If it did, it is in the War Department now, possibly, and seeable. I got

° If you could see Franklin and talk with him—then he would unbosom.

all this from a regular army man but I can't name him to save me.

The only time General Grant ever mentioned liquor to me was about last April or possibly May. He said:

"If I could only build up my strength! The doctors urge whisky and champagne but I can't take them. I can't abide the taste of any kind of liquor."

Had he made a conquest so complete that even the *taste* of liquor was become an offense? Or was he so sore over what had been said about his habit that he wanted to persuade others and likewise himself that he hadn't even ever *had* any taste for it? It *sounded* like the latter but that's no evidence.

He told me in the fall of '84 that there was something the matter with his throat and that at the suggestion of his physicians he had reduced his smoking to one cigar a day. Then he added in a casual fashion that he didn't care for *that* one and seldom smoked it.

I could understand that feeling. He had set out to conquer not the *habit* but the *inclination*—the *desire*. He had gone at the root, not the trunk. It's the *perfect* way and the only true way (I speak from experience). How I do hate those enemies of the human race who go around enslaving God's free people with *pledges*—to quit drinking instead of to quit wanting to drink.

But Sherman and Van Vliet know *everything* concerning Grant, and if you tell them how you want to use the facts, both of them will testify. Regular army men have no concealments about each other and yet they make their awful statements without shade or color or malice—with a frankness and a child-like naivete, indeed, which is enchanting—and stupefying. West Point seems to teach them that, among other priceless things not to be got in any other college in this world. If we talked about our guild-mates as I have heard Sherman, Grant, Van Vliet and others talk about theirs—mates with whom they were on the best possible terms—we could never expect them to speak to us again.

I am reminded now of another matter. The day of the funeral I sat an hour over a single drink and several cigars with Van Vliet and Sherman and Senator Sherman, and among other things Gen. Sherman said, with impatient scorn:

"The idea of all this nonsense about Grant not being able to stand rude language and indelicate stories! Why Grant was *full* of humor, and full of the appreciation of it. I have sat with him by the hour listening to Jim Nye's yarns, and I reckon you know the style of Jim Nye's histories, Clemens. It makes me sick—that newspaper nonsense. Grant was no namby-pamby fool, he was a *man*—all over—rounded and complete."

I wish I had thought of it! I would have said to General Grant: "Put the drunkenness in the *Memoirs*—and the repentance and reform. Trust the people."

But I will wager there is not a hint in the book. He was sore, there. As much of the book as I have read gives no hint, as far as I recollect.

The sick-room brought out the points of Gen. Grant's character—some of them particularly, to wit:

His patience. His indestructible equability of temper. His exceeding gentleness, kindness, forbearance, lovingness, charity. His *loyalty:* to friends, to convictions, to promises, half-promises, infinitesimal fractions and shadows of promises. (There was a requirement of him which I considered an atrocity, an injustice, an outrage. I wanted to implore him to repudiate it. Fred Grant said, "Save your labor, I *know* him. He is in doubt as to whether he made that half-promise or not—and he will give the thing the benefit of the doubt. He will fulfill that half-promise or kill himself trying." Fred Grant was right—he *did* fulfill it.) His aggravatingly trustful nature. His genuineness, simplicity, modesty, diffidence, self-depreciation, poverty in the quality of vanity. And, in no contradiction of this last, his simple pleasure in the flowers and general ruck sent to him by Tom, Dick and Harry from everywhere, a pleasure that suggested a perennial surprise that he should be the object of so much fine attention. He *was* the most lovable great child in the world.

I mentioned his loyalty. You remember Harrison, the colored body-servant? The whole family hated him but that did not make any difference, the General always stood at his back, wouldn't allow him to be scolded, always excused his failures and deficiencies with the one unvarying formula, "We are responsible for these things in his race. It is not fair to visit our fault upon them. Let him *alone*." So they did let him alone, under compulsion, until the great heart that was his shield was taken away. Then—well they simply couldn't *stand* him, and so they were excusable for determining to discharge him, a thing which they mortally hated to do and by lucky accident were saved from the necessity of doing.

His toughness as a bargainer when doing business for other people or for his country. Witness his "terms" at Donelson, Vicksburg, etc. Fred Grant told me his father wound up an estate for the widow and orphans of a friend in St. Louis. It took several years. At the end every complication had been straightened out and the property put upon a prosperous basis. Great sums had passed through his hands, and when he handed over the papers there were vouchers to show what had been done with every penny. And his trusting, easy, unexacting fashion when doing business for himself. At that same time he was paying out money in driblets to a man who was running his farm for him. And in his first Presidency he paid every one of those driblets again (total $3,000, F said), for he hadn't a scrap of paper to show that he had ever paid them before.

In his dealings with me he would *not* listen to terms which would place my money at risk and leave him protected. The thought plainly gave him *pain* and he put it from him, waved it off with his *hands* as one does accounts of crushings and mutilations—wouldn't listen, changed the subject.

And his fortitude! He was under sentence of death last spring. He sat thinking, musing, several days, nobody knows what about. Then he pulled himself together and set to work to finish that book, a colossal task for a dying man. Presently his hand gave out. Fate seemed to have got him checkmated. Dictation was suggested. No, he never could do that, had never tried it, too old to learn now. By and by—if he could only do Appomattox—well. So he sent for a stenographer and dictated 9,000 words at a single sitting!—never pausing, never hesitating for a word, never repeating—and in the written-out copy he made hardly a correction. He dictated again every two or three days. The intervals were intervals of exhaustion and slow recuperation. And at last he was able to tell me that he had written more matter than could be got into the book.

I then enlarged the book—had to. Then he lost his voice. He was not quite done yet, however. There was no end of little plums and spices to be stuck in here and there. And this work he patiently continued a few lines a day with pad and pencil till far into July, at Mt. McGregor.

One day he put his pencil aside and said he was done—there was nothing more to do. If I had been there I could have foretold the shock that struck the world three days later.

Well, I've written all this, and it doesn't seem to amount to anything. But I do want to help, if I only could. I will enclose some scraps from my Autobiography—scraps about General Grant—they may be of some trifle of use and they may not—they at least verify known traits of his character. My Autobiography is pretty freely dictated, but my idea is to jack-plane it a little before I die, some day or other; I mean the rude construction and rotten grammar. It is the only dictating I ever did and it was most troublesome and awkward work. You may return it to Hartford.

Sincerely Yours
S. L. Clemens

Oliver Wendell Holmes wrote a poem on the occasion of Clemens's fiftieth birthday. It appeared in the *Critic*.

To Oliver Wendell Holmes, Boston

Dear Mr. Holmes,

I shall never be able to tell you the half of how proud you have made me. If I could, you would say you were nearly paid for the trouble you took. And then the family. If I can convey the electrical surprise and gratitude and exaltation of the wife and the children last night when they happened upon that *Critic* where I had, with artful artlessness, spread it open and retired out of view to see what would happen—well, it was great and fine and beautiful to see, and made me feel as the victor feels when the shouting hosts march by. And if you also could have seen it you would have said the account was squared. For I have brought them up in your company, as in the company of a warm and friendly and beneficent but far-distant sun. And so for you to do this thing was for the sun to send down out of the skies the miracle of a special ray and transfigure me before their faces. I knew what that poem would be to them. I knew it would raise me up to remote and shining heights in their eyes, to very fellowship with the chambered Nautilus itself, and that from that fellowship they could never more dissociate me while they should live. And so I made sure to be by when the surprise should come.

Charles Dudley Warner is charmed with the poem for its own felicitous sake, and so indeed am I, but more because it has drawn the sting of my fiftieth year, taken away the pain of it, the grief of it, the somehow *shame* of it, and made me glad and proud it happened.

With reverence and affection,

Sincerely yours,

S. L. Clemens

To Howells, Boston

Hartford, *May 19, '86*

My dear Howells,

. . . Here's a secret. A most curious and pathetic romance, which has just come to light. Read these things but don't mention them. Last fall my old mother, then 82, took a notion to attend a convention of old settlers of the Mississippi Valley in an Iowa town. My brother's wife was astonished and represented to her the hardships and fatigues of such a trip and said my mother might possibly not even survive them, and said there could be no possible interest for her in such a meeting and such a crowd. But my mother insisted and persisted and finally gained her point.

They started, and all the way my mother was young again with excitement, interest, eagerness, anticipation.

They reached the town and the hotel. My mother strode with the same eagerness in her eye and her step, to the counter, and said:

"Is Dr. Barrett of St. Louis here?"

"No. He was here but he returned to St. Louis this morning."

"Will he come again?"

"No."

My mother turned away, the fire all gone from her, and said, "Let us go home."

They went straight back to Keokuk.

My mother sat silent and thinking for many days, a thing which had never happened before. Then one day she said:

"I will tell you a secret. When I was eighteen a young medical student named Barrett lived in Columbia (Ky.) eighteen miles away and he used to ride over to see me. This continued for some time. I loved him with my whole heart and I knew that he felt the same toward me, though no words had been spoken. He was too bashful to speak, he could not do it. Everybody supposed we were engaged, took it for granted we were, but we were not. By and by there was to be a party in a neighboring town, and he wrote my uncle telling him his feelings and asking him to drive me over in his buggy and let him (Barrett) drive me back, so that he might have that opportunity to propose. My uncle should have done as he was asked, without explaining anything to me, but instead he read me the letter and then, of course, I could not go, and did not. He (Barrett) left the country presently and I, to stop the clacking tongues and to show him that *I* did not care, *married* in a pet. In all these sixty-four years I have not seen him since. I saw in a paper that he was going to attend that Old Settlers' Convention. Only three hours before we reached that hotel, he had been standing there!"

Since then her memory is wholly faded out and gone and now she writes letters to the schoolmates who have been dead forty years, and wonders why they neglect her and do not answer.

Think of her carrying that pathetic burden in her old heart sixty-four years, and no human being ever suspecting it!

Yrs ever,
Mark

Jane Clemens now lived with Orion and his wife.

To Jane Clemens, Keokuk, Iowa

Elmira, *Aug. 7, '86*

Dear Ma,

I heard that Molly and Orion and Pamela had been sick but I see by your letter that they are much better now or nearly well. When we visited you a month ago it seemed to us that your Keokuk weather was pretty hot. Jean and Clara sat up in bed at Mrs. McElroy's and cried about it and so did I. But I judge by your letter that it has cooled down now, so that a person is comparatively comfortable with his skin off. Well it did need cooling. I remember that I burnt a hole in my shirt there, with some ice cream that fell on it. And Miss Jenkins told me they never used a stove, but cooked their meals on a marble-topped table in the drawing room just with the natural heat. If anybody else had told me I would not have believed it. I was told by the Bishop of Keokuk that he did not allow crying at funerals because it scalded the furniture. If Miss Jenkins had told me that I would have believed it.

This reminds me that you speak of Dr. Jenkins and his family as if they were strangers to me. Indeed they are not. Don't you suppose I remember gratefully how tender the doctor was with Jean when she hurt her arm, and how quickly he got the pain out of the hurt, whereas I supposed it was going to last at least an hour? No, I don't forget some things as easily as I do others.

Yes, it was pretty hot weather. Now here, when a person is going to die, he is always in a sweat about where he is going to, but in Keokuk of course they don't care, because they are fixed for everything. It has set me reflecting, it has taught me a lesson. By and by, when my health fails, I am going to put all my affairs in order and bid goodbye to my friends here and kill all the people I don't like, and go out to Keokuk and prepare for death.

They are all well in this family, and we all send love.

Affly Your Son
Sam

TEN

[1886-87]

Mailed and unmailed letters contrasted — on unearned
credentials — his opinion of his work — his work habits —
"How stunning are the changes which age makes in a man
while he sleeps" — apology to Mrs. Grover Cleveland

To a gas and electric company, Hartford

Gentlemen,

There are but two places in our whole street where lights could be of any value, by any accident, and you have measured and appointed your intervals so ingeniously as to leave each of those places in the center of a couple of hundred yards of solid darkness. When I noticed that you were setting one of your lights in such a way that I could almost see how to get into my gate at night, I suspected that it was a piece of carelessness on the part of the workmen and would be corrected as soon as you should go around inspecting and find it out. My judgment was right. It is always right when you are concerned. For fifteen years, in spite of my prayers and tears, you persistently kept a gas lamp exactly half-way between my gates so that I couldn't find either of them after dark, and then furnished such execrable gas that I had to hang a danger signal on the lamp post to keep teams from running into it, nights. Now I suppose your present idea is to leave us a little more in the dark.

Don't mind us—out our way. We possess but one vote apiece, and no rights which you are in any way bound to respect. Please take your electric light and go to—but never mind, it is not for me to suggest. You will probably find the way. And anyway you can reasonably count on divine assistance if you lose your bearings.

S. L. Clemens

Paine has explained that Clemens often received very curious letters, asking for one thing or another from him. For example, there was a woman who requested that he send her a single day's income, which she "conservatively estimated at $5,000." He rarely replied to these, but on one occasion he started a series of unmailed answers whose sole function was to give him a chance to let off steam, and he actually wrote an introduction for the series.

"You receive a letter. You read it. It will be tolerably sure to produce one of three results: (1) pleasure, (2) displeasure, (3) indifference. I do not need to say anything about Nos. 1 and 3. Everybody knows what to do with those breeds of letters. It is breed No. 2 that I am after. It is the one that is loaded up with trouble.

"When you get an exasperating letter, what happens? If you are young you answer it promptly, instantly, and mail the thing you have written. At forty what do you do? By that time you have found out that a letter written in a passion is a mistake in ninety-nine cases out of a hundred, that it usually wrongs two persons and *always* wrongs one—yourself. You have grown weary of wronging yourself and repenting, so you manacle, you fetter, you log-chain the frantic impulse to write a pulverizing answer. You will wait a day or die. But in the mean time what do you *do*?

"Why, if it is about dinner time you sit at table in a deep distraction all through the meal. You try to throw it off and help do the talking. You get a start three of four times but conversation dies on your lips every time. Your mind isn't on it, your heart isn't in it. You give up and subside into a bottomless deep of silence permanently. People must speak to you two or three times to get your attention, and then say it over again to make you understand.

"This kind of thing goes on all the rest of the evening. Nobody can interest you in anything. You are useless, a depressing influence, a burden. You go to bed at last, but at three in the morning you are as wide awake as you were in the beginning.

"Thus we see what you have been doing for nine hours—on the outside. But what were you doing on the inside? You were *writing letters* in your mind. And enjoying it, that is quiet true, that is not to be denied. You have been flaying your correspondent alive with your incorporeal pen. You have been braining him, disemboweling him, carving him into little bits, and then—doing it all over again. For nine hours.

"It was wasted time, for you had no intention of putting any of this insanity on paper and mailing it. Yes, you know that and confess it, but what were you to do? Where was your remedy? Will anybody contend that a man can say to such masterful anger as that, 'Go, and be obeyed'?

"No, he cannot. That is certainly true. Well then, what is he to do? I will explain by the suggestion contained in my opening paragraph. During the nine hours he has written as many as forty-seven furious letters—

in his mind. If he had put just *one* of them on paper it would have brought him relief, saved him eight hours of trouble, and given him an hour's red-hot pleasure besides.

"He is not to *mail* this letter. He understands that. And so he can turn on the whole volume of his wrath. There is no harm. He is only writing to get the bile out. So to speak, he is a volcano. Imagining himself erupting does no good. He must open up his crater and pour out in reality his intolerable charge of lava if he would get relief.

"Before he has filled his first sheet sometimes the relief is there. He degenerates into good nature from that point.

"Sometimes the load is so hot and so great that one writes as many as three letters before he gets down to a mailable one, a very angry one, a less angry one, and an argumentative one with hot embers in it here and there. He pigeonholes these and then does one of two things—dismisses the whole matter from his mind or writes the proper sort of letter and mails it.

"To this day I lose my balance and send an overwarm letter—or more frequently a telegram—two or three times a year. But that is better than doing it a hundred times a year, as I used to do years ago. Perhaps I write about as many as ever, but I pigeonhole them. They ought not to be thrown away. Such a letter a year or so old is as good as a sermon to the man who wrote it. It makes him feel small and shabby but—well, that wears off. Any sermon does. But the sermon does some little good anyway. An old cold letter like that makes you wonder how you could ever have got into such a rage about nothing."

The following specimen of an unmailed reply was written to the chairman of a hospital committee.

Dear Sir,

If I were Smithfield I would certainly go out and get behind something and blush. According to your report, "the politicians are afraid to tax the people for the support" of so humane and necessary a thing as a hospital. And do your "people" propose to stand that?—at the hands of vermin officials whom the breath of their votes could blow out of official existence in a moment if they had the pluck to band themselves together and blow? Oh, come, these are not "people"—they are cowed schoolboys with backbones made of boiled macaroni.

If you are not misreporting those "people" you are just in the right business passing the mendicant hat for them. Dear sir, communities where anything like citizenship exists are accustomed to hide their shames, but here we have one proposing to get up a great "exposition" of its dishonor and advertise it all it can.

It has been eleven years since I wrote anything for one of those graveyards called a "Fair paper," and so I have doubtless lost the knack of it somewhat. Still, I have done the best I could for you.

On one occasion Clemens received a letter intended for a Samuel Clements of Elma, New York, informing Clements that his pension had been granted. Clemens forwarded the letter, then sent the following to the appropriate commissioner in Washington.

Dear Sir,

I have not applied for a pension. I have often wanted a pension— often—ever so often—I may say, but inasmuch as the only military service I performed during the war was in the Confederate army, I have always felt a delicacy about asking you for it. However, since you have suggested the thing yourself, I feel strengthened.

I haven't any very pensionable diseases myself but I can furnish a substitute—a man who is just simply a chaos, a museum, of all the different kinds of aches and pains, fractures, dislocations and malformations there are; a man who would regard "rheumatism and sore eyes" as mere recreation and refreshment after the serious occupations of his day.

If you grant me the pension, dear sir, please hand it to General Jos. Hawley, United States Senator—I mean hand him the certificate, not the money, and he will forward it to me. You will observe by this postal card which I inclose that he takes a friendly interest in the matter. He thinks I've already got the pension, whereas I've only got the rheumatism; but didn't want that—I had that before. I wish it were catching. I know a man that I would load up with it pretty early. Lord, but we all feel that way sometimes. I've seen the day when—but never mind that. You may be busy. Just hand it to Hawley—the certificate, you understand, is not transferable.

"Clemens was all the time receiving application from people who wished him to recommend one article or another—books, plays, tobacco and what not," Paine wrote. "They were generally persistent people, unable to accept a polite or kind denial. Once he set down some remarks on this particular phase of correspondence."

1

No doubt Mr. Edison has been offered a large interest in many and many an electrical project for the use of his name to float it withal. And no doubt all men who have achieved for their names, in any line of activity whatever, a sure market value have been familiar with this sort of solicitation. Reputation is a hallmark. It can remove doubt from pure silver and it can also make the plated article pass for pure.

And so, people without a hallmark of their own are always trying to get the loan of somebody else's.

As a rule, that kind of a person sees only one side of the case. He sees that his invention or his painting or his book is—apparently—a trifle better than you yourself can do, therefore why shouldn't you be willing to put your hallmark on it? You will be giving the purchaser his full money's worth, so who is hurt and where is the harm? Besides, are you not helping a struggling fellow craftsman, and is it not your duty to do that?

That side is plenty clear enough to him but he can't and won't see the other side, to wit: that you are a rascal if you put your hallmark upon a thing which you did not produce yourself, howsoever good it may be. How simple that is and yet there are not two applicants in a hundred who can be made to see it.

When one receives an application of this sort his first emotion is an indignant sense of insult. His first deed is the penning of a sharp answer. He blames nobody but that other person. That person is a very base being. He *must* be. He would degrade himself for money, otherwise it would not occur to him that you would do such a thing. But all the same, that application has done its work and taken you down in your own estimation. You recognize that everybody hasn't as high an opinion of you as you have of yourself, and in spite of you there ensues an interval during which you are not in your own estimation as fine a bird as you were before.

However, being old and experienced, you do not mail your sharp letter, but leave it lying a day. That saves you. For by that time you have begun to reflect that you are a person who deals in exaggerations—and exaggerations are lies. You meant yours to be playful, and thought you made them unmistakably so. But you couldn't make them playfulnesses to a man who has no sense of the playful and can see nothing but the serious side of things. You rattle on quite playfully and with measureless extravagance about how you wept at the tomb of Adam, and all in good time you find to your astonishment that no end of people took you at your word and believed you. And presently they find out that you were not in earnest. They have been deceived. Therefore (as they argue—and there is a sort of argument in it) you are a deceiver. If you will deceive in one way, why shouldn't you in another? So they apply for the use of your trademark. You are amazed and affronted. You retort that you are not that kind of person. Then *they* are amazed and affronted, and wonder "since when?"

By this time you have got your bearings. You realize that perhaps there is a little blame on both sides. You are in the right frame now. So you write a letter void of offense, declining. You mail this one. You pigeon-hole the other.

That is, *being* old and experienced, you do, but early in your career you don't: you mail the first one.

2

An enthusiast who had a new system of musical notation wrote to me and suggested that a magazine article from me, contrasting the absurdities of the old system with the simplicities of his new one, would be sure to make a "rousing hit." He shouted and shouted over the marvels wrought by his system and quoted the handsome compliments which had been paid it by famous musical people but he forgot to tell me what his notation was like or what its simplicities consisted in. So I could not have written the article if I had wanted to—which I didn't, because I hate strangers with axes to grind. I wrote him a courteous note explaining how busy I was—I always explain how busy I am—and casually dropped this remark:

"I judge the X-X notation to be a rational mode of representing music, in place of the prevailing fashion, which was the invention of an idiot."

Next mail he asked permission to print that meaningless remark. I answered no—courteously but still no, explaining that I could not afford to be placed in the attitude of trying to influence people with a mere worthless *guess*. What a scorcher I got, next mail! Such irony! Such sarcasm, such caustic praise of my superhonorable loyalty to the public! And withal, such compassion for my stupidity, too, in not being able to understand my own language. I cannot remember the words of this letter broadside but there was about a page used up in turning this idea round and round and exposing it in different lights.

Unmailed Answer

Dear Sir,

What is the trouble with you? If it is your viscera, you cannot have them taken out and reorganized a moment too soon. I mean, if they are inside. But if you are composed of them, that is another matter. Is it your brain? But it could not be your brain. Possibly it is your skull: you want to look out for that. Some people, when they get an idea, it pries the structure apart. Your system of notation has got in there and couldn't find room. Without a doubt that is what the trouble is. Your skull was not made to put ideas in, it was made to throw potatoes at.

Yours Truly

Mailed Answer

Dear Sir,

Come, come—take a walk. You disturb the children.

Yours Truly

Clemens was frequently asked by newspapers to express himself on some subject of the day—without payment.

Unmailed Answer

Dear Sir,

I have received your proposition, which you have imitated from a pauper London periodical which had previously imitated the *idea* of this sort of mendicancy from seventh-rate American journalism, where it originated as a variation of the inexpensive "interview."

Why do you buy Associated Press dispatches? To make your paper the more salable, you answer. But why don't you try to beg them? Why do you discriminate? I can sell my stuff. Why should I give it to you? Why don't you ask me for a shirt? What is the difference between asking me for the worth of a shirt and asking me for the shirt itself? Perhaps you didn't know you were begging. I would not use that argument—it makes the user a fool. The passage of poetry—or prose, if you will—which has taken deepest root in my thought and which I oftenest return to and dwell upon with keenest no matter what, is this: That the proper place for journalists who solicit literary charity is on the street corner with their hats in their hands.

Mailed Answer

Dear Sir,

Your favor of recent date is received, but I am obliged by press of work to decline.

"The manager of a traveling theatrical company wrote that he had taken the liberty of dramatizing *Tom Sawyer*," Paine has written, "and would like also the use of the author's name, the idea being to convey to the public that it was a Mark Twain play. In return for this slight favor the manager sent an invitation for Mark Twain to come and see the play—to be present on the opening night, as it were, at his (the manager's) expense. He added that if the play should be a go in the cities there might be some 'arrangement' of profits."

Unmailed Answer

Hartford, *Sept. 8, '87*

Dear Sir,

And so it has got around to you at last, and you also have "taken the liberty." You are No. 1365. When 1364 sweeter and better people, including the author, have "tried" to dramatize *Tom Sawyer* and did not arrive, what sort of show do you suppose you stand? That is a book, dear sir, which cannot be dramatized. One might as well try to dramatize any other hymn. *Tom Sawyer* is simply a hymn put into prose form to give it a wordly air.

Why the pale doubt that flitteth dim and nebulous athwart the forecastle of your third sentence? Have no fears. Your piece will be a Go. It will go out the back door on the first night. They've all done it—the 1364. So will—1365. Not one of us ever thought of the simple device of half-soling himself with a stove-lid. Ah, what suffering a little hindsight would have saved us. Treasure this hint.

How kind of you to invite me to the funeral. Go to. I have attended a thousand of them. I have seen Tom Sawyer's remains in all the different kinds of dramatic shrouds there are. You cannot start anything fresh. Are you serious when you propose to pay my expence— if that is the Susquehannian way of spelling it? And can you be aware that I charge a hundred dollars a mile when I travel for pleasure? Do you realize that it is 432 miles to Susquehanna? Would it be handy for you to send me the $43,200 first, so I could be counting it as I come along, because railroading is pretty dreary to a sensitive nature when there's nothing sordid to buck at for Zeitvertreib.

Now as I understand it, dear and magnanimous 1365, you are going to recreate *Tom Sawyer* dramatically and then do me the compliment to put me in the bills as father of this shady offspring. Sir, do you know that this kind of a compliment has destroyed people before now? Listen.

Twenty-four years ago I was strangely handsome. The remains of it are still visible through the rifts of time. I was so handsome that human activities ceased as if spellbound when I came in view, and even inanimate things stopped to look—like locomotives and district messenger boys and so on. In San Francisco in the rainy season I was often mistaken for fair weather.

Upon one occasion I was traveling in the Sonora region and stopped for an hour's nooning to rest my horse and myself. All the town came out to look. The tribes of Indians gathered to look. A Piute squaw named her baby for me, a voluntary compliment which pleased me greatly. Other attentions were paid me.

Last of all arrived the president and faculty of Sonora University and offered me the post of Professor of Moral Culture and the Dogmatic Humanities, which I accepted gratefully, and entered at once upon my duties. But my name had pleased the Indians, and in the deadly kindness of their hearts they went on naming their babies after me. I tried to stop it but the Indians could not understand why I should object to so manifest a compliment. The thing grew and grew and spread and spread and became exceedingly embarrassing. The University stood it a couple of years but then for the sake of the college they felt obliged to call a halt although I had the sympathy of the whole faculty.

The president himself said to me, "I am as sorry as I can be for you, and would still hold out if there were any hope ahead, but you see how it is. There are a hundred and thirty-two of them already, and fourteen precincts to hear from. The circumstance has brought your name into most wide and unfortunate renown. It causes much comment. I believe that that is not an overstatement. Some of this comment is palliative but some of it—by patrons at a distance who only know the statistics without the explanation—is offensive, and in some cases even violent. Nine students have been called home. The trustees of the college have been growing more and more uneasy all these last months—steadily along with the implacable increase in your census—and I will not conceal from you that more than once they have touched upon the expediency of a change in the Professorship of Moral Culture. The coarsely sarcastic editorial in yesterday's *Alta*—headed Give the Moral Acrobat a Rest—has brought things to a crisis and I am charged with the unpleasant duty of receiving your resignation."

I know you only mean me a kindness, dear 1365, but it is a most deadly mistake. Please do not name your Injun for me. Truly Yours

Mailed Answer

New York, *Sept. 8, 1887*

Dear Sir,

Necessarily I cannot assent to so strange a proposition. And I think it but fair to warn you that if you put the piece on the stage, you must take the legal consequences.

Yours respectfully,
S. L. Clemens

Before the days of international copyright, Clemens's books were sometimes printed by Canadian publishers, whose cheaply printed editions made their way into the U.S., where they competed with books on which he received a royalty.

Unmailed letter to H. C. Christiancy, on book piracy

Hartford, *Dec. 18,* '87

H. C. Christiancy, Esq.

Dear Sir,

As I understand it, the position of the U. S. Government is this. If a person be captured on the border with counterfeit bonds in his hands—bonds of the N. Y. Central Railway, for instance—the procedure in his case shall be as follows:

1. If the N. Y. C. have not previously filed in the several police offices along the border proof of ownership of the originals of the bonds, the government officials must collect a *duty* on the counterfeits and then let them go ahead and circulate in this country.

2. But if there *is* proof already on file, then the N. Y. C. may pay the duty and take the counterfeits.

But in no case will the United States consent to go without its share of the swag.

It is delicious. The biggest and proudest government on earth turned sneak thief. Collecting pennies on stolen property and pocketing them with a greasy and libidinous leer. Going into partnership with foreign thieves to rob its own children, and when the child escapes the foreigner, descending to the abysmal baseness of hanging on and robbing the infant all alone by itself!

Dear sir, this is not any more respectable than for a father to collect toll on the forced prostitution of his own daughter. In fact it is the same thing. Upon these terms, what is a U.S. custom house but a "fence?" That is all it is: a legalized trader in stolen goods.

And this nasty law, this filthy law, this unspeakable law, calls itself a "regulation for the protection of owners of copyright!" Can sarcasm go further than that? In what way does it protect them? Inspiration itself could not furnish a rational answer to that question. Whom does it protect, then? Nobody, as far as I can see, but the foreign thief—sometimes—and his fellow-footpad the U. S. government all the time. What could the Central Company do with the counterfeit bonds after it had bought them of the star spangled banner Master-thief? Sell them at a dollar apiece and fetch down the market for the genuine hundred-dollar bond? What could I do with that 20-cent copy of *Roughing It* which the United States has collared on the border and is waiting to release to me for cash in case I am willing to come down to its moral level and help rob myself? Sell it at ten or fifteen cents—duty added—and destroy the market for the original $3.50 book? Who ever did invent that law? I would like to know the name of that immortal jackass.

Dear sir, I appreciate your courtesy in stretching your authority in the desire to do me a kindness, and I sincerely thank you for it. But I have no use for that book, and if I were even starving for it I would not pay duty on it either to get it or suppress it. No doubt there are ways in which I might consent to go into partnership with thieves and fences but this is not one of them. This one revolts the remains of my self-respect; turns my stomach. I think I could companion with a highwayman who carried a shotgun and took many risks. Yes, I think I should like that if I were younger. But to go in with a big rich government that robs paupers and the widows and orphans of paupers and takes no risk—why the thought just gags me.

Oh, no, I shall never pay any duties on pirated books of mine. I am much too respectable for that—yet awhile. But here, one thing that gravels me is this, as far as I can discover—while freely granting that the U. S. copyright laws are far and away the most idiotic that exist anywhere on the face of the earth, *they* don't authorize the government to admit pirated books into this country, toll or no toll. And so I think that that regulation is the invention of one of those people—as a rule, early stricken of God, intellectually—the departmental *interpreters* of the laws, in Washington. They can always be depended on to take any reasonably good law and interpret the common sense all out of it. They can be depended on, every time, to defeat a good law and make it inoperative—yes and utterly grotesque too, mere matter for laughter and derision.

Take some of the decisions of the Post Office Department, for instance, though I do not mean to suggest that that asylum is any worse than the others for the breeding and nourishing of incredible lunatics—I merely instance it because it happens to be the first to come into my mind. Take that case of a few years ago where the P. M. General suddenly issued an edict requiring you to add the name of the *State* after Boston, New York, Chicago, &c, in your superscriptions, on pain of having your letter stopped and forwarded to the deadletter office. Yes, and I believe he required the county too. He made one little concession in favor of New York: you could say "New York *City*" and stop there. But if you left off the "city," you must add "N. Y." to your "New York." Why, it threw the business of the whole country into chaos and brought commerce almost to a standstill.

Now think of that! When that man goes to—to—well, wherever he is going to—we shan't want the microscopic details of his address. I guess we can find him.

Well, as I was saying, *I* believe that this whole paltry and ridiculous swindle is a pure creation of one of those cabbages that used to be at the head of one of those Retreats down there—Departments, you know—and that you will find it so if you look into it. And moreover—but land, I reckon we are both tired by this time.

Truly Yours,
Mark Twain

Clemens once remarked, "The symbol of the human race ought to be an ax. Every human being has one concealed about him somewhere." He told Paine that "when a stranger called on him, or wrote to him, in nine cases out of ten he could distinguish the gleam of the ax almost immediately." The following letter is a specimen of the kind that was mailed.

To Mrs. T, concerning unearned credentials, etc.

Hartford, *1887*

My dear Madam,

It is an idea which many people have had but it is of no value. I have seen it tried out many and many a time. I have seen a lady lecturer urged and urged upon the public in a lavishly complimentary document signed by Longfellow, Whittier, Holmes and some others of supreme celebrity, but—there was nothing in her and she failed. If there had been any great merit in her she never would have needed those men's help and (at her rather mature age) would never have consented to ask for it.

There is an unwritten law about human successes, and your sister must bow to that law, she must submit to its requirements. In brief this law is:

1. No occupation without an apprenticeship.

2. No pay to the apprentice.

This law stands right in the way of the subaltern who wants to be a general before he has smelt powder. And it stands (and should stand) in everybody's way who applies for pay or position before he has served his apprenticeship and *proved* himself. Your sister's course is perfectly plain. Let her enclose this letter to Maj. J. B. Pond and offer to lecture a year for $10 a week and her expenses, the contract to be annullable by him at any time after a month's notice, but not annullable by her at all. The second year he to have her services, if he wants them, at a trifle under the best price offered her by anybody else.

She can learn her trade in those two years and then be entitled to remuneration, but she cannot learn it in any less time than that unless she is a human miracle.

Try it and do not be afraid. It is the fair and right thing. If she wins, she will win squarely and righteously and never have to blush.

Truly yours,
S. L. Clemens

In February, Howells offered to take the *Library of Humor,* a project of Clemens's publishing company, off Clemens's hands. Howells had received $2,600 for work he had put in on it, and he was troubled because he thought the book might never be used. His letter also referred to "one of the disastrous inventions in which Clemens had invested—a method of casting brass dies for stamping book covers and wall paper," as Paine has described it.

Hartford, *Feb. 15, '87*

Dear Howells,

I was in New York five days ago, and Webster mentioned the *Library* and proposed to publish it a year or a year and half hence. I have written him your proposition today. (The *Library* is part of the property of the C. L. W. & Co. firm.)

I don't remember what that technical phrase was but I think you will find it in any Cyclopedia under the head of "Brass." The thing I best remember is that the self-styled "inventor" had a very ingenious way of keeping me from seeing him *apply* his invention. The first appointment was spoiled by his burning down the man's shop in which it was to be done, the night before. The second was spoiled by his burning down his own shop the night before. He unquestionably did both of these things. He really had no invention. The whole project was a blackmailing swindle and cost me several thousand dollars.

The slip you sent me from the May "Study" has delighted Mrs. Clemens and me to the marrow. To think that thing might be possible to many, but to be brave enough to say it is possible to you only, I certainly believe. The longer I live the clearer I perceive how unmatchable, how unapproachable, a compliment one pays when he says of a man, "He has the courage to utter his convictions." Haven't you had reviewers *talk* Alps to you and then print potato hills?

I haven't as good an opinion of my work as you hold of it but I've always done what I could to secure and enlarge my good opinion of it. I've always said to myself, "Everybody reads it and that's something. It surely isn't pernicious, or the most acceptable people would get pretty tired of it." And when a critic said by implication that it wasn't high and fine, through the remark, "High and fine literature is wine," I retorted (confidentially, to myself), "Yes, high and fine literature is wine, and mine is only water. But everybody likes water."

You didn't tell me to return that proof slip, so I have pasted it into my private scrapbook. None will see it there. With a thousand thanks.

Ys Ever
Mark

Jeannette Gilder was on the staff of the *Critic*. "Rest-and-be-Thankful" was the official name of the Clemens place in Elmira which was better known as "Quarry Farm."

To Jeannette Gilder (not mailed)

Hartford, *May 14*, '87

My dear Miss Gilder,

We shall spend the summer at the same old place, the remote farm called "Rest-and-be-Thankful," on top of the hills three miles from Elmira, N. Y. Your other question is harder to answer. It is my habit to keep four or five books in process of erection all the time, and every summer add a few courses of bricks to two or three of them. But I cannot forecast which of the two or three it is going to be. It takes seven years to complete a book by this method but still it is a good method: gives the public a rest. I have been accused of "rushing into print" prematurely, moved thereto by greediness for money, but in truth I have never done that.

Do you care for trifles of information? Well then, *Tom Sawyer* and *The Prince and the Pauper* were each on the stocks two or three years, and *Old Times on the Mississippi* eight. One of my unfinished books has been on the stocks sixteen years; another seventeen. This latter book could have been finished in a day at any time during the past five years. But as in the first of these two narratives all the action takes place in Noah's ark, and as in the other the action takes place in heaven, there seemed to be no hurry and so I have not hurried. Tales of stirring adventure in those localities do not need to be rushed to publication lest they get stale by waiting.

In twenty-one years, with all my time at my free disposal, I have written and completed only eleven books, whereas with half the labor that a journalist does I could have written sixty in that time. I do not greatly mind being accused of a proclivity for rushing into print, but at the same time I don't believe that the charge is really well founded. Suppose I did write eleven books. Have you nothing to be grateful for? Go to—remember the forty-nine which I din't write.

Truly Yours
S. L. Clemens

Notes (added twenty-two years later)

Stormfield, April 30, 1909. It seems the letter was not sent. I probably feared she might print it, and I couldn't find a way to say so without running a risk of hurting her. No one would hurt Jeannette Gilder purposely, and no one would want to run the risk of doing it unintentionally. She is my neighbor, six miles away, now, and I must ask her about this ancient letter.

I note with pride and pleasure that I told no untruths in my unsent answer. I still have the habit of keeping unfinished books lying around years and years, waiting. I have four or five novels on hand at present in a half-finished condition, and it is more than three years since I have looked at any of them. I have no intention of finishing them. I could complete all of them in less than a year if the impulse should come powerfully upon me. Long, long ago money-*necessity* furnished that impulse once (*Following the Equator*) but mere desire for money has never furnished it, so far as I remember. Not even money-necessity was able to overcome me on a couple of occasions when perhaps I ought to have allowed it to succeed. While I was a bankrupt and in debt, two offers were made me for weekly literary contributions to continue during a year, and they would have made a debtless man of me but I declined them, with my wife's full approval, for I had known of no instance where a man had pumped himself out once a week and failed to run "emptyings" before the year was finished.

As to that "Noah's Ark" book, I began it in Edinburgh in 1873. I don't know where the manuscript is now. It was a diary which professed to be the work of Shem but wasn't. I began it again several months ago but only for recreation. I hadn't any intention of carrying it to a finish, or even to the end of the first chapter, in fact.

As to the book whose action "takes place in Heaven." That was a small thing, "Captain Stormfield's Visit to Heaven." It lay in my pigeon-holes 40 years, then I took it out and printed it in *Harper's Monthly* last year.

S. L. C.

To Mollie Clemens, Keokuk, Iowa

On the hill near Elmira, *July 10*, '87

Dear Mollie,

This is a superb Sunday for weather—very cloudy, and the thermometer as low as 65. The city in the valley is purple with shade as seen from up here at the study. The Cranes are reading and loafing in the canvas-curtained summer house 50 yards away on a higher (the highest) point. The cats are loafing over at "Ellerslie," which is the children's estate and dwelling house in their own private grounds (by deed from Susie Crane) a hundred yards from the study, amongst the clover and young oaks and willows. Livy is down at the house but I shall now go and bring her up to the Cranes to help us occupy the lounges and hammocks—whence a great panorama of distant hill and valley and city is seeable. The children have gone on a lark through the neighboring hills and woods. It is a perfect day indeed.

With love to you all.
Sam

To Howells, Boston

Elmira, Aug. 22, '87

My dear Howells,

How stunning are the changes which age makes in a man while he sleeps. When I finished Carlyle's French Revolution in 1871, I was a Girondin. Every time I have read it since, I have read it differently, being influenced and changed little by little, by life and environment (and Taine and St. Simon). And now I lay the book down once more and recognize that I am a Sansculotte! And not a pale, characterless Sansculotte but a Marat. Carlyle teaches no such gospel, so the change is in *me*—in my vision of the evidences.

People pretend that the Bible means the same to them at 50 that it did at all former milestones in their journey. I wonder how they can lie so. It comes of practice, no doubt. They would not say that of Dickens's or Scott's books. *Nothing* remains the same. When a man goes back to look at the house of his childhood it has always *shrunk*. There is no instance of such a house being as big as the picture in memory and imagination call for. Shrunk how? Why, to its correct dimensions. The house hasn't altered. This is the first time it has been in focus.

Well, that's loss. To have house and Bible shrink so under the disillusioning corrected angle is loss—for a moment. But there are compensations. You tilt the tube skyward and bring planets and comets and corona flames a hundred and fifty thousand miles high into the field. Which I see you have done and found Tolstoi. I haven't got him in focus yet but I've got Browning. . . .

Ys Ever

Mark

To Mrs. Grover Cleveland, Washington

Hartford, *Nov. 6, 1887*

My dear Madam,

I do not know how it is in the White House, but in this house of ours whenever the minor half of the administration tries to run itself without the help of the major half it gets aground. Last night when I was offered the opportunity to assist you in the throwing open the Warner brothers superb benefaction in Bridgeport to those fortunate women, I naturally appreciated the honor done me, and promptly seized my chance. I had an engagement but the circumstances washed it out of my mind. If I had only laid the matter before the major half of the administration on the spot, there would have been no blunder. But I never thought of that. So when I did lay it before her later, I realized once more that it will not do for the literary fraction of a combination to try to manage affairs which properly belong in the office of the business bulk of it.

I suppose the President often acts just like that: goes and makes an impossible promise, and you never find it out until it is next to impossible to break it up and set things straight again. Well, that is just our way exactly—one half of the administration always busy getting the family into trouble, and the other half busy getting it out again. And so we do seem to be all pretty much alike, after all.

The fact is, I had forgotten that we were to have a dinner party on that Bridgeport date. I thought it was the next day, which is a good deal of an improvement for me, because I am more used to being behind a day or two than ahead. But that is just the difference between one end of this kind of an administration and the other end of it, as you have noticed yourself—the other end does not forget these things.

Just so with a funeral. If it is the man's funeral, he is most always there, of course—but that is no credit to him, he wouldn't be there if you depended on *him* to remember about it. Whereas if on the other hand—but I seem to have got off from my line of argument somehow. Never mind about the funeral. Of course I am not meaning to say anything *against* funerals—that is, as occasions—mere occasions—for as diversions I don't think they amount to much. But as I was saying—if you are not busy I will look back and see what it was I was saying.

I don't seem to find the place. But anyway she was as sorry as ever anybody could be that I could not go to Bridgeport, but there was no help for it. And I, I have been not only sorry but very sincerely ashamed of having made an engagement to go without first making sure that I could keep it, and I do not know how to apologize enough for my heedless breach of good manners.

With the sincerest respect,
S. L. Clemens

To Mr. Chatto of Chatto & Windus, London

Hartford, *Dec.* 5, '87

My dear Chatto,

Look here, I don't mind paying the tax, but don't you let the Inland Revenue Office send me any more receipts for it, for the postage is something perfectly demoralizing. If they feel obliged to print a receipt on a horse blanket, why don't they hire a ship and send it over at their own expense?

Wasn't it good that they caught me out with an old book instead of a new one? The tax on a new book would bankrupt a body. It was my purpose to go to England next May and stay the rest of the year, but I've found that tax office out just in time. My new book would issue in March, and they would tax the sale in both countries. Come, we must get up a compromise somehow. You go and work in on the good side of those revenue people and get them to take the profits and give me the tax. Then I will come over and we will divide the swag and have a good time.

I wish you to thank Mr. Christmas for me. But we won't resist. The country that allows me copyright has a right to tax me.

Sincerely Yours
S. L. Clemens

ELEVEN

[1888-90]

River nostalgia — on being interviewed — typesetting euphoria — to the death of monarchy — "Indeed I have been misjudged from the very first"

In June 1888 Clemens received his first honorary degree: Master of Arts, conferred by Yale. He was notified of this honor by his friend Charles H. Clarke, editor of the *Hartford Courant*, to whom he wrote, "I feel mighty proud of that degree. In fact, I could squeeze the truth a little closer and say vain of it. And why shouldn't I be? I am the only literary animal of my particular subspecies who has ever been given a degree by any College in any age of the world, as far as I know."

Being busy in Elmira, he was unable to attend the award ceremony in June. However, he expressed his thanks to Yale in an address later in the year in the following manner.

"I was sincerely proud and grateful to be made a Master of Arts by this great and venerable university and I would have come last June to testify this feeling, as I do now testify it, but that the sudden and unexpected notice of the honor done me found me at a distance from home and unable to discharge that duty and enjoy that privilege.

"Along at first, say for the first month or so, I did not quite know how to proceed because of my not knowing just what authorities and privileges belonged to the title which had been granted me, but after that I consulted some students of Trinity in Hartford and they made everything clear to me. It was through them that I found out that my title made me head of the Governing Body of the university and lodged in me very broad and severely responsible powers.

"I was told that it would be necessary to report to you at this time, and of course I comply, though I would have preferred to put it off till I could make a better showing, for indeed I have been so pertinaciously hindered and obstructed at every turn by the faculty that it would be difficult to prove that the university is really in any better shape now than it was when I first took charge.

"By advice, I turned my earliest attention to the Greek Department. I told the Greek professor I had concluded to drop the use of Greek written character because it is so hard to spell with and so impossible to read after you get it spelt. Let us draw the curtain there. I saw by what followed that nothing but early neglect saved him from being a very profane man.

"I ordered the professor of mathematics to simplify the whole system, because the way it was I couldn't understand it, and I didn't want things going on in the college in what was practically a clandestine fashion. I told him to drop the conundrum system. It was not suited to the dignity of a college, which should deal in facts, not guesses and suppositions. We didn't want any more cases of *if* A and B stand at opposite poles of the earth's surface and C at the equator of Jupiter, at what variations of angle will the left limb of the moon appear to these different parties? I said you just let that thing alone. It's plenty of time to get in a sweat about it when it happens. As like as not it ain't going to do any harm, anyway. His reception of these instructions bordered on insubordination, insomuch that I felt obliged to take his number and report him.

"I found the astronomer of the university gadding around after comets and other such odds and ends—tramps and derelicts of the skies. I told him pretty plainly that we couldn't have that. I told him it was no economy to go on piling up and piling up raw material in the way of new stars and comets and asteroids that we couldn't ever have any use for till we had worked off the old stock. At bottom I don't really mind comets so much, but somehow I have always been down on asteroids. There is nothing mature about them. I wouldn't sit up nights the way that man does if I could get a basketful of them. He said it was the best line of goods he had. He said he could trade them to Rochester for comets, and trade the comets to Harvard for nebulae, and trade the nebulae to the Smithsonian for flint hatchets. I felt obliged to stop this thing on the spot. I said we couldn't have the university turned into an astronomical junkyard. And while I was at it I thought I might as well make the reform complete. The astronomer is extraordinarily mutinous, and so, with your approval, I will transfer him to the Law Department and put one of the law students in his place. A boy will be more biddable, more tractable, also cheaper. It is true he cannot be intrusted with the important work at first, but he can comb the skies for nebulae till he gets his hand in.

"I have other changes in mind but as they are in the nature of surprises I judge it politic to leave them unspecified at this time."

Jack Downing of the following had been a Mississippi pilot in the old days and had long ago retired to a comfortable life in an Ohio town. Clemens had not heard from him for years.

To Major Jack Downing, Middleport, Ohio

Elmira, N. Y., [no month] *1888*

Dear Major,

And has it come to this that the dead rise up and speak? For I supposed that you were dead, it has been so long since I heard your name.

And how young you've grown! I was a mere boy when I knew you on the river, where you had been piloting for 35 years, and now you are only a year and a half older than I am! I mean to go to Hot Springs myself and get 30 or 40 years knocked off my age. It's manifestly the place that Ponce de Leon was striking for, but the poor fellow lost the trail.

Possibly I may see you, for I shall be in St. Louis a day or two in November. I propose to go down the river and "note the changes" once more before I make the long crossing, and perhaps you can come there. Will you? I want to see all the boys that are left alive.

And so Grant Marsh, too, is flourishing yet? A mighty good fellow, and smart too. When we were taking that wood flat down to the *Chambers*, which was aground, I soon saw that I was a perfect lubber at piloting such a thing. I saw that I could never hit the *Chambers* with it, so I resigned in Marsh's favor, and he accomplished the task to my admiration. We should all have gone to the mischief if I had remained in authority. I always had good judgment, more judgment than talent, in fact.

No, the nom de plume did not originate in that way. Capt. Sellers used the signature, "Mark Twain," himself when he used to write up the antiquities in the way of river reminiscences for the *New Orleans Picayune*. He hated me for burlesquing them in an article in the *True Delta*. So four years later, when he died, I robbed the corpse—that is, I confiscated the nom de plume. I have published this vital fact 3,000 times now. But no matter, it is good practice. It is about the only fact that I can tell the same way every time. Very glad, indeed, to hear from you, Major, and shall be gladder still to see you in November.

Truly yours,
S. L. Clemens

The Paige typesetting machine and Clemens's typesetting fever were a constant financial drain on Clemens. At a time when type was set entirely by hand, James W. Paige was designing and building a machine which was intended to revolutionize type composition. It would set, justify and distribute type at such a speed that it would do the work of half a dozen men. But his product was too complicated, too delicate, and had the disastrous habit of breaking type. Furthermore, Paige was a tinkerer who couldn't let well enough alone. He was a persuasive talker. Clemens once remarked that Paige could persuade fish to leave the water and go for a walk with him. Paine described him as "a small, bright-eyed, alert, smartly dressed man, with a crystal-clear mind, but a dreamer and a visionary." The promoters of the Mergenthaler Linotype machine, which was to prove very successful, offered to swap half their interests for a half interest in the Paige patent but Clemens, convinced the Paige machine was the wave of the future, turned them down and thus declined a fortune.

To Orion, Keokuk, Iowa

Private

Oct. 3, '88

. . . Saturday 29th, by a closely calculated estimate, there were 85 days work to do on the machine.

We can use 4 men but not constantly. If they could work constantly it would complete the machine in 21 days, of course. They will all be on hand and under wages, and each will get in all the work there is opportunity for, but by how much they can reduce the 85 days toward the 21 days, nobody can tell.

Today I pay Pratt & Whitney $10,000. This squares back indebtedness and everything to date. They began about May or April or March 1886—along there somewhere—and have always kept from a dozen to two dozen master hands on the machine.

That outgo is done. 4 men for a month or two will close up that leak and caulk it. Work on the patents is also kind of drawing toward a conclusion.

Love to you both. All well here.

And give our love to Ma if she can get the idea.

Sam

Clemens was working steadily and well on *The Connecticut Yankee*, which he had begun two years earlier. On returning from Elmira to Hartford, he found a good deal of confusion at home, so he moved temporarily to Twichell's, where he seemed to be happy despite some carpenter work going on.

To Theodore W. Crane, at Quarry Farm, Elmira, N.Y.

Friday, Oct. 5, '88

Dear Theo,

I am here in Twichell's house at work, with the noise of the children and an army of carpenters to help. Of course they don't help but neither do they hinder. It's like a boiler-factory for racket, and in nailing a wooden ceiling onto the room under me the hammering tickles my feet amazingly sometimes, and jars my table a good deal. But I never am conscious of the racket at all, and I move my feet into position of relief without knowing when I do it. I began here Monday morning and have done eighty pages since. I was so tired last night that I thought I would lie abed and rest today, but I couldn't resist. I mean to try to knock off tomorrow but it's doubtful if I do. I want to finish the day the machine finishes, and a week ago the closest calculations for that indicated Oct. 22—but experience teaches me that their calculations will miss fire as usual.

The other day the children were projecting a purchase, Livy and I to furnish the money—a dollar and a half. Jean discouraged the idea. She said: "We haven't got any money. Children, if you would think, you would remember the machine isn't done."

It's billiards tonight. I wish you were here.

With love to you both—

S. L. C.

Will Bowen was both a schoolmate and a Mississippi pilot colleague.

To Will Bowen, Hannibal, Missouri

Hartford, Nov. 4, '88

Dear Will,

I received your letter yesterday evening just as I was starting out of town to attend a wedding, and so my mind was privately busy all the evening in the midst of the maelstrom of chat and chaff and laughter, with the sort of reflections which create themselves, examine themselves and continue themselves unaffected by surroundings—unaffected, that is *understood*, by the surroundings, but not

uninfluenced by them. Here was the near presence of the two supreme events of life: marriage, which is the beginning of life, and
death which is the end of it. I found myself seeking chances to shirk
into corners where I might think, undisturbed. And the most I got
out of my thought was this. Both marriage and death ought to be
welcome: the one promises happiness, doubtless the other assures it.
A long procession of people filed through my mind, people whom
you and I knew so many years ago, so many centuries ago, it seems
like, and these ancient dead marched to the soft marriage music of a
band concealed in some remote room of the house. And the content-
ed music and the dreaming shades seemed in right accord with each
other, and fitting. Nobody else knew that a procession of the dead
was passing through this noisy swarm of the living, but there it was,
and to me there was nothing uncanny about it. No, they were welcome faces to me. I would have liked to bring up every creature we
knew in those days—even the dumb animals—it would be bathing
in the fabled Fountain of Youth.

We all feel your deep trouble with you, and we would hope, if we
might, but your words deny us that privilege. To die one's self is a
thing that must be easy and of light consequence, but to lose a *part*
of one's self—well, we know how deep that pang goes, we who have
suffered that disaster, received that wound which cannot heal.

Sincerely your friend
S. L. Clemens

To Orion, Keokuk, Iowa

Nov. 29, '88

Jesus *Christ!*

It is perilous to write such a man. You can go crazy on less material than anybody that ever lived. What in hell has produced all these
maniacal imaginings? You told me you *had* hired an attendant for
ma. Now hire one instantly and stop this nonsense of wearing Mollie
and yourself out trying to do that nursing yourselves. Hire the attendant and tell me her cost so that I can instruct Webster & Co. to add
it every month to what they already send. Don't fool away any more
time about this. And don't write me any more damned rot about

"storms," and inability to pay trivial sums of money and—and—hell
and *damnation!* You see I've read only the first page of your letter. I
wouldn't read the rest for a million dollars.

Yr Sam

P. S. Don't imagine that I have lost my temper because I swear. I
swear all day but I do not lose my temper. And don't imagine that I
am on my way to the poorhouse, for I am not; or that I am uneasy,
for I am not; or that I am uncomfortable or unhappy—for *I never
am.* I don't know what it is to be unhappy or uneasy, and I am not
going to try to learn how at this late day.

Sam

Of the following, Paine has written: "Few men were ever interviewed
oftener than Mark Twain, yet he never welcomed interviewers and was
seldom satisfied with them. 'What I say in an interview loses its character
in print,' he often remarked, 'all its life and personality. The reporter
realizes this himself and tries to improve upon me but he doesn't help
matters any.'

"Edward W. Bok, before he became editor of the *Ladies' Home Journal,* was conducting a weekly syndicate column under the title of 'Bok's
Literary Leaves.' It usually consisted of news and gossip of writers, comment, etc., literary odds and ends, and occasional interviews with distinguished authors. He went up to Hartford one day to interview Mark
Twain. The result seemed satisfactory to Bok, but wishing to be certain
that it would be satisfactory to Clemens, he sent him a copy for approval."

To Edward W. Bok, New York

My dear Mr. Bok,
    No, no. It is like most interviews, pure twaddle and valueless.
    For several quite plain and simple reasons, an "interview" must,
as a rule, be an absurdity, and chiefly for this reason. It is an attempt
to use a boat on land or a wagon on water, to speak figuratively.
Spoken speech is one thing, written speech is quite another. Print is
the proper vehicle for the latter but it isn't for the former. The moment "talk" is put into print you recognize that it is not what it was
when you heard it. You perceive that an immense something has

disappeared from it. That is its soul. You have nothing but a dead carcass left on your hands. Color, play of feature, the varying modulations of the voice, the laugh, the smile, the informing inflections, everything that gave that body warmth, grace, friendliness and charm and commended it to your affections—or at least to your tolerance—is gone and nothing is left but a pallid, stiff and repulsive cadaver.

Such is "talk" almost invariably as you see it lying in state in an "interview." The interviewer seldom tries to tell one *how* a thing was said, he merely puts in the naked remark and stops there. When one writes for print his methods are very different. He follows forms which have but little resemblance to conversation, but they make the reader understand what the writer is trying to convey. And when the writer is making a story and finds it necessary to report some of the talk of his characters, observe how cautiously and anxiously he goes at that risky and difficult thing.

"If he had dared to say that thing in my presence," said Alfred, taking a mock heroic attitude and casting an arch glance upon the company, "blood would have flowed."

"If he had dared to say that thing in my presence," said Hawkwood, with that in his eye which caused more than one heart in that guilty assemblage to quake, "blood would have flowed."

"If he had dared to say that thing in my presence," said the paltry blusterer, with valor on his tongue and pallor on his lips, "blood would have flowed."

So painfully aware is the novelist that naked talk in print conveys no meaning, that he loads and often overloads almost every utterance of his characters with explanations and interpretations. It is a loud confession that print is a poor vehicle for "talk." It is a recognition that uninterpreted talk in print would result in confusion to the reader, not instruction.

Now, in your interview you have certainly been most accurate. You have set down the sentences I uttered as I said them. But you have not a word of explanation. What my manner was at several points is not indicated. Therefore, no reader can possibly know where I was in earnest and where I was joking, or whether I was joking altogether or in earnest altogether. Such a report of a conversation has no value. It can convey many meanings to the reader but never the right one. To add interpretations which would convey the right meaning is a something which would require—what? An art so high and fine and difficult that no possessor of it would ever be allowed to waste it on interviews.

No. Spare the reader and spare me. Leave the whole interview out. It is rubbish. I wouldn't talk in my sleep if I couldn't talk better than that.

If you wish to print anything, print this letter. It may have some value, for it may explain to a reader here and there why it is that in interviews, as a rule, men seem to talk like anybody but themselves.

Very sincerely yours,
Mark Twain

Perhaps I may be allowed to note that when I was a boy growing up in Richmond, Virginia, I was much influenced by Bok's kindness to me. I was born in Odessa, Russia, and came to the U.S. in December 1920, just before I turned six. Bok was born in the Netherlands and emigrated to the U.S. when he was six. I was much impressed and moved by his autobiography, *The Americanization of Edward Bok*, which won the Pulitzer Prize in 1921. I was living on St. James Street in a black ghetto of Richmond when I wrote to Bok, thanking him for his book, and when I received a gracious reply, which unfortunately is no longer extant. That was more than half a century ago. Bok died in 1930.

To Orion, Keokuk

Hartford, *Jan. 5, '89*

Dear Orion,

At 12:20 this afternoon a line of movable types was spaced and justified by machinery for the first time in the history of the world! And I was there to see. It was done *automatically*—instantly—perfectly. This is indeed the first line of movable types that ever *was* perfectly spaced and perfectly justified on this earth.

This was the last function that remained to be tested, and so by long odds the most amazing and extraordinary invention ever born of the brain of man stands completed and perfect. Livy is downstairs celebrating.

But it's a cunning devil, is that machine, and knows more than any man that ever lived. You shall see. We made the test in this way. We set up a lot of random letters in a stick—three-fourths of a line—then filled out the line with quads representing 14 spaces, each space to be 35/1000 of an inch thick. Then we threw aside the quads and put the letters into the machine and formed them into 15 two-letter words, leaving the words separated by two-inch vacancies. Then we started up the machine slowly, by hand, and fastened our eyes on the space-selecting pins. The first pin-block projected its third pin as the first word came traveling along the race-way. Second block did the same. But the third block projected its *second* pin!

"Oh, hell! Stop the machine—something wrong—it's going to set a 30/1000 space!"

General consternation. "A foreign substance has got into the spacing plates." This from the head mathematician.

"Yes, that is the trouble," assented the foreman.

Paige examined. "No—look in, and you can see that there's nothing of the kind." Further examination. "*Now* I know what it is—what it *must* be. One of those plates projects and binds. It's too bad—the first test is a failure." A *pause*. "Well, boys, no use to cry. Get to work—take the machine down.—No—Hold on! Don't touch a thing! Go right ahead! We are fools, the machine isn't. The machine knows what it's about. There is a *speck of dirt* on one of those types, and the machine is putting in a thinner space to *allow* for it!"

That was just it. The machine went right ahead, spaced the line, justified it to a hair, and shoved it into the galley complete and perfect! We took it out and examined it with a glass. You could not tell by your eye that the third space was thinner than the others but the glass and the calipers showed the difference. Paige had always said that the machine would measure invisible particles of dirt and allow for them but even he had forgotten that vast fact for the moment.

All the witnesses made written record of the immense historical birth—the first justification of a line of movable type by machinery—and also set down the hour and the minute. Nobody had drunk anything and yet everybody seemed drunk. Well—dizzy, stupefied, stunned.

All the other wonderful inventions of the human brain sink pretty nearly into commonplace contrasted with this awful mechanical miracle. Telephones, telegraphs, locomotives, cotton gins, sewing machines, Babbage calculators, Jacquard looms, perfecting presses, Arkwright's frames—all mere toys, simplicities! The Paige Compositor marches alone and far in the lead of human inventions.

In two or three weeks we shall work the stiffness out of her joints and have her performing as smoothly and softly as human muscles, and then we shall speak out the big secret and let the world come and gaze.

Return me this letter when you have read it.

Sam

To Mrs. Theodore Crane, Elmira, N. Y.

Hartford, *May 28, '89*

Susie dear,

I want you to tell this to Theodore. You know how absent-minded Twichell is and how desolate his face is when he is in that frame. At such times he passes the word with a friend on the street and is not aware of the meeting at all. Twice in a week our Clara had this latter experience with him within the past month. But the second instance was too much for her and she woke him up in his tracks with a reproach. She said:

"Uncle Joe, *why* do you always look as if you were just going down into the grave when you meet a person on the street?"

And then went on to reveal to him the funereal spectacle which he presented on such occasions.

Well, she has met Twichell three times since then, and would swim the Connecticut to avoid meeting him the fourth. As soon as he sights her, no matter how public the place nor how far off she is, he makes a bound into the air, heaves arms and legs into all sorts of frantic gestures of delight, and so comes prancing, skipping and pirouetting for her like a drunken Indian entering heaven.

With a full invoice of love from us all to you and Theodore.

S.L.C.

That summer Rudyard Kipling, a great admirer of Clemens's work, visited him in Elmira and described the visit in the *New York Herald*.

"You are a contemptible lot out there, over yonder. Some of you are Commissioners and some Lieutenant Governors and some have the V.C., and a few are privileged to walk about the Mall arm in arm with the Viceroy; but I have seen Mark Twain this golden morning, have shaken his hand and smoked a cigar—no, two cigars—with him, and talked with him for more than two hours! Understand clearly that I do not despise you, indeed I don't. I am only very sorry for you all, from the Viceroy downward. . . .

"Morning revealed Elmira, whose streets were desolated by railway tracks, and whose suburbs were given up to the manufacture of door sashes and window frames. It was surrounded by pleasant, fat little hills trimmed with timber and topped with cultivation. The Chemung River flowed generally up and down the town and had just finished flooding a few of the main streets. . . .

"It was a very pretty house, anything but Gothic, clothed with ivy, standing in a very big compound and fronted by a veranda full of all sorts of chairs and hammocks for lying in all sorts of positions. The roof of the veranda was a trellis work of creepers and the sun peeped through and moved on the shining boards below. . . .

"A big, darkened drawing room, a huge chair, a man with eyes, a mane of grizzled hair, a brown mustache covering a mouth as delicate as a woman's, a strong, square hand shaking mine, and the slowest, calmest, levellest voice in all the world saying:

" 'Well, you think you owe me something and you've come to tell me so. That's what I call squaring a debt handsomely.' . . .

"The thing that struck me first was that he was an elderly man, yet after a minute's thought I perceived that it was otherwise, and in five minutes, the eyes looking at me, I saw that the gray hair was an accident of the most trivial kind. He was quite young. I had shaken his hand. I was smoking his cigar, and I was hearing him talk—this man I had learned to love and admire fourteen thousand miles away. . . .

"He spoke always through his eyes, a light under the heavy eyebrows; anon crossing the room with a step as light as a girl's to show me some book or other; then resuming his walk up and down the room puffing at the cob pipe. I would have given much for nerve enough to demand the gift of that pipe, value five cents when new. . . .

"Once indeed he put his hand on my shoulder. It was an investiture of the Star of India, blue silk, trumpets and diamond studded jewel, all complete. If hereafter among the changes and chances of this mortal life I fall to cureless ruin I will tell the superintendent of the workhouse that Mark Twain once put his hand on my shoulder, and he shall give me a room to myself and a double allowance of paupers' tobacco."

To Joseph T. Goodman, Nevada

Private.

Hartford, *Oct. 7,* '89

Dear Joe,

I had a letter from Aleck Badlam day before yesterday, and in answering him I mentioned a matter which I asked him to consider a secret except to you and John McComb,° as I am not ready yet to get into the newspapers.

I have come near writing you about this matter several times but it wasn't ripe, and I waited. It is ripe now. It is a typesetting machine which I undertook to build for the inventor (for a consideration). I have been at it three years and seven months without losing a day, at a cost of $3,000 a month, and in so private a way that Hartford has known nothing about it. Indeed only a dozen men have known of the matter. I have reported progress from time to time to the proprietors of the *N. Y. Sun, Herald, Times, World,* Harper Brothers and John F. Trow; also to the proprietors of the *Boston Herald* and the *Boston Globe.* Three years ago I asked all these people to squelch their frantic desire to load up their offices with the Mergenthaler (*N. Y. Tribune*) machine and wait for mine and then choose between the two. They have waited—with no very gaudy patience—but still they have waited, and I could prove to them today that they have not lost anything by it. But I reserve the proof for the present except in the case of the *N. Y. Herald.* I sent an invitation there the other day, a courtesy due a paper which ordered $240,000 worth of our machines long ago when it was still in a crude condition. The *Herald* has ordered its foreman to come up here next Thursday, but that is the only invitation which will go out for some time yet.

The machine was finished several weeks ago and has been running ever since in the machine shop. It is a magnificent creature of steel, all of Pratt & Whitney's superbest workmanship, and as nicely adjusted and as accurate as a watch. In construction it is as elaborate and complex as that machine which it ranks *next* to, by every right—Man—and in performance it is as simple and sure.

°Of the *Alta-California,* who had sent Mark Twain on the *Quaker City* excursion.

Anybody can set type on it who can read, and can do it after only 15 minutes instruction. The operator does not need to leave his seat at the keyboard, for the reason that he is not required to do anything but strike the keys and set type—merely one function. The spacing, justifying, emptying into the galley, and distributing of dead matter are all done by the machine without anybody's help—four functions.

The ease with which a cub can learn is surprising. Day before yesterday I saw our newest cub set, perfectly space and perfectly justify 2,150 ems of solid nonpareil in an hour and distribute the like amount in the same hour—and six hours previously he had never seen the machine or its keyboard. It was a good hour's work for 3-year *veterans* on the other typesetting machines to do. We have 3 cubs. The dean of the trio is a school youth of 18. Yesterday morning he had been an apprentice on the machine 16 working days (8-hour days), and we speeded him to see what he could do in an hour. In the hour he set 5,900 ems solid nonpareil, and the machine perfectly spaced and justified it, and of course distributed the like amount in the same hour. Considering that a good fair compositor sets 700 and distributes 700 in the one hour, this boy did the work of about 8½ compositors in that hour. This fact sends all other typesetting machines a thousand miles to the rear, and the best of them will never be heard of again after we publicly exhibit in New York.

We shall put on 3 more cubs. We have one school boy and two compositors now and we think of putting on a type writer, a stenographer, and perhaps a shoemaker, to show that no special gifts or training are required with this machine. We shall train these beginners two or three months, or until some one of them gets up to 7,000 an hour. Then we will show up in New York and run the machine 24 hours a day 7 days in the week for several months—to prove that this is a machine which will never get out of order or cause delay, and can stand anything an anvil can stand. You know there is no other typesetting machine that can run two hours on a stretch without causing trouble and delay with its incurable caprices.

We own the whole field—every inch of it—and nothing can dislodge us.

Now then, above is my preachment, and here follows the reason and purpose of it. I want you to run over here, roost over the machine a week and satisfy yourself, and then go to John P. Jones or to whom you please and sell me a hundred thousand dollars worth of this property and take ten per cent in cash or the "property" for your trouble—the latter, if you are wise, because the price I ask is a long way short of the value.

What I call "property" is this. A small part of my ownership consists of a royalty of $500 on every machine marketed under the American patents. My selling terms are, a permanent royalty of one dollar on every American-marketed machine for a thousand dollars cash to me in hand paid. We shan't market any fewer than 15,000 machines in 15 years—a return of fifteen thousand dollars for one thousand. A royalty is better than stock, in one way—*it* must be paid every six months rain or shine. It is a debt and must be paid before dividends are declared. By and by, when we become a stock company, I shall buy these royalties back for stock if I can get them for anything like reasonable terms.

I have never borrowed a penny to use on the machine, and never sold a penny's worth of the property until the machine was entirely finished and proven by the severest tests to be what she started out to be—perfect, permanent, and occupying the position, as regards all kindred machines, which the City of Paris occupies as regards the canvas-backs of the mercantile marine.

It is my purpose to sell two hundred dollars of my royalties at the above price during the next two months and keep the other $300.

Mrs. Clemens begs Mrs. Goodman to come with you, and asks pardon for not writing the message herself—which would be a pathetically welcome spectacle to me, for I have been her amanuensis for 8 months, now, since her eyes failed her.

Yours as always
Mark

The Baxter of the following was Sylvester Baxter of the *Boston Herald*. The Brazilian monarchy had fallen.

Dear Mr. Baxter,

Another throne has gone down, and I swim in oceans of satisfaction. I wish I might live fifty years longer. I believe I should see the thrones of Europe selling at auction for old iron. I believe I should really see the end of what is surely the grotesquest of all the swindles ever invented by man—monarchy. It is enough to make a graven image laugh, to see apparently rational people, away down here in this wholesome and merciless slaughter-day for shams, still mouthing empty reverence for those moss-backed frauds and scoundrelisms: hereditary kingship and so-called "nobility." It is enough to make the monarchs and nobles themselves laugh, and in private they do, there can be no question about that.

I think there is only one funnier thing, and that is the spectacle of these bastard Americans, these Hamersleys and Huntingtons and such, offering cash, encumbered by themselves, for rotten carcases and stolen titles.

When our great brethren the disenslaved Brazilians frame their Declaration of Independence, I hope they will insert this missing link: "We hold these truths to be self-evident: that all monarchs are usurpers and descendants of usurpers, for the reason that no throne was ever set up in this world by the will, freely exercised, of the only body possessing the legitimate right to set it up—the numerical mass of the nation."

You already have the advance sheets of my forthcoming book in your hands. If you will turn to about the five hundredth page you will find a state paper of my *Connecticut Yankee* in which he announces the dissolution of King Arthur's monarchy and proclaims the English Republic. Compare it with the state paper which announces the downfall of the Brazilian monarchy and proclaims the Republic of the United States of Brazil, and stand by to defend the *Yankee* from plagiarism. There is merely a resemblance of ideas, nothing more. The *Yankee's* proclamation was already in print a week ago. This is merely one of those odd coincidences which are always turning up. Come, protect the *Yank* from that cheapest and easiest of all charges—plagiarism. Otherwise, you see, he will have to protect himself by charging approximate and indefinite plagiarism upon the official servants of our majestic twin down yonder, and then there might be war, or some similar annoyance.

Have you noticed the rumor that the Portuguese throne is unsteady and that the Portuguese slaves are getting restive? Also, that the head slave-driver of Europe, Alexander III, has so reduced his usual monthly order for chains that the Russian foundries are running on only half time now? Also that other rumor, that English nobility acquired an added stench the other day and had to ship it to India and the continent because there wasn't any more room for it at home? Things are working. By and by there is going to be an emigration, maybe. Of course we shall make no preparation. We never do. In a few years from now we shall have nothing but played-out kings and dukes on the police, and driving the horse-cars, and whitewashing fences, and in fact overcrowding all the avenues of unskilled labor. And then we shall wish, when it is too late, that we had taken common and reasonable precautions and drowned them at Castle Garden.

Paine has written, "The *Yankee* did not find a very hearty welcome in England. English readers did not fancy any burlesque of their Arthurian tales, or American strictures on their institutions. Mark Twain's publishers had feared this, and asked that the story be especially edited for the English edition. Clemens, however, would not listen to any suggestions of the sort."

To Messrs. Chatto & Windus, London

Gentlemen,

Concerning *The Yankee,* I have already revised the story twice, and it has been read critically by W. D. Howells and Edmund Clarence Stedman, and my wife has caused me to strike out several passages that have been brought to her attention and to soften others. Furthermore, I have read chapters of the book in public where Englishmen were present and have profited by their suggestions.

Now, mind you, I have taken all this pains because I wanted to say a Yankee mechanic's say against monarchy and its several natural props, and yet make a book which you would be willing to print exactly as it comes to you, without altering a word.

We are spoken of (by Englishmen) as a thin-skinned people. It is you who are thin-skinned. An Englishman may write with the most brutal frankness about any man or institution among us and we republish him without dreaming of altering a line or a word. But England cannot stand that kind of a book written about herself. It is England that is thin-skinned. It causeth me to smile when I read the modifications of my language which have been made in my English editions to fit them for the sensitive English palate.

Now, as I say, I have taken laborious pains to so trim this book of offense that you might not lack the nerve to print is just as it stands. I am going to get the proofs to you just as early as I can. I want you to read it carefully. If you can publish it without altering a single word, go ahead. Otherwise, please hand it to J. R. Osgood in time for him to have it published at my expense.

This is important, for the reason that the book was not written for America, it was written for England. So many Englishmen have done their sincerest best to teach us something for our betterment that it seems to me high time that some of us should substantially recognize the good intent by trying to pry up the English nation to a little higher level of manhood in turn.

Very truly yours,
S. L. Clemens

After the book's unfriendly reception in England, Clemens apparently decided that something should be done in its favor. He stated his case to a leading English critic, who was an admirer and a friend of his.

To Andrew Lang, London

[*First page missing.*]

1889

They vote but do not print. The head tells you pretty promptly whether the food is satisfactory or not, and everybody hears, and thinks the whole man has spoken. It is a delusion. Only his taste and his smell have been heard from—important, both, in a way, but these do not build up the man and preserve his life and fortify it.

The little child is permitted to label its drawings "This is a cow, this is a horse," and so on. This protects the child. It saves it from the sorrow and wrong of hearing its cows and its horses criticized as kangaroos and workbenches. A man who is whitewashing a fence is doing a useful thing. So also is the man who is adorning a rich man's house with costly frescoes. And all of us are sane enough to judge these performances by standards proper to each. Now, then, to be fair, an author ought to be allowed to put upon his book an explanatory line: "This is written for the Head." "This is written for the Belly and the Members." And the critic ought to hold himself in honor bound to put away from him his ancient habit of judging all books by one standard, and thenceforth follow a fairer course.

The critic assumes, every time, that if a book doesn't meet the cultivated-class standard it isn't valuable. Let us apply his law all around, for if it is sound in the case of novels, narratives, pictures and such things, it is certainly sound and applicable to all the steps which lead up to culture and make culture possible. It condemns the spelling book, for a spelling book is of no use to a person of culture. It condemns all school books and all schools which lie between the child's primer and Greek, and between the infant school and the university. It condemns all the rounds of art which lie between the cheap terra cotta groups and the Venus de Medici, and between the chromo and the Transfiguration. It requires Whitcomb Riley to sing no more till he can sing like Shakespeare. And it forbids all amateur music and will grant its sanction to nothing below the "classic."

Is this an extravagant statement? No, it is a mere statement of fact. It is the fact itself that is extravagant and grotesque. And what is the result? This—and it is sufficiently curious: the critic has actually imposed upon the world the superstition that a painting by Raphael is more valuable to the civilizations of the earth than is a chromo; and the august opera than the hurdy-gurdy and the villagers' singing society; and Homer than the little everybody's-poet whose rhymes are in all mouths today and will be in nobody's mouth next generation; and the Latin classics than Kipling's far-reaching bugle note; and Jonathan Edwards than the Salvation Army; and the Venus de Medici than the plaster-cast peddler; the superstition, in a word, that the vast and awful comet that trails its cold luster through the remote abysses of space once a century and interests and instructs a cultivated handful of astronomers is worth more to the world than the sun which warms and cheers all the nations every day and makes the crops to grow.

If a critic should start a religion it would not have any object but to convert angels, and they wouldn't need it. The thin top crust of humanity—the cultivated—are worth pacifying, worth pleasing, worth coddling, worth nourishing and preserving with dainties and delicacies, it is true. But to be caterer to that little faction is no very dignified or valuable occupation, it seems to me. It is merely feeding the over-fed, and there must be small satisfaction in that. It is not that little minority who are already saved that are best worth trying to uplift, I should think, but the mighty mass of the uncultivated who are underneath. That mass will never see the Old Masters—that sight is for the few. But the chromo maker can lift them all one step upward toward appreciation of art. They cannot have the opera, but the hurdy-gurdy and the singing class lift them a little way toward that far light. They will never know Homer, but the passing rhymester of their day leaves them higher than he found them. They may never even hear of the Latin classics, but they will strike step with Kipling's drum-beat, and they will march. For all Jonathan Edwards's help, they would die in their slums, but the Salvation Army will beguile some of them up to pure air and a cleaner life. They know no sculpture, the Venus is not even a name to them, but they are a grade higher in the scale of civilization by the ministrations of the plaster cast than they were before it took its place upon their mantel and made it beautiful to their unexacting eyes.

Indeed I have been misjudged from the very first. I have never tried in even one single instance to help cultivate the cultivated classes. I was not equipped for it, either by native gifts or training. And I never had any ambition in that direction, but always hunted for bigger game—the masses. I have seldom deliberately tried to instruct them, but have done my best to entertain them. To simply amuse them would have satisfied my dearest ambition at any time, for they could get instruction elsewhere, and I had two chances to help to the teacher's one: for amusement is a good preparation for study and a good healer of fatigue after it. My audience is dumb, it has no voice in print, and so I cannot know whether I have won its approbation or only got its censure.

Yes, you see, I have always catered for the Belly and the Members but have been served like the others—criticized from the culture-standard—to my sorrow and pain, because, honestly, I never cared what became of the cultured classes. They could go to the theater and the opera. They had no use for me and the melodeon.

And now at last I arrive at my object and tender my petition, making supplication to this effect: that the critics adopt a rule recognizing the Belly and the Members, and formulate a standard whereby work done for them shall be judged. Help me, Mr. Lang. No voice can reach further than yours in a case of this kind, or carry greater weight of authority.

Lang did not take the hint and come to the aid of the *Yankee*. Instead he wrote an appreciative article, "The Art of Mark Twain," for the *Illustrated London News*, in which he glorified *Huck Finn*, calling it the "great American novel which had escaped the eyes of those who watched to see this new planet swim into their ken."

To Joe Goodman, Washington

Hartford, *June 22, '90*

Dear Joe,

I have been sitting by the machine 2½ hours this afternoon and my admiration of it towers higher than ever. There is no sort of mistake about it, it is the Big Bonanza. In the 2½ hours, the time lost by type breakage was 3 minutes.

This machine is totally without a rival. Rivalry with it is impossible. Last Friday, Fred Whitmore (it was the 28th day of his apprenticeship on the machine) stacked up 49,700 ems of solid nonpareil in 8 hours, and the type breaking delay was only 6 minutes for the day.

I claim yet, as I have always claimed, that the machine's market (abroad and here together) is today worth $150,000,000, without saying anything about the doubling and trebling of this sum that will follow within the life of the patents. Now here is a queer fact: I am one of the wealthiest grandees in America—one of the Vanderbilt gang, in fact—and yet if you asked me to lend you a couple of dollars I should have to ask you to take my note instead.

It makes me cheerful to sit by the machine. Come up with Mrs. Goodman and refresh yourself with a draught of the same.

Ys ever
Mark

TWELVE

[1890–93]

*On the Czar's inhumanity — reviewing his own life —
typesetting blues — boating down the Rhone — "I am terribly
tired of business"*

During the summer of 1890, when Clemens and his family were
spending several weeks in the Catskills, he wrote the following letter in
response to an editorial invitation. The letter was never mailed.

A letter on the Czar

Onteora, *1890*

To the Editor of *Free Russia,*

I thank you for the compliment of your invitation to say something, but when I ponder the bottom paragraph on your first page
and then study your statement on your third page, of the objects of
the several Russian liberation parties, I do not quite know how to
proceed. Let me quote here the paragraph referred to:

"But men's hearts are so made that the sight of one voluntary
victim for a noble idea stirs them more deeply than the sight of a
crowd submitting to a dire fate they cannot escape. Besides, foreigners could not see so clearly as the Russians how much the Government was responsible for the grinding poverty of the masses; nor
could they very well realize the moral wretchedness imposed by that
Government upon the whole of educated Russia. But the atrocities
committed upon the defenceless prisoners are there in all their baseness, concrete and palpable, admitting of no excuse, no doubt or
hesitation, crying out to the heart of humanity against Russian tyranny. And the Czar's Government, stupidly confident in its apparently
unassailable position, instead of taking warning from the first re-
bukes, seems to mock this humanitarian age by the aggravation of

brutalities. Not satisfied with slowly killing its prisoners and with burying the flower of our young generation in the Siberian desserts, the Government of Alexander III resolved to break their spirit by deliberately submitting them to a regime of unheard-of brutality and degradation."

When one reads that paragraph in the glare of George Kennan's revelations and considers how much it means, considers that all earthly figures fail to typify the Czar's government and that one must descend into hell to find its counterpart, one turns hopefully to your statement of the objects of the several liberation parties—and is disappointed. Apparently none of them can bear to think of losing the present hell entirely, they merely want the temperature cooled down a little.

I now perceive why all men are the deadly and uncompromising enemies of the rattlesnake: it is merely because the rattlesnake has not speech. Monarchy has speech, and by it has been able to per-suade men that it differs somehow from the rattlesnake, has some-thing valuable about it somewhere, something worth preserving, something even good and high and fine when properly "modified," something entitling it to protection from the club of the first comer who catches it out of its hole. It seems a most strange delusion and not reconcilable with our superstition that man is a reasoning being.

If a house is afire, we reason confidently that it is the first comer's plain duty to put the fire out in any way he can—drown it with water, blow it up with dynamite, use any and all means to stop the spread of the fire and save the rest of the city. What is the Czar of Russia but a house afire in the midst of a city of eighty millions of inhabitants? Yet instead of extinguishing him, together with his nest and system, the liberation parties are all anxious to merely cool him down a little and keep him.

It seems to me that this is illogical—idiotic, in fact. Suppose you had this granite-hearted, bloody-jawed maniac of Russia loose in your house, chasing the helpless women and little children—your own. What would you do with him, supposing you had a shotgun? Well, he *is* loose in your house—Russia. And with your shotgun in your hand, you stand trying to think up ways to "modify" him.

Do these liberation parties think that they can succeed in a project which has been attempted a million times in the history of the world

and has never in one single instance been successful—the "modifica-
tion" of a despotism by other means than bloodshed? They seem to
think they can. My privilege to write these sanguinary sentences in
soft security was bought for me by rivers of blood poured upon
many fields, in many lands, but I possess not one single little paltry
right or privilege that come to me as a result of petition, persuasion,
agitation for reform, or any kindred method of procedure. When we
consider that not even the most responsible English monarch ever
yielded back a stolen public right until it was wrenched from him by
bloody violence, is it rational to suppose that gentler methods can
win privileges in Russia?

Of course I know that the properest way to demolish the Russian
throne would be by revolution. But it is not possible to get up a
revolution there, so the only thing left to do, apparently, is to keep
the throne vacant by dynamite until a day when candidates shall
decline with thanks. Then organize the Republic. And on the whole
this method has some large advantages, for whereas a revolution de-
stroys some lives which cannot well be spared, the dynamite way
doesn't.

Consider this: the conspirators against the Czar's life are caught in
every rank of life, from the low to the high. And consider: if so
many take an active part where the peril is so dire, is this not evidence that the sympathizers who keep still and do not show their
hands are countless for multitudes? Can you break the hearts of
thousands of families with the awful Siberian exodus every year for
generations and not eventually cover all Russia from limit to limit
with bereaved fathers and mothers and brothers and sisters who secretly hate the perpetrator of this prodigious crime and hunger and
thirst for his life? Do you not believe that if your wife or your child
or your father was exiled to the mines of Siberia for some trivial
utterances wrung from a smarting spirit by the Czar's intolerable
tyranny, and you got a chance to kill him and did not do it, that you
would always be ashamed to be in your own society the rest of your
life?

Suppose that that refined and lovely Russian lady who was lately
stripped bare before a brutal soldiery and whipped to death by the
Czar's hand in the person of the Czar's creature had been your wife,
or your daughter or your sister, and today the Czar should pass with-

in reach of your hand how would you feel—and what would you do? Consider that all over vast Russia, from boundary to boundary, a myriad of eyes filled with tears when that piteous news came, and through those tears that myriad of eyes saw, not that poor lady, but lost darlings of their own whose fate her fate brought back with new access of grief out of a black and bitter past never to be forgotten or forgiven.

If I am a Swinburnian—and clear to the marrow I am—I hold human nature in sufficient honor to believe there are eighty million mute Russians that are of the same stripe, and only one Russian family that isn't.

Mark Twain

In August, Clemens was summoned to his mother's bedside in Keokuk. She had been ailing for some time and it was now thought she was dying. She rallied, and he returned to the Catskills. She died October 27th in her eighty-eighth year. She was buried in Hannibal. A month later Livy's mother died in Elmira.

In his autobiography Clemens wrote of his mother: "I knew her well during the first twenty-five years of my life; but after that I saw her only at wide intervals, for we lived many days' journey apart. . . . She had a slender, small body but a large heart—a heart so large that everybody's grief and everybody's joys found welcome in it and hospitable accommodation. The greatest difference which I find between her and the rest of the people whom I have known is this, and it is a remarkable one: those others felt a strong interest in a few things, whereas to the very day of her death she felt a strong interest in the whole world and everything and everybody in it. In all her life she never knew such a thing as a half-hearted interest in affairs and people, or an interest which drew a line and left out certain affairs and was indifferent to certain people. The invalid who takes a strenuous and indestructible interest in everything and everybody but himself, and to whom a dull moment is an unknown thing and an impossibility, is a formidable adversary for disease and a hard invalid to vanquish. I am certain that it was this feature of my mother's make-up that carried her so far toward ninety." (Earlier in the autobiography he had characterized her as "one who at forty was so delicate of body as to be accounted a confirmed invalid and destined to pass soon away.")

What with the money that kept being consumed by the Paige typesetting machine and by Clemens's publishing house, Clemens's financial situation was becoming critical, and the year ended gloomily. Writing a brief letter to Fred J. Hall, manager of his publishing house, Clemens closed with, "Merry Xmas to you!—and I wish to God I could have one myself before I die."

Paine has written, "He had always enjoyed writing and felt now that he was equipped better than ever for authorship, at least so far as material was concerned. There exists a fragmentary copy of a letter to some unknown correspondent, in which he recites his qualifications."

Fragment of Letter to _____, *1891*

... I confine myself to life with which I am familiar when pretending to portray life. But I confined myself to the boy life out on the Mississippi because that had a peculiar charm for me and not because I was not familiar with other phases of life. I was a *soldier* two weeks once in the beginning of the war and was hunted like a rat the whole time. Familiar? My splendid Kipling himself hasn't a more burnt-in, hard-baked and unforgetable familiarity with that death-on-the-pale-horse-with-hell-following-after which is a raw soldier's first fortnight in the field and which, without any doubt, is the most tremendous fortnight and the vividest he is ever going to see.

Yes, and I have shoveled silver tailings in a quartz mill a couple of weeks and acquired the last possibilities of culture in *that* direction. And I've done "pocket mining" during three months in the one little patch of ground in the whole globe where Nature conceals gold in pockets—or *did* before we robbed all of those pockets and exhausted, obliterated, annihilated the most curious freak Nature ever indulged in. There are not thirty men left alive who, being told there was a pocket hidden on the broad slope of a mountain, would know how to go and find it or have even the faintest idea of how to set about it, but I am one of the possible 20 or 30 who possess the secret, and I could go and put my hand on that hidden treasure with a mostly deadly precision.

And I've been a prospector, and know pay rock from poor when I find it—just with a touch of the tongue. And I've been a *silver* miner and know how to dig and shovel and drill and put in a blast. And so I know the mines and the miners interiorly as well as Bret Harte knows them exteriorly.

And I was a newspaper reporter four years in cities, and so saw the inside of many things, and was reporter in a legislature two sessions and the same in Congress one session, and thus learned to know personally three sample bodies of the smallest minds and the selfishest souls and the cowardliest hearts that God makes.

And I was some years a Mississippi pilot, and familiarly knew all the different kinds of steamboatmen—a race apart and not like other folk.

And I was for some years a traveling "jour" printer and wandered from city to city—and so I know *that* sect familiarly.

And I was a lecturer on the public platform a number of seasons and was a responder to toasts at all the different kinds of banquets, and so I know a great many secrets about the audiences, secrets not to be got out of books but only acquirable by experience.

And I watched over one dear project of mine for years, spent a fortune on it and failed to make it go—and the history of that would make a large book in which a million men would see themselves as in a mirror, and they would testify and say, Verily, this is not imagination, this fellow has been there—and after would cast dust upon their heads, cursing and blaspheming.

And I am a publisher, and did pay to one author's widow (General Grant's) the largest copyright checks this world has seen—aggregating more than £80,000 in the first year.

And I have been an author for 20 years and an ass for 55.

Now then. As the most valuable capital or culture or education usable in the building of novels is personal experience, I ought to be well equipped for that trade.

I surely have the equipment, a wide culture, and all of it real, none of it artificial, for I don't know anything about books.

[*No signature*]

The Library of American Literature, mentioned in the following, was edited by Edmund Clarence Stedman and Ellen Mackay Hutchinson. It consisted of many volumes. Jones was Senator John Percival Jones, whom at one time Clemens regarded as a potential capitalist savior.

To Joe T. Goodman

April [?] 1891

Dear Joe,

Well, it's all right, anyway. Diplomacy couldn't have saved it—diplomacy of mine—at that late day. I hadn't any diplomacy in stock anyway. In order to meet Jones's requirements I had to surrender the old contract (a contract which made me boss of the situation and gave me the whip-hand of Paige) and allow the new one to be drafted and put in its place. I was running an immense risk but it was justified by Jones's promises—promises made to me not merely once but every time I talked with him. When February arrived I saw signs which were mighty plain reading. Signs which meant that Paige was hoping and praying that Jones would go back on me—which would leave Paige boss and me robbed and out in the cold. His prayers were answered and I am out in the cold. If I ever get back my nine-twentieths interest it will be by lawsuit, which will be instituted in the indefinite future, when the time comes.

I am at work again—on a book. Not with a great deal of spirit but with enough—yes, plenty. And I am pushing my publishing house. It has turned the corner after clearing $50,000 a year for three consecutive years, and piling every cent of it into one book—*Library of American Literature*—and from next January onward it will resume dividends. But I've got to earn $50,000 for it between now and then, which I will do if I keep my health. This additional capital is needed for that same book because its prosperity is growing so great and exacting.

It is dreadful to think of you in ill health. I can't realize it. You are always to me the same that you were in those days when matchless health and glowing spirits and delight in life were commonplaces with us. Lord save us all from old age and broken health and a hope-tree that has lost the faculty of putting out blossoms.

With love to you both from us all.

Mark

Livy's health was such now that several doctors, agreeing she had a heart disturbance, recommended a European stay. Clemens was plagued by rheumatism in his writing arm. She too was bothered by rheumatism. A large change of scene; European baths; and above all the simpler and vastly cheaper life of Europe beckoned. Toward the end of May 1891 Clemens agreed to write a series of six European letters for the McClure Syndicate and for his old friend William F. Laffan of the *New York Sun.*

After closing the Hartford house, in which they had lived seventeen years—closing it permanently, as it would turn out—the Clemens family, with their maid Katy Leary, sailed June 6th for France on the *Gascogne.* Eventually Clemens settled his family at the Hotel Beau Rivage in Ouchy, Switzerland, then hired Joseph Very, a courier who had served him on an earlier European trip, and proceeded to boat down the Rhone in a flat-bottom boat purchased by Very for $5. The pilot was the boat's former owner. The boating journey began the morning of September 20th, a Sunday.

Five Letters to Livy, Ouchy, Switzerland

On the Rhone below Villebois, *Tuesday noon*

Good morning, sweetheart. Night caught us yesterday where we had to take quarters in a peasant's house which was occupied by the family and a lot of cows and calves—also several rabbits.° The latter had a ball and I was the ballroom but they were very friendly and didn't bite.

The peasants were mighty kind and hearty and flew around and did their best to make us comfortable. This morning I breakfasted on the shore in the open air with two sociable dogs and a cat. Clean cloth, napkin and table furniture, white sugar, a vast hunk of excellent butter, good bread, first class coffee with pure milk, fried fish just caught. Wonderful that so much cleanliness should come out of such a phenomenally dirty house.

An hour ago we saw the Falls of the Rhone, a prodigiously rough and dangerous looking place. Shipped a little water but came to no harm. It was one of the most beautiful pieces of piloting and boat management I ever saw. Our admiral knew his business.

We have had to run ashore for shelter every time it has rained heretofore, but Joseph has been putting in his odd time making a waterproof sun-bonnet for the boat, and now we sail along dry although we had many heavy showers this morning.

° His word for fleas.

With a world of love to you all and particularly you,

Saml

On the Rhone below Vienne

I salute you, my darling. Your telegram reached me in Lyons last night and was very pleasant news indeed.

I was up and shaved before 8 this morning but we got delayed and didn't sail from Lyons till 10:30—an hour and a half lost. And we've lost another hour—two of them, I guess—since, by an error. We came in sight of Vienne at 2 o'clock, several miles ahead, on a hill, and I proposed to walk down there and let the boat go ahead of us. So Joseph and I got out and struck through a willow swamp along a dim path, and by and by came out on the steep bank of a slough or inlet or something, and we followed that bank forever and ever trying to get around the head of that slough. Finally I noticed a twig standing up in the water, and by George it had a distinct and even vigorous quiver to it! I don't know when I have felt so much like a donkey. On an island! I wanted to drown somebody but I hadn't anybody I could spare. However, after another long tramp we found a lonely native, and he had a scow and soon we were on the mainland—yes, and a blamed sight further from Vienne than we were when we started.

Notes—I make millions of them, and so I get no time to write to you. If you've got a pad there, please send it poste-restante to Avignon. I may not need it but I fear I shall.

I'm straining to reach St. Pierre de Boef, but it's going to be a close fit, I reckon.

Afloat, *Friday, 3 p.m., '91*

Livy darling, we sailed from St. Pierre de Boef six hours ago and are now approaching Tournon, where we shall not stop but go on and make Valence, a city of 25,000 people. It's too delicious, floating with the swift current under the awning these superb sunshiny days in deep peace and quietness. Some of these curious old historical towns strangely persuade me but it is so lovely afloat that I don't stop, but view them from the outside and sail on. We get abundance of grapes and peaches for next to nothing.

Joseph is perfect. He is at his very best—and never was better in his life. I guess he gets discouraged and feels disliked and in the way when he is lying around, but here he is perfection and brim full of useful alacrities and helps and ingenuities.

When I woke up an hour ago and heard the clock strike 4, I said "I seem to have been asleep an immensely long time. I must have gone to bed mighty early. I wonder what time I did go to bed." And I got up and lit a candle and looked at my watch to *see.*

Afloat—
2 Hours Below Bourg St. Andeol
Monday, 11 a.m., Sept. 28

Livy darling, I didn't write yesterday. We left La Voulte in a driving storm of cold rain—couldn't write in it—and at 1 p.m., when we were not thinking of stopping, we saw a picturesque and mighty ruin on a high hill back of a village, and I was seized with a desire to explore it. So we landed at once and set out with rubbers and umbrella, sending the boat ahead to St. Andeol. And we spent 3 hours clambering about those cloudy heights among those worn and vast and idiotic ruins of a castle built by two crusaders 650 years ago. The work of these asses was full of interest, and we had a good time inspecting, examining and scrutinizing it. All the hills on both sides of the Rhone have peaks and precipices, and each has its gray and wasted pile of mouldy walls and broken towers.

The Romans displaced the Gauls, the Visigoths displaced the Romans, the Saracens displaced the Visigoths, the Christians displaced the Saracens, and it was these pious animals who built these strange lairs and cut each other's throats in the name and for the glory of God, and robbed and burned and slew in peace and war. And the pauper and the slave built churches, and the credit of it went to the Bishop who racked the money out of them. These are pathetic shores and they make one despise the human race.

We came down in an hour by rail but I couldn't get your telegram till this morning, for it was Sunday and they had shut up the post office to go to the circus. I went too. It was all one family— parents and 5 children—performing in the open air to 200 of these enchanted villagers, who contributed coppers when called on. It was a most gay and strange and pathetic show. I got up at 7 this morning to see the poor devils cook their poor breakfast and pack up their sordid fineries.

This is a 9 km current and the wind is with us. We shall make Avignon before 4 o'clock. I saw watermelons and pomegranates for sale at St. Andeol.

With a power of love, Sweetheart,
Saml

Hotel d'Europe, Avignon, *Monday, 6 p.m., Sept. 28*

Well, Livy darling, I have been having a perfect feast of letters for an hour, and I thank you and dear Clara with all my heart. It's like hearing from home after a long absence.

It is early to be in bed but I'm always abed before 9 on this voyage and up at 7 or a trifle later every morning. If I ever take such a trip again I will have myself called at the first tinge of dawn and get to sea as soon after as possible. The early dawn on the water—nothing can be finer, as I know by old Mississippi experience. I did so long for you and Sue yesterday morning—the most superb sunrise!— the most marvelous sunrise!—and I saw it *all*—from the very faintest suspicion of the coming dawn all the way through to the final explosion of glory. But it had interest private to itself and not to be found elsewhere in the world, for between me and it, in the far distant eastward, was a silhouette mountain range in which I had discovered, the previous afternoon, a most noble face upturned to the sky, and mighty form outstretched, which I had named Napoleon Dreaming of Universal Empire. And now, this prodigious face, soft, rich, blue, spirituelle, asleep, tranquil, reposeful, lay against that giant conflagration of ruddy and golden splendors all rayed like a wheel with the upstreaming and far-reaching lances of the sun. It made one want to cry for delight, it was so supreme in its unimaginable majesty and beauty.

We had a curious experience today. A little after I had sealed and directed my letter to you, in which I said we should make Avignon before 4, we *got lost*. We ceased to encounter any village or ruin mentioned in our "particularizes" and detailed Guide of the Rhone—went drifting along by the hour in a wholly unknown land and on an uncharted river! Confound it, we stopped talking and did nothing but stand up in the boat and search the horizons with the glass and wonder what in the devil had happened. And at last, away yonder at 5 o'clock when some vast towers and fortresses hove in sight we couldn't recognize them for Avignon—yet we knew by the broken bridge that it *was* Avignon.

Then we saw what the trouble was. At some time or other we had drifted down the wrong side of an island and followed a sluggish branch of the Rhone not frequented in modern times. We lost an hour and a half by it and missed one of the most picturesque and gigantic and history-sodden masses of castellated medieval ruin that Europe can show.

It was dark by the time we had wandered through the town and got the letters and found the hotel, so I went to bed.

We shall leave here at noon tomorrow and float down to Arles, arriving about dark, and there bid goodbye to the boat, the river trip finished. Between Arles and Nimes (and Avignon again) we shall be till Saturday morning, then rail it through on that day to Ouchy, reaching the hotel at 11 at night if the train isn't late.

Next day (Sunday) if you like, go to Basel, and Monday to Berlin. But I shall be at your disposal to do exactly as you desire and prefer.

With no end of love to all of you and twice as much to you, sweetheart,

Saml

I believe my arm is a trifle better than it was when I started.

To Clara Clemens, Ouchy, Switzerland

Afloat, 11:20 a.m., Sept. 29, Tuesday

Dear old Ben,

The vast stone masses and huge towers of the ancient papal palace of Avignon are projected above an intervening wooded island a mile up the river behind me, for we are already on our way to Arles. It is a perfectly still morning with a brilliant sun and very hot—outside. But I am under cover of the linen hood and it is cool and shady in here.

Please tell mamma I got her very last letter this morning and I perceive by it that I do not need to arrive at Ouchy before Saturday midnight. I am glad, because I couldn't do the railroading I am proposing to do during the next two or three days and get there earlier. I *could* put in the time till Sunday midnight, but shall not venture it without telegraphic instructions from her to Nimes day after tomorrow, Oct. 1, care Hotel Manivet.

The only adventures we have is in drifting into rough seas now and then. They are not dangerous but they go through all the motions of it. Yesterday when we shot the Bridge of the Holy Spirit it was probably in charge of some inexperienced deputy spirit for the day, for we were allowed to go through the wrong arch, which brought us into a tourbillon below which tried to make this old scow stand on its head. Of course I lost my temper and blew it off in a way to be heard above the roar of the tossing waters. I lost it because the admiral had taken that arch in deference to *my* opinion that it was the best one, while his own judgment told him to take the one nearest the other side of the river. I could have poisoned him, I was so mad to think I had hired such a turnip. A boatman in command should obey nobody's orders but his own and yield to nobody's suggestions.

It was very sweet of you to write me, dear, and I thank you ever so much. With greatest love and kisses,

Papa

The Clemenses spent the winter in Berlin, where, not unexpectedly, Clemens received a great deal of attention socially. For a while he was down with pneumonia. Livy was not feeling well either. They were advised by physicians to move, at least temporarily, to a warmer climate. Leaving the children behind, they went to the south of France with his old courier, Joseph Very.

To Susy Clemens, Berlin

Mentone [France], *March 22, '92*

Susy dear,

I have been delighted to note your easy facility with your pen and proud to note also your literary superiorities of one kind and another—clearness of statement, directness, felicity of expression, photographic ability in setting forth an incident—style—good style—no barnacles on it in the way of unnecessary, retarding words (the shipman scrapes off the barnacles when he wants his racer to go her best gait and straight to the buoy). You should write a letter every day, long or short, and so ought I but I don't.

Mamma says, tell Clara yes, she *will* have to write a note if the fan comes back mended.

We couldn't go to Nice today—had to give it up, on various accounts—and this was the last chance. I am sorry for Mamma. I wish she could have gone. She got a heavy fall yesterday evening and was pretty stiff and lame this morning but is working it off trunk packing.

Joseph is gone to Nice to educate himself in Kodacking and to get the pictures mounted which Mamma thinks she took here. But I noticed she didn't take the plug out, as a rule. When she did she took nine pictures on top of each other—composites.

With lots of love.

Papa

In the course of their journeying, Clemens and Livy came upon the Villa Viviani near Settignano, Italy, "an old palace beautifully located on the hilltops east of Florence, commanding a wonderful view of the ancient city," as Paine has written. "Clemens felt that he could work there, and time proved that he was right."

The Clemenses, however, spent the summer in Bad Nauheim, Germany, where they were visited by the Twichells. By late September the Clemens family were ensconced in the Villa Viviani, about which Clemens wrote: "It is a plain, square building, like a box, and is painted light green and has green window shutters. It stands in a commanding position on the artificial terrace of liberal dimensions, which is walled around with masonry. From the walls the vineyards and olive groves of the estate slant away toward the valley.... Roses overflow the retaining walls and the battered and mossy stone urn on the gate post, in pink and yellow cataracts, exactly as they do on the drop curtains in the theaters. The house is a very fortress for strength."

To Susy Crane, Livy's sister, now in Elmira, Clemens wrote, "This present house is modern. It is not much more than two centuries old. But parts of it, and also its foundation, are of high antiquity. The fine beautiful family portraits—the great carved ones in the large ovals over the doors of the big hall—carry one well back into the past. One of them is dated 1305—he could have known Dante, you see. Another is dated 1343—he could have known Boccaccio and spent his afternoons in Fiesole listening to the Decameron tales. Another is dated 1463—he could have met Columbus."

To Susie Crane, Elmira

Villa Viviani
Settignano, Florence
Oct. 22, '92

Dear Sue,

We are getting wonted. The open fires have driven away the cold and the doubt, and now a cheery spirit pervades the place. Livy and the Kings and Mademoiselle having been taking their tea a number of times lately on the open terrace with the city and the hills and the sunset for company. I stop work a few minutes as a rule when the sun gets down to the hilltops west of Florence, and join the tea group to wonder and exclaim. There is always some new miracle in the view, a new and exquisite variation in the show, a variation which occurs every 15 minutes between dawn and night. Once, early in the morning, a multitude of white villas, not before perceived, revealed themselves on the far hills. Then we recognized that all those great hills are snowed *thick* with them clear to the summit.

The variety of lovely effects, the infinitude of change, is something not to be believed by anyone who has not seen it. No view that I am acquainted with in the world is at all comparable to this for delicacy, charm, exquisiteness, dainty coloring and bewildering rapidity of change. It keeps a person drunk with pleasure all the time. Sometimes Florence ceases to be substantial and becomes just a faint soft dream, with domes and towers of air, and one is persuaded that he might blow it away with a puff of his breath.

Livy is progressing admirably. This is just the place for her.

[Remainder missing]

Clemens's financial affairs were worsening, in large measure due to the *Library of American Literature,* which increasingly demanded large infusions of capital. Nor did the Paige typesetter situation look promising. Financially, 1893 was a hard year for the U.S. as a whole. Clemens made a feverish trip to the U.S. but it did not improve matters for him. The Whitmore of the following was F. G. Whitmore of Hartford, Clemens's financial agent.

To Fred J. Hall, New York

Florence, *May 30,* '93

Dear Mr. Hall,

You were to cable me if you sold any machine royalties, so I judge you have not succeeded.

This has depressed me. I have been looking over the past year's letters and statements and am depressed still more.

I am terribly tired of business. I am by nature and disposition unfitted for it and I want to get out of it. I am standing on the Mount Morris volcano with help from the machine a long way off, doubtless a long way further off than the Connecticut Co. imagines.

Now here is my idea for getting out.

The firm owes Mrs. Clemens and me—I do not know quite how much but it is about $170,000 or $175,000, I suppose (I make this guess from the documents here, whose technicalities confuse me terribly).

The firm owes other sums but there are stock and cash assets to cover the entire indebtedness and $116,679.20 over. Is that it? In addition we have the L. A. L. plates and copyright, worth more than $130,000—is that correct?

That is to say, we have property worth about $250,000 above indebtedness, I suppose—or, by one of your estimates, $300,000? The greater part of the first debts to me is in notes paying 6 percent. The rest (the old $70,000 or whatever it is) pays no interest.

Now then, will Harper or Appleton or Putnam give me $200,000 for those debts and my two-thirds interest in the firm? (The firm of course taking the Mount Morris and all such obligations off my hands and leaving me clear of all responsibility.)

I don't want much money. I only want first class notes, $200,000 worth of them at 6 per cent, payable *monthly;* yearly notes, renewable annually for 3 years, with $5,000 of the principal payable at the beginning and middle of each year. After that the notes renewable annually and (perhaps) a larger part of the principal payable semi-annually.

Please advise me and suggest alterations and emendations of the above scheme, for I need that sort of help, being ignorant of business and not able to learn a single detail of it.

Such a deal would make it easy for a big firm to pour in a big cash capital and jump L. A. L. up to enormous prosperity. Then your one-third would be a fortune—and I hope to see that day!

I enclose an authority to use with Whitmore in case you have sold any royalties. But if you can't make this deal don't make any. Wait a little and see if you can't make the deal. Do make the deal if you possibly can. And if my presence shall be necessary in order to complete it, I will come over, though I hope it can be done without that.

Get me out of business!

And I will be yours forever gratefully,

S. L. Clemens

My idea is that I am offering my ⅔ of L. A. L. and the business for thirty or forty thousand dollars. Is that it?

P. S. S. The new firm could retain my books and reduce them to a 10 percent royalty.

S.L.C.

In June the Clemenses left the Villa Viviani for Munich, where Livy was able to visit some of the baths.

To Fred J. Hall, New York

Aug. 6, '93

Dear Mr. Hall,

I am very sorry. It was thoughtless in me. Let the reports go. Send me once a month two items, and two only:

Cash liabilities—(so much).

Cash assets—(so much).

I can perceive the condition of the business at a glance then, and that will be sufficient.

Here we never see a newspaper but even if we did I could not come anywhere near appreciating or correctly estimating the tempest you have been buffeting your way through. Only the man who is in it can do that. But I have tried not to burden you thoughtlessly or wantonly. I have been wrought and unsettled in mind by apprehensions, and that is a thing that is not helpable when one is in a strange land and sees his resources melt down to a two months' supply and can't see any sure daylight beyond. The bloody machine offered but a doubtful outlook and will still offer nothing much better for a long time to come, for when Davis's "three weeks" is up there's three months tinkering to follow, I guess. That is unquestionably the boss machine of the world but is the toughest one on prophets, when it is in an incomplete state, that has ever seen the light. Neither Davis nor any other man can foretell with any considerable approach to certainty when it will be ready to get down to actual work in a printing office.

[No signature]

On August 29th Clemens sailed again for the U.S. He lived in New York, where, one evening at the Murray Hill Hotel, he was introduced to Henry H. Rogers, "of the Standard Oil group of financiers," as Paine characterized him. It was a very eventful moment for Clemens. Rogers was not only an admirer of Clemens's work. He was to become Clemens's financial savior.

To Livy, Europe

Oct. 18, '93

Dear, dear Sweetheart,

I don't seem to get even half a chance to write you these last two days and yet there's lots to say.

Apparently everything is at last settled as to the giveaway of L. A. L., and the papers will be signed and the transfer made tomorrow morning.

Meantime I have got the best and wisest man in the whole Standard Oil group of multimillionaires a good deal interested in looking into the typesetter (this is private, don't mention it). He has been searching into that thing for three weeks, and yesterday he said to me, "I find the machine to be all you represented it. I have here exhaustive reports from my own experts and I know every detail of its capacity, its immense value, its construction, cost, history, and all about its inventor's character. I know that the New York Co. and the Chicago Co. are *both* stupid and that they are unbusinesslike people, destitute of money and in a hopeless boggle."

Then he told me the scheme he had planned, then said: "If I can arrange with these people on this basis—it will take several weeks to find out—I will see to it that they get the money they need. Then the thing will move right along and your royalties will cease to be waste paper. I will post you the minute my scheme fails or succeeds. In the meantime, *you stop walking the floor.* Go off to the country and try to be gay. You may have to go to walking again but don't begin till I tell you my scheme has failed." And he added: "Keep me posted always as to where you are, for if I need you and can use you I want to know where to put my hand on you."

If I should even divulge the fact that the Standard Oil is merely *talking* remotely about going into the typesetter, it would send my royalties up.

With worlds and worlds of love and kisses to you all,

Saml

To Livy, Paris

Livy darling,

Last night at John Mackay's the dinner consisted of soup, raw oysters, corned beef and cabbage, and something like a custard. I ate without fear or stint and yet have escaped all suggestion of indigestion. The men present were old gray Pacific-coasters whom I knew when I and they went young and not gray. The talk was of the days when we went gypsying a long time ago—thirty years. Indeed it was a talk of the dead. Mainly that. And of how they looked, and the harum-scarum things they did and said. For there were no cares in that life, no aches and pains, and not time enough in the day (and three-fourths of the night) to work off one's surplus vigor and energy. Of the midnight highway robbery joke played upon me with revolvers at my head on the windswept and desolate Gold Hill Divide, no witness is left but me, the victim. All the friendly robbers are gone. These old fools last night laughed till they cried over the particulars of that old forgotten crime.

John Mackay has no family here but a pet monkey, a most affectionate and winning little devil. But he makes trouble for the servants, for he is full of curiosity and likes to take everything out of the drawers and examine it minutely, and he puts nothing back. The examinations of yesterday count for nothing today, he makes a new examination every day. But he injures nothing.

I went with Laffan to the Racquet Club the other night and played billiards two hours without starting up any rheumatism. I suppose it was all really taken out of me in Berlin.

Richard Harding Davis spoke yesterday of Clara's impersonations at Mrs. Van Rensselaer's here and said they were a wonderful piece of work.

Livy dear, I do hope you are comfortable as to quarters and food at the Hotel Brighton. But if you're not, don't stay there. Make one more effort, don't give it up. Dear heart, this is from one who loves you—which is Saml.

THIRTEEN

[1894-97]

Gentleman Jim Corbett — living it up in New York — "There is temporary defeat but no dishonor" — on tour around the world — the untimely death of Susy Clemens — on behalf of Helen Keller

To Livy, Paris

Sunday, 9:30 a.m.

Livy dear, when we got out to the house last night Mrs. Rogers, who is up and around now, didn't want to go downstairs to dinner but Mr. R persuaded her and we had a very good time indeed. By 8 o'clock we were down again and bought a fifteen-dollar box in the Madison Square Garden (Rogers bought it, not I), then he went and fetched Dr. Rice while I went to the Players and picked up two artists, Reid and Simmons. And thus we filled 5 of the 6 seats.

There was a vast multitude of people in the brilliant place. Stanford White came along presently and invited me to go the the World Champion's dressing room, which I was very glad to do. Corbett has a fine face and is modest and diffident, besides being the most perfectly and beautifully constructed human animal in the world. I said,

"You have whipped Mitchell and maybe you will whip Jackson in June but you are not done then. You will have to tackle me."

He answered, so gravely that one might easily have thought him in earnest,

"No—I am not going to meet you in the ring. It is not fair or right to require it. You might chance to knock me out by no merit of your own but by a purely accidental blow, and then my reputation would be gone and you would have a double one. You have got fame enough and you ought not to want to take mine away from me."

Corbett was for a long time a clerk in the Nevada Bank in San Francisco.

There were lots of little boxing matches to entertain the crowd. Then at last Corbett appeared in the ring and the 8,000 people present went mad with enthusiasm. My two artists went mad about his form. They said they had never seen anything that came reasonably near equaling its perfection except Greek statues, and *they* didn't surpass it.

Corbett boxed 3 rounds with the middleweight Australian champion—oh, beautiful to see!—then the show was over and we struggled out through a perfect *wash* of humanity. When we reached the street I found I had left my arctics in the box. I had to have them, so Simmons said he would go back and get them, and I didn't dissuade him. I couldn't see how he was going to make his way a single yard into that solid oncoming wave of people, yet he must plow through it full 50 yards. He was back with the shoes in 3 minutes!

How do you reckon he accomplished that miracle? By saying,

"Way, gentlemen, please. Coming to fetch Mr. Corbett's overshoes."

The word flew from mouth to mouth, the Red Sea divided and Simmons walked comfortably through and back, dry shod. Simmons (this was revealed to me under seal of secrecy by Reid) is the hero of "Gwen," and he and Gwen's author were once engaged to marry. This is "fire-escape" Simmons, the inveterate talker, you know: *"Exit—in case of Simmons."*

I had an engagement at a beautiful dwelling close to the Players for 10:30. I was there by 10:45. Thirty cultivated and very musical ladies and gentlemen present, all of them acquaintances and many of them personal friends of mine. That wonderful Hungarian Band was there (they charge $500 for an evening). Conversation and Band until midnight. Then a bite of supper. Then the company was compactly grouped before me and I told about Dr. B. E. Martin and the etchings, and followed it with the Scotch-Irish Christening. My, but the Martin is a darling story! Next, the head tenor from the Opera sang half a dozen great songs that set the company wild, yes, mad with delight, that nobly handsome young Damrosch accompanying on the piano.

Just a little pause. Then the Band burst out into an explosion of weird and tremendous dance music. A Hungarian celebrity and his wife took the floor. I followed. I couldn't help it. The others drifted in one by one and it was Onteora over again.

By half past 4 I had danced all those people down and yet was not tired, merely breathless. I was in bed at 5 and asleep in ten minutes. Up at 9 and presently at work on this letter to you. I think I wrote until 2 or half past. Then I walked leisurely out to Mr. Rogers's (it is called 3 miles but it is short of it), arriving at 3:30, but he was out, to return at 5:30 (and a person was *in*, whom I don't particularly like), so I didn't stay, but dropped over and chatted with the Howellses until 6.

First Howells and I had a chat together. I asked about Mrs. H. He said she was fine, still steadily improving and nearly back to her old best health. I asked (as if I didn't know):

"What do you attribute this strange miracle to?"

"Mind-cure—simply mind-cure."

"Lord, what a conversion! You were a scoffer three months ago."

"I? I wasn't."

"You were. You made elaborate fun of me in this very room."

"I did *not*, Clemens."

"It's a lie. Howells, you *did*."

I detailed to him the conversation of that time—with the stately argument furnished by Boyesen in the fact that a patient had actually been killed by a mind-curist, and Howells's own smart remark that when the mind-curist is done with you, you *have* to call in a "regular" at last because the former can't procure you a burial permit.

At last he gave in. He said he remembered that talk but had now been a mind-curist so long it was difficult for him to realize that he had ever been anything else.

Mrs. H came skipping in presently, the very person to a dot that she used to be so many years ago.

Mrs. H said, "People may *call* it what they like but it is just *hypnotism* and that's *all* it is—hypnotism pure and simple. Mind-cure!—the *idea!* Why, this woman that cured me hasn't got any mind. She's a good creature but she's dull and dumb and illiterate and—"

"Now *Eleanor!*"

"I know what I'm talking about! Don't I go there twice a week? And Mr. Clemens, if you could only *see* her wooden and satisfied face when she snubs me for forgetting myself and showing by a thoughtless remark that to *me* weather is still *weather*, instead of being just an abstraction and a superstition—oh, it's the *funniest* thing you *ever* saw! A-n-d—when she tilts up her nose—well, it's—it's—Well it's that kind of a nose that—"

"Now *Eleanor!*—the woman is not *responsible* for her nose—" and so on and so on. It didn't seem to me that I had any right to be having this feast and you not there.

She convinced *me*, before she got through, that she and William James are right, hypnotism and mind-cure are the same thing, no difference between them. Very well. The very source, the very *center* of hypnotism is *Paris*. Dr. Charcot's pupils and disciples are right there and ready to your hand without fetching poor dear old Susy across the stormy sea. Let Mrs. Mackay (to whom I send my best respects) tell you whom to go to to learn all you need to learn and how to proceed. *Do*, do it, honey. Don't lose a minute.

. . . At 11 o'clock last night Mr. Rogers said:

"*I* am able to feel physical fatigue and I feel it now. You never show any, either in your eyes or your movements. Do you ever feel any?"

I was able to say that I had forgotten what that feeling was like. Don't you remember how almost impossible it was for me to tire myself at the Villa? Well, it is just so in New York. I go to bed unfatigued at 3, I get up fresh and fine six hours later. I believe I have taken only one daylight nap since I have been here.

When the anchor is down then I shall say:

"Farewell—a long farewell—to *business!* I will *never* touch it again!"

I will live in literature, I will wallow in it, revel in it, I will swim in ink! Joan of Arc—but all this is premature. The anchor is not down yet.

Tomorrow (Tuesday) I will add a P. S. if I've any to add. But, whether or no, I must mail this tomorrow, for the mail steamer goes next day.

5:30 p.m. Great Scott, *this* is Tuesday! I must rush this letter into the mail instantly.

Tell that sassy Ben I've got her welcome letter and I'll write her as soon as I get a daylight chance. I've most time at night but I'd druther write daytimes.

Saml

Rice was Clarence C. Rice, who had introduced Rogers to Clemens. The Players was and is a famous New York club. Reid and Simmons were Robert Reid and Edward Simmons, painters. Paine has described Simmons as "a brilliant, fluent and industrious talker. The title, 'Fire-escape Simmons,' . . . originated when Oliver Herford . . . one day pinned up by the back door of the Players the notice: 'Exit in case of Simmons.'"

Stanford White was a famous American architect of the late nineteenth century who designed Madison Square Garden, in the tower of which he built himself an apartment where he threw parties. He also designed the Washington Arch in Washington Square, New York, the New York Herald Building and a number of buildings at the University of Virginia in Charlottesville. He was shot and killed in 1906 by Harry K. Thaw, who has been described as the jealous and wealthy playboy husband of a woman with whom White was involved. A great trial ensued, the conclusion of which was that Thaw was found innocent by reason of insanity.

James J. Corbett became the world's heavyweight boxing champion when he defeated John L. Sullivan in 1892. He lost the title to Bob Fitzsimmons in 1897. He is considered to be one of the first scientific boxers, and the first boxer to win a championship under the Queensberry rules. After retiring from boxing he became an actor. In his day he was often referred to as Gentleman Jim.

Gwen, a popular novel of the time, was written by Blanche Willis Howard. Damrosch was Walter Damrosch, who later became a well-known orchestra conductor. The Jamie Dodge of the next letter was the son of Mary Mapes Dodge, editor of *St. Nicholas* magazine.

To Clara Clemens, Paris

Mr. Rogers's Office, *Feb. 5, '94*

Dear Benny,

I was intending to answer your letter today but I am away downtown and will simply whirl together a sentence or two for good fellowship. I have bought photographs of Coquelin and Jane Hading and will ask them to sign them. I shall meet Coquelin tomorrow night, and if Hading is not present I will send her picture to her by somebody.

I am to breakfast with Madame Nordica in a few days, and meantime I hope to get a good picture of her to sign. She was of the breakfast company yesterday but the picture of herself which she signed and gave me does not do her majestic beauty justice.

I am too busy to attend to the photo-collecting right, because I have to live up to the name which Jamie Dodge has given me—the "Belle of New York"—and it just keeps me rushing. Yesterday I had engagements to breakfast at noon, dine at 3 and dine again at 7. I got away from the long breakfast at 2 p.m., went and excused myself from the 3 o'clock dinner, then lunched with Mrs. Dodge in 58th street, returned to the Players and dressed, dined out at 7 and was back at Mrs. Dodge's at 10 p.m., where we had magic lantern views of a superb sort, and a lot of yarns until an hour after midnight, and got to bed at 2 this morning—a good deal of a gain on my recent hours. But I don't get tired. I sleep as sound as a dead person and always wake up fresh and strong, usually at exactly 9.

I was at breakfast lately where people of seven separate nationalities sat and the seven languages were going all the time. At my side sat a charming gentleman who was a delightful and active talker, and interesting. He talked glibly to those folks in all those seven languages and still had a language to spare! I wanted to kill him for very envy.

I greet you with love and kisses.

Papa

To Livy, Paris

Feb.—

Livy dear, last night I played billiards with Mr. Rogers until 11, then went to Robert Reid's studio and had a most delightful time until 4 this morning. No ladies were invited this time. Among the people present were:

Coquelin; Richard Harding Davis; Harrison, the great outdoor

painter; Wm. H. Chase, the artist; Bettini, inventor of the new pho-
nograph; Nikola Tesla, the worldwide illustrious electrician; see article about him in Jan. or Feb. *Century;* John Drew, actor; James
Barnes, a marvelous mimic; my, you should see him!; Smedley the
artist; Zorn the artist; Zogbaum the artist; Reinhart the artist; Met-
calf the artist; Ancona, head tenor at the Opera.

Oh, a great lot of others. Everybody there had done something
and was in his way famous.

Somebody welcomed Coquelin in a nice little French speech. John
Drew did the like for me in English. And then the fun began. Coquelin did some excellent French monologues, one of them an un-
grammatical Englishman telling a colorless historiette in French. It
nearly killed the fifteen or twenty people who understood it.

I told a yarn. Ancona sang half a dozen songs. Barnes did his
darling imitations. Harding Davis sang the hanging of Danny Deever, which was of course good, but he followed it with that most
fascinating (for what reason I don't know) of all Kipling's poems,
"On the Road to Mandalay," sang it tenderly, and it searched me
deeper and charmed me more than the Deever.

Young Gerrit Smith played some ravishing dance music and we
all danced about an hour. There couldn't be a pleasanter night than
that one was. Some of those people complained of fatigue but I don't
seem to know what the sense of fatigue is.

Coquelin talks quite good English now. He said:

"I have a brother who has the fine mind—ah, a charming and
delicate fancy. And he knows your writings so well, and loves
them—and that is the same with me. It will *stir* him so when I write
and tell him I have seen you!"

Wasn't that nice? We talked a good deal together. He is as winning as his own face. But he wouldn't sign that photograph for
Clara. "*That?* No! She shall have a better one. I will send it to you."

He is much driven and will forget it but Reid has promised to get
the picture for me, and I will try and keep him reminded.

Oh, dear, my time is all used up and your letters are not answered.

Mama dear, I don't go everywhere, I decline most things. But
there are plenty that I can't well get out of. I will remember what
you say and not make my yarning too common.

I am so glad Susy has gone on that trip and that you are trying the electric. May you both prosper. For you are mighty dear to me and in my thoughts always.

Saml

The affairs of Clemens's firm, Charles L. Webster & Co., were now in a very bad way, which was not helped by the lingering effects of the national financial depression of the previous year. Creditors were increasingly pressing their claims. Finally, on the afternoon of April 18, 1894, the firm executed assignment papers and went out of business through voluntary bankruptcy. At meetings of the creditors, Rogers represented Clemens. Some of the creditors seemed relatively lenient. Others, hard-nosed, wanted Clemens to turn over to them his literary copyrights, his home in Hartford, and whatever other assets could be found.

Rogers insisted that Livy was the chief creditor (she had lent the firm more than $60,000 of her own money) and that therefore the copyrights would go to her. He added that the Hartford house was already hers. Aside from her claim, the firm's debts amounted to about $100,000. It was agreed that Clemens would pay fifty cents on the dollar. Thus ended Clemens's publishing business after less than a decade, during which its most notable publication was the General Grant *Memoirs*.

Despite these realities, for a little while, as the following shows, Clemens was under the illusion that the company would be able to resume business.

To Livy, Paris

April 22, '94

Dear old darling, we all think the creditors are going to allow us to resume business, and if they do we shall pull through and pay the debts. I am prodigiously glad we made an assignment. And also glad that we did *not* make it sooner. Earlier we should have made a poor showing but now we shall make a good one.

I meet flocks of people and they all shake me cordially by the hand and say, "I was so sorry to hear of the assignment but so glad you did it. It was around, this long time, that the concern was tottering, and all your friends were afraid you would delay the assignment too long."

John Mackay called yesterday and said, "Don't let it disturb you,

Sam. We all have to do it at one time or another. It's nothing to be ashamed of."

One stranger out in New York State sent me a dollar bill and thought he would like to get up a dollar subscription for me. And Poultney Bigelow's note came promptly, with his check for $1,000. I had been meeting him every day at the Club and liking him better and better all the time. I couldn't take his money, of course, but I thanked him cordially for his goodwill.

Now and then a good and dear Joe Twichell or Susy Warner condoles with me and says, "Cheer up. Don't be downhearted," and some other friend says, "I am glad and surprised to see how cheerful you are and how bravely you stand it"—and none of them suspect what a burden has been lifted from me and how blithe I am inside. *Except* when I think of you, dear heart—then I am not blithe, for I seem to see you grieving and ashamed, and dreading to look people in the face. For in the thick of the fight there is cheer, but you are far away and cannot hear the drums nor see the wheeling squadrons. You only seem to see rout, retreat, and dishonored colors dragging in the dirt—whereas none of these things exist. There is temporary defeat but no dishonor, and we will march again. Charley Warner said today, "Sho, Livy isn't worrying. So long as she's got you and the children she doesn't care what happens. She knows it isn't her affair." Which didn't convince *me*.

Goodbye my darling, I love you and all of the kids—and you can tell Clara I am *not* a spitting gray kitten.

Saml

Clemens sailed for Europe in May and soon joined Livy in Paris. In the fall, under Rogers's guidance, the Paige typesetting machine was tested in Chicago. It proved finally and without question to be too complicated and fragile: a failure.

To H. H. Rogers, New York

[No date]

Dear Mr. Rogers,

Yours of Dec. 21 has arrived, containing the circular to stockholders, and I guess the Co. will really quit. There doesn't seem to be any other wise course.

There's one thing which makes it difficult for me to soberly realize that my ten-year dream is actually disolved, and that is, that it reverses my horoscope. The proverb says, "Born lucky, *always* lucky," and I am very superstitious. As a small boy I was notoriously lucky. It was usual for one or two of our lads (per annum) to get drowned in the Mississippi or in Bear Creek, but I was pulled out in a ⅔ drowned condition 9 times before I learned to swim, and was considered to be a cat in disguise.

When the *Pennsylvania* blew up and the telegraph reported my brother as fatally injured (with 60 others) but made no mention of me, my uncle said to my mother, "It means that Sam was somewhere else after being on that boat a year and a half. He was born lucky."

Yes, I *was* somewhere else. I am so superstitious that I have always been afraid to have business dealings with certain relatives and friends of mine because they were unlucky people. All my life I have stumbled upon lucky chances of large size, and whenever they were wasted it was because of my own stupidity and carelessness. And so I have felt entirely certain that that machine would turn up trumps eventually. It disappointed me lots of times but I couldn't shake off the confidence of a lifetime in my luck.

Well, whatever I get out of the wreckage will be due to good luck—the good luck of getting you into the scheme—for but for that there wouldn't be any wreckage. It would *be* total loss.

I wish you had been in at the beginning. Then we should have had the good luck to step promptly ashore.

Miss Harrison has had a dream which promises me a large bank account, and I want her to go ahead and dream it twice more so as to make the prediction sure to be fulfilled.

I've got a first-rate subject for a book. It kept me awake all night, and I began it and completed it in my mind. The minute I finish *Joan* I will take it up.

Love and Happy New Year to you all.

> Sincerely yours,
> S. L. Clemens

Paine has written: "In February [1895] Clemens returned to New York to look after matters connected with his failure and to close arrangements for a reading tour around the world. He was nearly sixty years old, and time had not lessened his loathing for the platform. More than once, however, in earlier years, he had turned to it as a debt payer, and never yet had his burden been so great as now."

In April, Clemens returned to Paris. By the latter part of May he and his family were back at Quarry Farm in Elmira. He embarked on his world tour in mid-July and sailed from Vancouver on August 23rd. He was accompanied by Livy and Clara. Jean and Susy stayed behind with their aunt at Quarry Farm.

To Rudyard Kipling, England

August, 1895

Dear Kipling,

It is reported that you are about to visit India. This has moved me to journey to that far country in order that I may unload from my conscience a debt long due to you. Years ago you came from India to Elmira to visit me, as you said at the time. It has always been my purpose to return that visit and that great compliment some day. I shall arrive next January and you must be ready. I shall come riding my ayah with his tusks adorned with silver bells and ribbons and escorted by a troop of native howdahs richly clad and mounted upon a herd of wild bungalows. And you must be on hand with a few bottles of ghee, for I shall be thirsty.

Affectionately,
S. L. Clemens

To Twichell, Hartford

Frank Moeller's Masonic Hotel, Napier, New Zealand
November 29, '95

Dear Joe,

Your welcome letter of two months and five days ago has just arrived and finds me in bed with another carbuncle. It is No. 3. Not a serious one this time. I lectured last night without inconvenience but the doctors thought best to forbid tonight's lecture. My second one kept me in bed a week in Melbourne.

... We are all glad it is you who is to write the article, it delights us all through.

I think it was a good stroke of luck that knocked me on my back here at Napier instead of some hotel in the center of a noisy city. Here we have the smooth and placidly complaining sea at our door, with nothing between us and it but 20 yards of shingle, and hardly a suggestion of life in that space to mar it or make a noise. Away down here fifty-five degrees south of the Equator this sea seems to murmur in an unfamiliar tongue—a foreign tongue—a tongue bred among the icefields of the Antarctic—a murmur with a note of melancholy in it proper to the vast unvisited solitudes it has come from. It was very delicious and solacing to wake in the night and find it still pulsing there. I wish you were here. Land, but it would be fine!

Livy and Clara enjoy this nomadic life pretty well, certainly better than one could have expected they would. They have tough experiences in the way of food and beds and frantic little ships but they put up with the worst that befalls with heroic endurance that resembles contentment.

No doubt I shall be on the platform next Monday. A week later we shall reach Wellington, talk there 3 nights, then sail back to Australia. We sailed *for* New Zealand October 30.

Day before yesterday was Livy's birthday (under world time) and tomorrow will be mine. I shall be 60—no thanks for it.

I and the others send worlds and worlds of love to all you dear ones.

Mark

The article mentioned above was one which Twichell had been assigned to write about Clemens for *Harper's Magazine*. It appeared in the May 1896 issue. Clemens read it when he reached South Africa after leaving Australia.

One of the great loves of Clemens's life was his daughter Susy, born March 19, 1872. He always felt she was special not only to himself but in general. Her childhood summers were spent at Quarry Farm, the other seasons in the Hartford home. He believed she was particularly gifted literarily, and he relished the little private biography she wrote about him. Speaking about her in his autobiography, he remarked:

"Like other children, she was blithe and happy, fond of play; unlike the average of children, she was at times much given to retiring within herself and trying to search out the hidden meanings of the deep things that make the puzzle and pathos of human existence and in all the ages have baffled the inquirer and mocked him. As a little child aged seven she was oppressed and perplexed by the maddening repetition of the stock incidents of our race's fleeting sojourn here, just as the same thing has oppressed and perplexed minds from the beginning of time."

During the summer of 1896 Katy Leary, the long-time Clemens maid, noticed an odd change in Susy, who was visiting in Hartford. Susy seemed unusually restless, nervous and in other ways unlike herself. Her health, Katy Leary thought, was failing. The doctor who was called said Susy was suffering from overwork and needed isolation and rest. But although Susy rested, she did not get better, so her aunt in Elmira was sent for, and Twichell came down to Hartford from his summer place in the Adirondacks.

On August 15th the doctor diagnosed Susy's illness as meningitis. That evening she ate for the last time. Next morning, a Sunday, she walked about a bit in pain and delirium, then felt very weak and returned to bed, but before doing so, rummaging in a closet, she came across a gown she had once seen her mother wear. She thought the gown was her dead mother and, kissing it, began to cry. At about noon she became blind. She spoke for the last time about an hour later when, groping with her hands and finding Katy Leary, she caressed Katy's face and said, "Mama."

A little later she fell into a coma and remained unconscious until the evening of Tuesday, the 18th, when she died. She was twenty-four.

Clemens wrote in his autobiography:

"The last thirteen days of Susy's life were spent in our own house in Hartford, the home of her childhood and always the dearest place in the earth to her. About her she had faithful old friends—her pastor, Mr. Twichell, who had known her from the cradle and who had come a long journey to be with her; her uncle and aunt, Mr. and Mrs. Theodore Crane; Patrick, the coachman; Katy, who had begun to serve us when Susy was a child of eight years; John and Ellen, who had been with us many years. Also Jean was there."

Of Susy's last word, "Mama," he wrote, "How gracious it was that in that forlorn hour of wreck and ruin, with the night of death closing around her, she should have been granted that beautiful illusion—that the latest vision which rested upon the clouded mirror of her mind should have been the vision of her mother, and the latest emotion she should know in life the joy and peace of that dear imagined presence."

Clemens, with Livy and Clara, sailed on the *Norman* from Capetown in mid-July, a year almost to the day since they had left Elmira. He had high hopes now of paying off all his debts dollar for dollar instead of the fifty cents on the dollar he had agreed upon with his creditors. And he looked forward to beginning work on his new travel book soon in England. The Clemenses arrived in Southampton on the 31st and proceeded to rent a house in Guildford, where they expected to await the arrival of Susy, Jean and Katy Leary no later than August 12th.

At first no news came. Then, on Friday the 14th, there was a letter saying that Susy was slightly ill—nothing to worry about. But the Clemenses, upset, cabled for later news. All that Friday there was no answer. A ship was due to leave from Southampton for New York next day at noon. Livy and Clara began to pack in order to be ready to depart in case bad news should come.

Finally there was a cable, saying, "Wait for cablegram in the morning."

This was not in the least reassuring. Clemens cabled again and asked that the reply be sent to Southampton. That night, in the hope that good news would still come, he waited in the local post office until the place closed around midnight. Still no further message.

Clemens wrote in his autobiography:

"We sat silent at home till one in the morning, waiting—waiting for we knew not what. Then we took the earliest morning train and when we reached Southampton the message was there. It said the recovery would be long but certain. This was a great relief to me but not to my wife. She was frightened. She and Clara went aboard the steamer at once and sailed for America to nurse Susy. I remained behind to search for another and larger house in Guildford.

"That was the 15th of August, 1896. Three days later, when my wife and Clara were about halfway across the ocean, I was standing in our dining room, thinking of nothing in particular, when a cablegram was put into my hand. It said, 'Susy was peacefully released today.'

"It is one of the mysteries of our nature that a man, all unprepared, can receive a thunder-stroke like that and live. There is but one reasonable explanation of it. The intellect is stunned by the shock and but gropingly gathers the meaning of the words. The power to realize their full import is mercifully wanting. The mind has a dumb sense of vast loss—that is all. . . .

"The 18th of August brought me the awful tidings. The mother and the sister were out there in mid-Atlantic, ignorant of what was happening, flying to meet this incredible calamity. All that could be done to protect them from the full force of the shock was done by relatives and good friends. They went down the Bay and met the ship at night but did not show themselves until morning, and then only to Clara. When she returned to the stateroom she did not speak and did not need to. Her mother looked at her and said, 'Susy is dead.'

"At half past ten o'clock that night Clara and her mother completed their circuit of the globe and drew up at Elmira by the same train and in the same car which had borne them and me westward from it one year, one month and one week before. And again Susy was there—not waving her welcome in the glare of the lights as she had waved her farewell to us thirteen months before, but lying white and fair in her coffin in the house where she was born. . . .

"On the 23rd her mother and her sisters saw her laid to rest—she that had been our wonder and our worship."

To Twichell, Hartford

Permanent address: c/o Chatto & Windus
111 St. Martin's Lane, London
Sept. 27, '96

Through Livy and Katy I have learned, dear old Joe, how loyally you stood poor Susy's friend and mine and Livy's. How you came all the way down twice from your summer refuge on your merciful errands to bring the peace and comfort of your beloved presence, first to that poor child and again to the broken heart of her poor desolate mother. It was like you, like your good great heart, like your matchless and unmatchable self.

It was no surprise to me to learn that you stayed by Susy long hours, careless of fatigue and heat. It was no surprise to me to learn that you could still the storms that swept her spirit when no other could, for she loved you, revered you, trusted you, and "Uncle Joe" was no empty phrase upon her lips.

I am grateful to you, Joe, grateful to the bottom of my heart, which has always been filled with love for you, and respect and admiration. And I would have chosen you out of all the world to take my place at Susy's side and Livy's in those black hours.

Susy was a rare creature, the rarest that has been reared in Hartford in this generation. And Livy knew it, and you knew it, and Charley Warner and George, and Harmony, and the Hillyers and the Dunhams and the Cheneys, and Susy and Lilly, and the Bunces, and Henry Robinson and Dick Burton, and perhaps others. And I also was of the number but not in the same degree, for she was above my duller comprehension. I merely knew that she was my superior in fineness of mind, in the delicacy and subtlety of her intellect. But to fully measure her I was not competent.

I know her better now, for I have read her private writings and sounded the deeps of her mind. And I know better now the treasure that was mine than I knew it when I had it. But I have this consolation: that dull as I was, I always knew enough to be proud when she commended me or my work—as proud as if Livy had done it herself—and I took it as the accolade from the hand of genius. I see now, as Livy always saw, that she had greatness in her and that she herself was dimly conscious of it.

And now she is dead—and I can never tell her.

God bless you Joe—and all of your house.

S.L.C.

To Henry C. Robinson, Hartford

London, *Sept. 28, '96*

It is as you say, dear old friend, "the pathos of it." Yes, it was a piteous thing, as piteous a tragedy as any the year can furnish. When we started westward upon our long trip at half-past ten at night, July 14, 1895, at Elmira, Susy stood on the platform in the blaze of the electric light waving her goodbyes to us as the train glided away, her mother throwing back kisses and watching her through her tears. One year, one month and one week later, Clara and her mother having exactly completed the circuit of the globe, drew up at that platform at the same hour of the night, in the same train *and the same car*—and again Susy had come a journey and was near at hand to meet them. She was waiting in the house she was born in, in her coffin.

All the circumstances of this death were pathetic. My brain is worn to rags rehearsing them. The mere death would have been cruelty enough, without overloading it and emphasizing it with that score of harsh and wanton details. The child was taken away when her mother was within three days of her, and would have given three decades for sight of her.

In my despair and unassuageable misery I upbraid myself for ever parting with her. But there is no use in that. Since it was to happen, it would have happened.

With love

S.L.C.

To Mrs. H. H. Rogers, New York

[London, late November]

For and in behalf
of Helen Keller,
stone blind and deaf,
and formerly dumb.

Dear Mrs. Rogers,

Experience has convinced me that when one wishes to set a hard-worked man at something which he mightn't prefer to be bothered with, it is best to move upon him behind his wife. If she can't convince him it isn't worth while for other people to try.

Mr. Rogers will remember our visit with that astonishing girl at Laurence Hutton's house when she was fourteen years old. Last July, in Boston, when she was 16 she underwent the Harvard examination for admission to Radcliffe College. She passed without a single condition. She was allowed the same amount of time that is granted to other applicants, and this was shortened in her case by the fact that the question papers had to be read to her. Yet she scored an average of 90 as against an average of 78 on the part of the other applicants.

It won't do for America to allow this marvelous child to retire from her studies because of poverty. If she can go on with them she will make a fame that will endure in history for centuries. Along her special lines she is the most extraordinary product of all the ages.

There is danger that she must retire from the struggle for a College degree for lack of support for herself and for Miss Sullivan, the teacher who has been with her from the start—Mr. Rogers will remember her. Mrs. Hutton writes to ask me to interest rich Englishmen in her case, and I would gladly try, but my secluded life will not permit it. I see *nobody*. Nobody knows my address. Nothing but the strictest hiding can enable me to write my long book in time.

So I thought of this scheme: Beg you to lay siege to your husband and get him to interest himself and John D. and William Rockefeller and the other Standard Oil chiefs in Helen's case. Get them to subscribe an annual aggregate of six or seven hundred or a thousand dollars, and agree to continue this for three or four years until she has completed her college course. I'm not trying to *limit* their generosity—indeed no, they may pile that Standard Oil, Helen Keller College Fund as high as they please, they have *my* consent.

Mrs. Hutton's idea is to raise a permanent fund the interest upon which shall support Helen and her teacher and put them out of the fear of want. I shan't say a word against it but she will find it a difficult and disheartening job, and meanwhile what is to become of that miraculous girl?

No, for immediate and sound effectiveness the thing is for you to plead with Mr. Rogers for this hampered wonder of your sex and send him clothed with plenary powers to plead with the other chiefs. They have spent mountains of money upon the worthiest benevolences, and I think that the same spirit which moved them to put their hands down through their hearts into their pockets in those cases will answer "Here!" when its name is called in this one.

There—I don't need to apologize to you or to H. H. for this appeal that I am making. I know you too well for that.

Goodbye, with love to all of you,

S. L. Clemens

Laurence Hutton is on the staff of *Harper's Monthly*—close by and handy when wanted.

To Twichell, Hartford

London, *Jan. 19,* '97

Dear Joe,

Do I want you to write to me? Indeed I do. I do not want most people to write but I do want you to do it. The others break my heart but you will not. You have a something divine in you that is not in other men. You have the touch that heals, not lacerates. And you know the secret places of our hearts. You know our life—the outside of it—as the others do—and the inside of it—which they do not. You have seen our whole voyage. You have seen us go to sea, a cloud of sail, and the flag at the peak. And you see us now, chartless, adrift—derelicts, battered, water-logged, our sails a ruck of rags, our pride gone. For it is gone. And there is nothing in its place. The vanity of life was all we had, and there is no more vanity left in us. We are even ashamed of that we had, ashamed that we trusted the promises of life and builded high—to come to this!

I did know that Susy was part of us. I did *not* know that she could go away. I did not know that she could go away and take our lives with her, yet leave our dull bodies behind. And I did not know what she was. To me she was but treasure in the bank, the amount known, the need to look at it daily, handle it, weigh it, count it, *realize* it, not necessary. And now that I would do it, it is too late. They tell me it is not there, has vanished away in a night, the bank is broken, my fortune is gone, I am a pauper. How am I to comprehend this? How am I to *have* it? Why am I robbed, and who is benefited?

Ah well, Susy died at *home*. She had that privilege. Her dying eyes rested upon nothing that was strange to them, but only upon things which they had known and loved always and which had made her young years glad. And she had you and Sue and Katy and John and Ellen. This was happy fortune. I am thankful that it was vouchsafed to her. If she had died in another house—well, I think I could not have borne that. To us, our house was not unsentient matter. It had a heart and a soul and eyes to see us with and approvals and solicitudes and deep sympathies. It was of us and we were in its confidence and lived in its grace and in the peace of its benediction. We never came home from an absence that its face did not light up and speak out its eloquent welcome. And we could not enter it unmoved. And could we now, oh now, in spirit we should enter it unshod.

I am trying to add to the "assets" which you estimate so generously. No, I am not. The thought is not in my mind. My purpose is other. I am working but it is for the sake of the work—the "surcease of sorrow" that is found there. I work all the days, and trouble vanishes away when I use that magic. This book will not long stand between it and me now. But that is no matter, I have many unwritten books to fly to for my preservation. The interval between the finishing of this one and the beginning of the next will not be more than an hour, at most. *Continuances,* I mean, for two of them are already well along. In fact have reached exactly the same stage in their journey: 19,000 words each. The present one will contain 130,000 words—130,000 are done. I am well protected.

But Livy! She has nothing in the world to turn to, nothing but housekeeping and doing things for the children and me. She does not see people and cannot. Books have lost their interest for her. She sits solitary, and all the day and all the days wonders how it all happened and why. We others were always busy with our affairs but Susy was her comrade—had to be driven from her loving persecutions—sometimes at 1 in the morning. To Livy the persecutions were welcome. It was heaven to her to be plagued like that. But it is ended now. Livy stands so in need of help, and none among us all could help her like you.

Some day you and I will walk again, Joe, and talk. I hope so. We could have *such* talks! We are all grateful to you and Harmony— *how* grateful it is not given to us to say in words. We pay as we can, in love, and in this coin practicing no economy. Goodbye, dear old Joe!

Mark

FOURTEEN

[1897-1900]

Lucerne — the Jubilee Singers — Vienna — "I couldn't get along without work now" — visit to a princess — peace by compulsion — on how to hold an audience — "This is a sordid and criminal war"

In a letter to Rogers, Clemens remarked, "I am going to write with all my might on this book, and follow it up with others as fast as I can in the hope that within three years I can clear out the stuff that is in me waiting to be written, and that I shall then die in the promptest kind of a way and no fooling around."

To Howells, New York

London, *Feb. 23,* '97

Dear Howells,

I find your generous article in the *Weekly,* and I want to thank you for its splendid praises, so daringly uttered and so warmly. The words stir the dead heart of me and throw a glow of color into a life which sometimes seems to have grown wholly wan. I don't mean that I am miserable. No—worse than that—indifferent. Indifferent to nearly everything but work. I like that. I enjoy it and stick to it. I do it without purpose and without ambition, merely for the love of it.

This mood will pass some day—there is history for it—but it cannot pass until my wife comes up out of the submergence. She was always so quick to recover herself before, but now there is no rebound and we are dead people who go through the motions of life. Indeed I am a mud image and it will puzzle me to know what it is in me that writes and has comedy fancies and finds pleasure in phrasing them. It is a law of our nature, of course, or it wouldn't happen. The thing in me forgets the presence of the mud image and goes its own way, wholly unconscious of it and apparently of no kinship with it. I have finished my book but I go on as if the end were indefinitely away—as indeed it is. There is no hurry. At any rate there is no limit.

Jean's spirits are good, Clara's are rising. They have youth, the only thing that was worth giving to the race.

These are sardonic times. Look at Greece and that whole shabby muddle. But I am not sorry to be alive and privileged to look on. If I were not a hermit I would go to the House every day and see those people scuffle over it and blether about the brotherhood of the human race. This has been a bitter year for English pride, and I don't like to see England humbled—that is, not too much. We are sprung from her loins, and it hurts me. I am for republics, and she is the only comrade we've got in that. We can't count France, and there is hardly enough of Switzerland to count. Beneath the governing crust England is sound-hearted—and sincere too, and nearly straight. But I am appalled to notice that the wide extension of the surface has damaged her manners and made her rather Americanly uncourteous on the lower levels.

Won't you give our love to the Howellses all and singular?

Sincerely yours
S. L. Clemens

The magazine referred to was *Harper's Weekly*, in which Howells had reviewed the first five volumes of the so-called "Uniform Edition" of Clemens's works. The book Clemens says he has finished is *Following the Equator*.

The travel book did not get finished as easily as Clemens expected. It was not until mid-May that the final chapters were sent to the printer. He wrote to Rogers, "A successful book is not made of what is in it, but what is left out of it."

The Clemenses went to Weggis, Switzerland, on the shore of Lake Lucerne, for the summer. Clemens called their rented house, "the charmingest place we ever lived in, for repose, and restfulness, and superb scenery." Their small house was on a hillside, and their meals were served in it from the inn on the shore below. They had a rowboat, bicycles, good roads and no visitors. The cost was six francs a day per person, house and food included. Clemens wrote to Rogers, "Nobody knows we are here. And Sunday in heaven is noisy compared to this quietness."

To Twichell, Hartford

Lucerne, *Aug. 22,* '97

Dear Joe,

Livy made a noble find on the Lucerne boat the other day on one of her shopping trips—George Williamson Smith—did I tell you about it? We had a lovely time with him and such intellectual refreshment as we had not tasted in many a month.

And the other night we had a detachment of the Jubilee Singers— 6. I had known one of them in London 24 years ago. Three of the 6 were born in slavery, the others were children of slaves. How charming they were—in spirit, manner, language, pronunciation, enunciation, grammar, phrasing, matter, carriage, clothes—in every detail that goes to make the real lady and gentleman and welcome guest. We went down to the village hotel and bought our tickets and entered the beer hall, where a crowd of German and Swiss men and women sat grouped at round tables with their beer mugs in front of them—selfcontained and unimpressionable looking people, an indifferent and unposted and disheartened audience—and up at the far end of the room sat the Jubilees in a row. The Singers got up and stood, the talking and glass jingling went on.

Then rose and swelled out above those common earthly sounds one of those rich chords the secret of whose make only the Jubilees possess, and a spell fell upon that house. It was fine to see the faces light up with the pleased wonder and surprise of it. No one was indifferent any more. And when the singers finished, the camp was theirs. It was a triumph. It reminded me of Launcelot riding in Sir Kay's armor and astonishing complacent Knights who thought they had struck a soft thing.

The Jubilees sang a lot of pieces. Arduous and painstaking cultivation has not diminished or artificialized their music, but on the contrary—to my surprise—has mightily reinforced its eloquence and beauty. Away back in the beginning, to my mind, their music made all other vocal music cheap, and that early notion is emphasized now. It is utterly beautiful to me and it moves me infinitely more than any other music can. I think that in the Jubilees and their songs America has produced the perfectest flower of the ages, and I wish it were a foreign product so that she would worship it and lavish money on it and go properly crazy over it.

Now, these countries are different. They would do all that if it were *native*. It is true they praise God but that is merely a formality and nothing in it. They open out their whole hearts to no foreigner.

The musical critics of the German press praise the Jubilees with great enthusiasm—acquired technique etc. included.

One of the Jubilee men is a son of General Joe Johnson and was educated by him after the war. The party came up to the house and we had a pleasant time.

This is paradise here—but of course we have got to leave it by and by. The 18th of August has come and gone, Joe, and we still seem to live.

> With love from us all
> Mark

The Clemens family spent the fall and winter at the Hotel Metropole in Vienna.

To Twichell, Hartford

> Hotel Metropole
> Vienna, *Oct. 23,* '97

Dear Joe,

We are gradually getting settled down and wonted. Vienna is not a cheap place to live in but I have made one small arrangement which has a distinctly economical aspect. The Vice Consul made the contract for me yesterday—to wit: a barber is to come every morning 8:30 and shave me and keep my hair trimmed for $2.50 a month. I used to pay $1.50 per shave in our house in Hartford.

Does it suggest to you reflections when you reflect that this is the most important event which has happened to me in ten days—unless I count in my handing a cabman over to the police day before yesterday with the proper formalities, and promised to appear in court when his case comes up.

If I had time to run around and talk I would do it, for there is much politics agoing and it would be interesting if a body could get the hang of it. It is Christian and Jew by the horns—the advantage with the superior man, as usual—the superior man being the Jew every time and in all countries. Land, Joe, what chance would the Christian have in a country where there were 3 Jews to 10 Christians! Oh, not the shade of a shadow of a chance. The difference between the brain of the average Christian and that of the average Jew—certainly in Europe—is about the difference between a tadpole's and an Archbishop's. It's a marvelous race, by long odds the most marvelous that the world has produced, I suppose.

And there's more politics—the clash between Czech and Austrian. I wish I could understand these quarrels but of course I can't.

With the abounding love of us all
Mark

Following the Equator had a large initial sale, but the profits for Clemens were not as vast as certain newspaper accounts claimed. Bliss, still Clemens's publisher, became worried that such stories would dampen public sympathy for Clemens and consequently hurt the book's sales. He cabled Clemens for a denial of his vast sudden riches.

To Frank E. Bliss, Hartford

Vienna, *Nov. 4, 1897*

Dear Bliss,

Your cablegram informing me that a report is in circulation which purports to come from me and which says I have recently made $82,000 and paid all my debts has just reached me, and I have cabled back my regret to you that it is not true. I wrote a letter, a private letter, a short time ago, in which I expressed the belief that I should be out of debt within the next twelvemonth. If you make as much as usual for me out of the book, that belief will crystallize into a fact and I shall be wholly out of debt. I am encoring you now.

It is out of that moderate letter that the Eighty-Two-Thousand-Dollar mare's nest has developed. But why do you worry about the various reports? They do not worry me. They are not unfriendly and I don't see how they can do any harm. Be patient. You have but a little while to wait. The possible reports are nearly all in.

It has been reported that I was seriously ill. It was another man. Dying—it was another man. Dead—the other man again. It has been reported that I have received a legacy—it was another man. That I am out of debt—it was another man. And now comes this $82,000—still another man. It has been reported that I am writing books for publication. I am not doing anything of the kind. It would surprise (and gratify) me if I should be able to get another book ready for the press within the next three years.

You can see yourself that there isn't anything more to be reported—invention is exhausted. Therefore don't worry, Bliss, the long night is breaking. As far as I can see, nothing remains to be reported except that I have become a foreigner. When you hear it don't you believe it. And don't take the trouble to deny it. Merely just raise the American flag on our house in Hartford and let it talk.

Truly yours,
Mark Twain

P. S. This is not a private letter. I am getting tired of private letters.

Orion died December 11 at the age of seventy-two. According to Paine, it was early in the morning, and Orion had just sat down at a table with pencil and paper "and was setting down the details of his latest project."

Clemens was finally out of debt the end of January 1898. There was universal praise for him. "Honest men must be pretty scarce," he said, "when they make so much fuss over even a defective specimen." The end of his debts was in sight when he wrote the following.

To Howells, New York

Hotel Metropole
Vienna, *Jan. 22, '98*

Dear Howells,

Look at those ghastly figures. I used to write it "Hartford, *1871.*" There was no Susy then, there is no Susy now. And how much lies between—one long lovely stretch of scented fields and meadows and shady woodlands, and suddenly Sahara! You speak of the glorious days of that old time—and they were. It is my quarrel that traps like that are set. Susy and Winnie given us in miserable sport and then taken away.

About the last time *I* saw you I described to you the culminating disaster in a book I was going to write (and will yet, when the stroke is further away)—a man's dead daughter brought to him when he had been through all other possible misfortunes—and I said it couldn't be done as it ought to be done except by a man who had lived it—it must be written with the blood out of a man's heart. I couldn't know then how soon I was to be made competent. I have thought of it many a time since. If you were here I think we could cry down each other's necks, as in your dream. For we *are* a pair of old derelicts drifting around now, with some of our passengers gone and the sunniness of the others in eclipse.

I couldn't get along without work now. I bury myself in it up to the ears. Long hours—8 and 9 on a stretch sometimes. And all the days, Sundays included. It isn't all for print, by any means, for much of it fails to suit me—50,000 words of it in the past year. It was because of the deadness which invaded me when Susy died. But I have made a change lately—into dramatic work—and I find it absorbingly entertaining. I don't know that I can write a play that will play, but no matter, I'll write half a dozen that won't, anyway. Dear me, I didn't know there was such fun in it. I'll write twenty that won't play.

I get into immense spirits as soon as my day is fairly started. Of course a good deal of this friskiness comes of my being in sight of land—on the Webster & Co. debts, I mean. (Private.) We've lived close to the bone and saved every cent we could, and there's no undisputed claim now that we can't cash. I have marked this "private" because it is for the friends who are attending to the matter for us in New York to reveal it when they want to and if they want to. There are only two claims which I dispute and which I mean to look into personally before I pay them. But they are small. Both together they amount to only $12,500.

I hope you will never get the like of the load saddled onto you that was saddled onto me 3 years ago. And yet there is such a solid pleasure in *paying* the things that I reckon maybe it is worth while to get into that kind of a hobble after all. Mrs. Clemens gets millions of delight out of it. And the children have never uttered one complaint about the scrimping, from the beginning.

We all send you and all of you our love.

Mark

Winnie is Howells's daughter Winifred, who died March 3, 1889.

According to Paine, the Clemens apartment in the Hotel Metropole was "much more like an embassy than the home of a mere literary man. Celebrities in every walk of life, persons of social and official rank, writers for the press, assembled there on terms hardly possible in any other home in Vienna. Wherever Mark Twain appeared in public he was a central figure. Now and then he read or spoke to aid some benefit, and these were great gatherings attended by members of the royal family."

To Twichell, Hartford

Hotel Metropole
Vienna, *Feb. 3, '98*

(*Private*)

Dear Joe,

There's that letter that I began so long ago. You see how it is: can't get time to finish anything. I pile up lots of work nevertheless. There may be idle people in the world but I'm not one of them. I say "Private" up there because I've got an adventure to tell and you mustn't let a breath of it get out. First I thought I would lay it up along with a thousand others that I've laid up for the same purpose—to talk to you about—but those others have vanished out of my memory, and that must not happen with this.

The other night I lectured for a Vienna charity, and at the end of it Livy and I were introduced to a princess who is aunt to the heir apparent of the imperial throne—a beautiful lady with a beautiful spirit and very cordial in her praises of my books and thanks to me for writing them, and glad to meet me face to face and shake me by the hand—just the kind of princess that adorns a fairy tale and makes it the prettiest tale there is.

Very well, we long ago found that when you are noticed by supremacies the correct etiquette is to go within a couple of days and pay your respects in the quite simple form of writing your name in the Visitors' Book kept in the office of the establishment. That is the end of it, and everything is squared up and shipshape.

So at noon today Livy and I drove to the Archducal palace and got by the sentries all right and asked the grandly uniformed porter for the book and said we wished to write our names in it. And he called a servant in livery and was sending us upstairs, and said her Royal Highness was out but would soon be in.

Of course Livy said, "No, no, we only want the book."

But he was firm and said, "You are Americans?"

"Yes."

"Then you are expected. Please go upstairs."

"But indeed we are not expected. Please let us have the book and—"

"Her Royal Higness will be back in a *very* little while. She commanded me to *tell* you so, and you must wait."

Well, the soldiers were there close by—there was no use trying to resist—so we followed the servant up. But when he tried to beguile us into a drawing-room, Livy drew the line, she wouldn't go in. And she wouldn't stay up there either. She said the princess might come in at any moment and catch us, and it would be too infernally ridiculous for anything. So we went downstairs again—to my unspeakable regret. For it was too darling a comedy to spoil. I was hoping and praying the princess would come and catch us up there, and that those other Americans who *were* expected would arrive and be taken for impostors by the portier and shot by the sentinels—and then it would all go into the papers and be cabled all over the world and make an immense stir and be perfectly lovely. And by that time the princess would discover that *we* were not the right ones, and the Minister of War would be ordered out, and the garrison, and they would come for us, and there would be another prodigious time, and *that* would get cabled too, and—well, Joe, I was in a state of perfect bliss.

But happily, oh so happily, that big portier wouldn't let us out. He was sorry but he must obey orders. We must go back upstairs and wait. Poor Livy. I couldn't help but enjoy her distress. She said we were in a fix and how *were* we going to explain if the princess should arrive before the rightful Americans came?

We went upstairs again, laid off our wraps and were conducted through one drawing-room and into another and left alone there, and the door closed upon us.

Livy was in a state of mind! She said it was too theatrically ridiculous and that I would never be able to keep my mouth shut, that I would be sure to let it out and it would get into the papers, and she tried to make me promise.

"Promise *what?*" I said. "To be quiet about this? Indeed I won't. It's the best thing that ever happened. I'll tell it, and add to it. And I wish Joe and Howells were here to make it perfect. I can't make all the rightful blunders myself. It takes all three of us to do justice to an opportunity like this. I would just like to see Howells get down to his work and explain and lie and work his futile and inventionless subterfuges when that princess comes raging in here and wanting to *know.*"

But Livy could not hear fun. It was not a time to be trying to be funny. We were in a most miserable and shameful situation, and if—

Just then the door spread wide and our princess and 4 more, and 3 little princes flowed in! Our princess and her sister the Archduchess Marie Therese (mother to the imperial Heir and to the young girl Archduchesses present, and aunt to the 3 little princes) and we shook hands all around and sat down and had a most sociable good time for half an hour. And by and by it turned out that we *were* the right ones, and had been sent for by a messenger who started too late to catch us at the hotel. We were invited for 2 o'clock but we beat that arrangement by an hour and a half.

Wasn't it a rattling good comedy situation? Seems a kind of pity we were the right ones. It would have been such nuts to see the right ones come and get fired out, and we chatting along comfortably and nobody suspecting us for impostors.

We send lots and lots of love.

Mark

Clemens and his family spent the summer of 1898 in Kaltenleutgeben, a village near Vienna. By the end of the year he was in easy circumstances again. The Clemenses spent the winter at the Hotel Krantz in Vienna.

When the Czar of Russia proposed a plan for world disarmament, William T. Stead, of the *Review of Reviews*, cabled Clemens for his opinion on the matter.

To Wm. T. Stead, London

No. 1

Vienna, Jan. 9

Dear Mr. Stead,

The Czar is ready to disarm. *I* am ready to disarm. Collect the *others*, it should not be much of a task now.

Mark Twain

To Wm. T. Stead, London

No. 2

Dear Mr. Stead,

Peace by compulsion. That seems a better idea than the other. Peace by persuasion has a pleasant sound but I think we should not be able to work it. We should have to tame the human race first, and history seems to show that that cannot be done.

Can't we reduce the armaments little by little on a pro rata basis by concert of the powers? Can't we get four great powers to agree to reduce their strength 10 per cent a year and thrash the others into doing likewise? For, of course, we cannot expect all of the powers to be in their right minds at one time. It has been tried. We are not going to try to get all of them to go into the scheme peaceably, are we? In that case I must withdraw my influence because for business reasons I must preserve the outward signs of sanity. Four is enough if they can be securely harnessed together. They can compel peace, and peace without compulsion would be against nature and not operative.

A sliding scale of reduction of 10 per cent a year has a sort of plausible look and I am willing to try that if three other powers will join. I feel sure that the armaments are now many times greater than necessary for the requirements of either peace or war.

Take wartime, for instance. Suppose circumstances made it necessary for us to fight another Waterloo, and that it would do what it did before—settle a large question and bring peace. I will guess that 400,000 men were on hand at Waterloo (I have forgotten the figures). In five hours they disabled 50,000 men. It took them that tedious, long time because the firearms delivered only two or three shots a minute.

But we would do the work now as it was done at Omdurman, with shower guns raining 600 balls a minute. Four men to a gun—is that the number? A hundred and fifty shots a minute per man. Thus a modern soldier is 149 Waterloo soldiers in one. Thus also we can now retain one man out of each 150 in service, disband the others and fight our Waterloos just as effectively as we did eighty-five years ago. We should do the same beneficent job with 2,800 men now that we did with 400,000 then. The allies could take 1400 of the men and give Napoleon 1400 and then whip him.

But instead, what do we see? In wartime, in Germany, Russia and France taken together, we find about 8 million men equipped for the field. Each man represents 149 Waterloo men in usefulness and killing capacity. Altogether they constitute about 350 million Waterloo men, and there are not quite that many grown males of the human race now on this planet. Thus we have this insane fact—that whereas those three countries could arm 18,000 men with modern weapons and make them the equals of 3 million men of Napoleon's day and accomplish with them all necessary war work, they waste their money and their prosperity creating forces of their populations in piling together 349,982,000 extra Waterloo equivalents which they would have no sort of use for if they would only stop drinking and sit down and cipher a little.

Perpetual peace we cannot have on any terms, I suppose. But I hope we can gradually reduce the war strength of Europe till we get it down to where it ought to be—20,000 men, properly armed. Then we can have all the peace that is worthwhile, and when we want a war, anybody can afford it.

Vienna, *January 9*

P. S.—In the article I sent, the figures are wrong—"350 million" ought to be 450 million. "349,982,000" ought to be 449,982,000. And the remark about the sum being a little more than the present number of males on the planet—that is wrong, of course. It represents really one and a half the existing males.

In the middle of May, Clemens was still in Vienna. The story mentioned in the following is "The Mysterious Stranger," which was not finished at the time. The closing chapter was found after Clemens's death, and six years later, in 1916, the tale was published serially in *Harper's Magazine* before it was issued in book form.

To Howells, New York

May 12, 1899

Dear Howells,

. . . For several years I have been intending to stop writing for print as soon as I could afford it. At last I can afford it, and have put the potboiler pen away. What I have been wanting is a chance to write a book without reserves, a book which should take account of no one's feelings and no one's prejudices, opinions, beliefs, hopes, illusions, delusions, a book which should say my say right out of my heart in the plainest language and without a limitation of any sort. I judged that that would be an unimaginable luxury, heaven on earth.

It is under way now and it *is* a luxury! an intellectual drunk. Twice I didn't start it right, and got pretty far in both times before I found it out. But I am sure it is started right this time. It is in tale form. I believe I can make it tell what I think of Man, and how he is constructed, and what a shabby poor ridiculous thing he is, and how mistaken he is in his estimate of his character and powers and qualities and his place among the animals.

So far, I think I am succeeding. I let the madam into the secret day before yesterday and locked the doors and read to her the opening chapters. She said:

"It is perfectly horrible—and perfectly beautiful!"

"Within the due limits of modesty, that is what *I* think."

I hope it will take me a year or two to write it and that it will turn out to be the right vessel to contain all the ordure I am planning to dump into it.

Yours ever

Mark

By the end of May the Clemenses were living in London. They summered in Sanna, Sweden, in order to avail themselves of Henrick Kellgren's osteopathic treatments. Soon Clemens was advertising to all his friends the marvels of the new panacea. When Howells informed him that he was going on a reading tour and asked for advice, Clemens responded with the following.

To Howells, New York

Sanna, Sweden, *Sept. 26, '99*

Dear Howells,

Get your lecture by heart—it will pay you. I learned a trick in Vienna by accident which I wish I had learned years ago. I meant to read from a Tauchnitz because I knew I hadn't well memorized the pieces, and I came on with the book and read a few sentences, then remembered that the sketch needed a few words of explanatory introduction. And so, lowering the book and now and then unconsciously using it to gesture with, I talked the introduction, and it happened to carry me into the sketch *itself*. And then I went on, pretending that I was merely talking extraneous matter and would come to the sketch *presently*. It was a beautiful success. I knew the substance of the sketch and the telling phrases of it, and so the throwing of the rest of it into informal talk as I went along limbered it up and gave it the snap and go and freshness of an impromptu.

I was to read several pieces, and I played the same game with all of them, and always the audience thought I was being reminded of outside things and throwing them in, and was going to hold up the book and begin on the sketch presently—and so I always got through the sketch before they were entirely sure that it had begun. I did the same thing in Budapest and had the same good time over again.

It's a new dodge and the best one that was ever invented. Try it. You'll never lose your audience, not even for a moment. Their attention is fixed and never wavers. And that is not the case where one reads from book or MS, or where he stands up without a note and frankly exposes the fact, by his confident manner and smooth phrasing, that he is not improvising, but reciting from memory.

And in the heat of telling a thing that is memorised in substance only, one flashes out the happiest suddenly begotten phrases every now and then! Try it. Such a phrase has a life and sparkle about it that twice as good a one could not exhibit if prepared beforehand, and it "fetches" an audience in such an enthusing and inspiring and uplifting way that that lucky phrase breeds another one, sure.

Your September instalment was delicious—every word of it. You haven't lost any of your splendid art. Callers have arrived.

With love
Mark

Tauchnitz is Christian Bernard von Tauchnitz of Leipzig, Germany, publisher of the Tauchnitz Editions of American and British authors, sold in Europe. Pond in the following is James B. Pond, American lecture agent and manager.

To Howells, Boston

Wellington Court, Knightsbridge, London
Jan. 25, 1900

Dear Howells,

If you got half as much as Pond prophesied, be content and praise God—it has not happened to another. But I am sorry he didn't go with you, for it is marvelous to hear him yarn. He is good company, cheery and hearty, and his mill is never idle. Your doing a lecture tour was heroic. It was the highest order of grit and you have a right to be proud of yourself. No amount of applause or money or both could save it from being a hell to a man constituted as you are. It is that even to me, who am made of courser stuff.

I knew the audiences would come forward and shake hands with you—that one infallible sign of sincere approval. In all my life, wherever it failed me I left the hall sick and ashamed, knowing what it meant.

Privately speaking, this is a sordid and criminal war, and in every way shameful and excuseless. Every day I write (in my head) bitter magazine articles about it but I have to stop with that. For England must not fall. It would mean an inundation of Russian and German political degradations which would envelop the globe and steep it in a sort of Middle Age night and slavery which would last till Christ comes again. Even wrong—and she is wrong—England must be upheld. He is an enemy of the human race who shall speak against her now.

Why *was* the human race created? Or at least why wasn't something creditable created in place of it? God had his opportunity. He could have made a reputation. But no, He must commit this grotesque folly—a lark which must have cost him a regret or two when He came to think it over and observe effects. For a giddy and unbecoming caprice there has been nothing like it till this war. I talk the war with both sides—always waiting until the other man introduces the topic. Then I say, "My head is with the Briton but my heart and such rags of morals as I have are with the Boer—now we will talk, unembarrassed and without prejudice." And so we discuss, and have no trouble.

Jan. 26

It was my intention to make some disparaging remarks about the human race and so I kept this letter open for that purpose, and for the purpose of telling my dream, wherein the Trinity were trying to guess a conundrum. But I can do better, for I can snip out of the *Times* various samples and sidelights which bring the race down to date and expose it as of yesterday. If you will notice, there is seldom a telegram in a paper which fails to show up one or more members and beneficiaries of our Civilization as promenading in his shirt-tail, with the rest of his regalia in the wash.

I love to see the holy ones air their smug pieties and admire them and smirk over them, and at the same moment frankly and publicly show their contempt for the pieties of the Boer—confidently expecting the approval of the country and the pulpit, and getting it.

I notice that God is on both sides in this war. Thus history repeats itself. But I am the only person who has noticed this. Everybody here thinks He is playing the game for this side, and for this side only.

With great love to you all
Mark

FIFTEEN

[1900–03]

London family hotels — the human race — "Life should begin with age . . . and end with youth" — the slowness of telegrams — Walter Scott's literary offenses

To Mr. Ann, London

Wellington Court, *Feb. 23, '00*

Dear Mr. Ann,

Upon sober second thought, it won't do!—I withdraw that letter. Not because I said anything in it which is not true, for I didn't, but because when I allow my name to be used in forwarding a stock scheme I am assuming a certain degree of responsibility as toward the investor, and I am not willing to do that. I have another objection, a purely selfish one: trading upon my name, whether the enterprise scored a success or a failure, would damage me. I can't afford that. Even the Archbishop of Canterbury couldn't afford it, and he has more character to spare than I have. (Ah, a happy thought! If *he* would sign the letter with me that would change the whole complexion of the thing, of course. I do not know him, yet I would sign any commercial scheme that he would sign. As he does not know me, it follows that he would sign anything that I would sign. This is unassailable logic—but really that is all that can be said for it.)

No, I withdraw the letter. This virgin is pure up to date, and is going to remain so.

Ys sincerely,
S.L.C.

In July, Clemens and his family moved from their small apartment at 30 Wellington Court to a summer house in Dollis Hill, a little way from London. Livy wrote to her sister that the place was "simply divinely beautiful. The great old trees are beyond everything. I believe nowhere in the world do you find such trees as in England."

Clemens wrote to Twichell, "From the house you can see little but spacious stretches of hay fields and green turf. . . . Yet the massed, brick blocks of London are reachable in three minutes on a horse. By rail we can be in the heart of London, in Baker Street, in seventeen minutes—by a smart train in five."

The Clemens family left Dollis Hill near the end of September and lived briefly in a London hotel.

To J. Y. M. MacAlister, London

Sep. 1900

My dear MacAlister,

We do really start next Saturday. I meant to sail earlier but waited to finish some studies of what are called Family Hotels. They are a London specialty. God has not permitted them to exist elsewhere. They are ramshackle clubs which were dwellings at the time of the Heptarchy. Dover and Albemarle Streets are filled with them. The once spacious rooms are split up into coops which afford as much discomfort as can be had anywhere out of jail for any money. All the modern inconveniences are furnished, and some that have been obsolete for a century. The prices are astonishingly high for what you get. The bedrooms are hospitals for incurable furniture. I find it so in this one. They exist upon a tradition. They represent the vanishing home-like inn of fifty years ago, and are mistaken by foreigners for it. Some quite respectable Englishmen still frequent them through inherited habit and arrested development; many Americans also, through ignorance and superstition. The rooms are as interesting as the Tower of London, but older I think. Older and dearer. The lift was a gift of William the Conqueror. Some of the beds are prehistoric. They represent geological periods.

Mine is the oldest. It is formed in strata of Old Red Sandstone, volcanic tufa, ignis fatuus, and bicarbonate of hornblende, superimposed upon argillaceous shale, and contains the prints of prehistoric man. It is in No. 149. Thousands of scientists come to see it. They consider it holy. They want to blast out the prints but cannot. Dynamite rebounds from it.

Finished studies and sail Saturday in *Minnehaha*.

Yours ever affectionately
Mark Twain

The Clemenses sailed for New York on October 6th, stayed for a while at the Earlington Hotel and debated whether to move back into the Hartford house. After a solitary visit to the house, Clemens wrote to Sylvester Baxter in Boston, "I realize that if we ever enter the house again to live, our hearts will break. I am not sure that we shall ever be strong enough to endure that strain."

Clemens rented a large, handsomely furnished house at 14 West Tenth Street in New York.

Early in 1901, an editorial in the *Louisville Courier-Journal* noted:

"A remarkable transformation, or rather development, has taken place in Mark Twain. The genial humorist of the earlier day is now a reformer of the vigorous kind, a sort of knight errant who does not hesitate to break a lance with either Church or State if he thinks them interposing on that broad highway over which he believes not a part but the whole of mankind has the privilege of passing in the onward march of the ages."

Paine has written of Clemens: "He did not believe [at this time] that he could reform the world, but at least he need not withhold his protest against those things which stirred his wrath. He began by causing the arrest of a cabman who had not only overcharged but insulted him. He continued by writing openly against the American policy in the Philippines, the missionary propaganda which had resulted in the Chinese uprising and massacre, and against Tammany politics. Not all his efforts were in the line of reform. He had become a sort of general spokesman which the public flocked to hear, whatever the subject. . . . He was obliged to attend more dinners than were good for his health."

To Twichell, Hartford

14 W. 10th *Jan. 29, '01*

Dear Joe,

. . . I'm not expecting anything but kicks for scoffing, and am expecting a diminution of my bread and butter by it, but if Livy will let me I will have my say. This nation is like all the others that have been spewed upon the earth—ready to shout for any cause that will tickle its vanity or fill its pocket. What a hell of a heaven it will be when they get all these hypocrites assembled there!

I can't understand it! You are a public guide and teacher, Joe, and are under a heavy responsibility to men, young and old. If you teach your people—as you teach me—to hide their opinions when they believe the flag is being abused and dishonored, lest the utterance do them and a publisher a damage, how do you answer for it to your conscience? You are sorry for me. In the fair way of give and take, I am willing to be a little sorry for you.

However, I seem to be going counter to my own Private Philosophy, which Livy won't allow me to publish because it would destroy me. But I hope to see it in print before I die. I planned it 15 years ago and wrote it in '98. I've often tried to read it to Livy but she won't have it, it makes her melancholy. The truth always has that effect on people. *Would* have, anyway, if they ever got hold of a rag of it. Which they don't.

You are supposing that I am supposing that I am moved by a Large Patriotism and that I am distressed because our President has blundered up to his neck in the Philippine mess, and that I am grieved because this great big ignorant nation, which doesn't know even the A B C facts of the Philippine episode, is in disgrace before the sarcastic world. Drop that idea! I care nothing for the rest. I am only distressed and troubled because I am befouled by these things. That is all. When I search myself away down deep, I find this out. Whatever a man feels or thinks or does, there is never any but one reason for it, and that is a selfish one.

At great inconvenience, and expense of precious time, I went to the chief synagogue the other night and talked in the interest of a charity school of poor Jew girls. I know to the finest shades the selfish ends that moved me but no one else suspects. I could give you the details if I had time. You would perceive how true they are.

I've written another article. You better hurry down and help Livy squelch it.

She's out pottering around somewhere, poor housekeeping slave. And Clara is in the hands of the osteopath, getting the bronchitis pulled and hauled out of her. It was a bad attack, and a little disquieting. It came day before yesterday and she hasn't sat up till this afternoon. She is getting along satisfactorily now.

Lots of love to you all.

Mark

Clemens and his family spent the summer of 1901 in a lodge in the Adirondacks, where he received an invitation to attend the celebration of Missouri's eightieth anniversary.

To Edward L. Dimmitt, St. Louis

Among the Adirondack Lakes, July 19, 1901

Dear Mr. Dimmitt,

By an error in the plans, things go wrong end first in this world and much precious time is lost and matters of urgent importance are fatally retarded. Invitations which a brisk young fellow should get and which would transport him with joy are delayed and impeded and obstructed until they are fifty years overdue when they reach him.

It has happened again in this case.

When I was a boy in Missouri I was always on the lookout for invitations but they always miscarried and went wandering through the aisles of time. And now they are arriving when I am old and rheumatic and can't travel and must lose my chance.

I have lost a world of delight through this matter of delaying invitations. Fifty years ago I would have gone eagerly across the world to help celebrate anything that might turn up. It would have made no difference to me what it was, so that I was there and allowed a chance to make a noise.

The whole scheme of things is turned wrong end to. Life should begin with age and its privileges and accumulations, and end with youth and its capacity to splendidly enjoy such advantages. As things are now, when in youth a dollar would bring a hundred pleasures, you can't have it. When you are old you get it and there is nothing worth buying with it then.

It's an epitome of life. The first half of it consists of the capacity to enjoy without the chance. The last half consists of the chance without the capacity.

I am admonished in many ways that time is pushing me inexorably along. I am approaching the threshold of age. In 1977 I shall be 142. This is no time to be flitting about the earth. I must cease from the activities proper to youth and begin to take on the dignities and gravities and inertia proper to that season of honorable senility which is on its way and imminent as indicated above.

Yours is a great and memorable occasion, and as a son of Missouri I should hold it a high privilege to be there and share your just pride in the state's achievements. But I must deny myself the indulgence, while thanking you earnestly for the prized honor you have done me in asking me to be present.

Very truly yours,
S. L. Clemens

The following refers to the assassination of President William McKinley early in September. As for Clemens's statement, "I bought a revolver once and traveled twelve hundred miles to kill a man," according to Paine "There is no other mention of it elsewhere in the records that survive him."

To Twichell, Hartford

Ampersand, *Tuesday, [Sept. 10, 1901]*

Dear Joe,

It is another off day, but tomorrow I shall resume work to a *certainty* and bid a long farewell to letter scribbling.

The news of the President looks decidedly hopeful and we are all glad, and the household faces are much improved as to cheerfulness. Oh, the *talk* in the newspapers! Evidently the Human Race is the same old Human Race. And how unjust and unreflectingly discriminating the talkers are. Under the unsettling effects of powerful emotion the talkers are saying wild things, crazy things—they are out of themselves and do not know it. They are temporarily insane, yet with one voice they declare the assassin *sane*—a man who has been entertaining fiery and reason-debauching maggots in his head for weeks and months.

Why, no one is sane, straight along, year in and year out, and we all know it. Our insanities are of varying sorts and express themselves in varying forms—fortunately harmless forms as a rule—but in whatever form they occur an immense upheaval of feeling can at any time topple us distinctly over the sanity line for a little while, and then if our form happens to be of the murderous kind we must look out—and so must the spectator.

This ass with the unpronounceable name was probably more insane than usual this week or two back, and may get back upon his bearings by and by, but he was over the sanity border when he shot the President. It is possible that it has taken him the whole interval since the murder of the King of Italy to get insane enough to attempt the President's life.

Without a doubt some thousands of men have been meditating the same act in the same interval, but new and strong interests have intervened and diverted their overexcited minds long enough to give them a chance to settle, and tranquilize, and get back upon a healthy level again. *Every* extraordinary occurrence unsettles the heads of hundreds of thouands of men for a few moments or hours or days. If there had been ten kings around when Humbert fell, they would have been in great peril for a day or more, and from men in whose presence they would have been quite safe after the excess of their excitement had had an interval in which to cool down.

I bought a revolver once and traveled twelve hundred miles to kill a man. He was away. He was gone a day. With nothing else to do, I *had* to stop and think—and did. Within an hour—within half of it— I was ashamed of myself and felt unspeakably ridiculous. I do not know what to call it if I was not insane. During a whole week my head was in a turmoil night and day fierce enough and exhausting enough to upset a stronger reason than mine.

All over the world, every day, there are some millions of men in that condition temporarily. And in that time there is always a moment—perhaps only a single one—when they would do murder if their man was at hand. If the opportunity comes a shade too late, the chances are that it has come permanently too late. Opportunity seldom comes exactly at the supreme moment. This saves a million lives a day in the world for sure.

No Ruler is ever slain but the tremendous details of it are ravenously devoured by a hundred thousand men whose minds dwell, unaware, near the temporary-insanity frontier—and over they go now! There is a day—two days—three—during which no Ruler would be safe from perhaps the half of them, and there is a single moment wherein he would not be safe from any of them, no doubt.

It may take this present shooting case six months to breed another ruler tragedy, but it will breed it. There is at least one mind somewhere which will brood and wear and decay itself to the killing point and produce that tragedy.

Every negro burned at the stake unsettles the excitable brain of another one—I mean the inflaming details of his crime and the lurid theatricality of his exit do it—and the duplicate crime follows. And that begets a repetition, and that one another one, and so on. Every lynching account unsettles the brains of another set of excitable white men, and lights another pyre—115 lynchings last year, 102 inside of 8 months this year. In ten years this will be *habit*, on these terms.

Yes, the wild talk you see in the papers! And from men who are sane when not upset by overwhelming excitement. A U. S. Senator—Cullom—wants this Buffalo criminal lynched! It would breed other lynchings—of men who are not dreaming of committing murders now and will commit none if Cullom will keep quiet and not provide the exciting cause.

And a District Attorney wants a law which shall punish with death *attempts* upon a President's life—this, mind you, as a deterrent. It would have no effect—or the opposite one. The lunatic's mind-space is *all* occupied—as mine was—with the matter in hand. There is no room in it for reflections upon what may happen to *him*. That comes after the crime.

It is the *noise* the attempt would make in the world that would breed the subsequent attempts, by unsettling the rickety minds of men who envy the criminal his vast notoriety. His obscure name tongued by stupendous Kings and Emperors. His picture printed everywhere. The trivialest details of his movements, what he eats, what he drinks, how he sleeps, what he says, cabled abroad over the whole globe at cost of fifty thousand dollars a day. And he only a lowly shoemaker yesterday! Like the assassin of the President of France. In debt three francs to his landlady and insulted by her. And today she is proud to be able to say she knew him "as familiarly as you know your own brother," and glad to stand till she drops and pour out columns and pages of her grandeur and her happiness upon the eager interviewer.

Nothing will check the lynchings and ruler-murder but absolute silence, the absence of pow-pow about them. How are you going to manage that? By gagging every witness and jamming him into a dungeon for life? By abolishing all newspapers? By exterminating all newspaper men? And by extinguishing God's most elegant invention, the Human Race? It is quite simple, quite easy, and I hope you will take a day off and attend to it, Joe.

I blow a kiss to you, and am

Lovingly Yours,
Mark

At the end of the summer the Clemens family moved to a spacious home in Riverdale, New York, from which Clemens had ample views of the Hudson and its ships.

In April of the following year Clemens returned to his native state to receive an LL.D. from the University of Missouri. It was his last visit to the Mississippi.

He rented a furnished house in York Harbor, Maine, for the summer of 1902. Livy was ailing, so H. H. Rogers moved the Clemenses in his yacht *Kanawha* from Riverdale to York Harbor. The Clemens house, low, wide, was in a pine grove overlooking York River. Howells, at Kittery Point, was just some miles away. The two friends used to chat in a corner of the Clemens veranda. Clemens worked in a rented room in a separate cottage, "the house of a friend and neighbor, a fisherman and a boatman," as Clemens once explained.

To the President of Western Union, New York

"The Pines"
York Harbor, Maine

Dear Sir,

I desire to make a complaint and I bring it to you, the head of the company, because by experience I know better than to carry it to a subordinate.

I have been here a month and a half, and by testimony of friends, reinforced by personal experience, I now feel qualified to claim as an established fact that the telegraphic service here is the worst in the world except that in Boston.

These services are actually slower than was the New York and Hartford service in the days when I last complained to you, which was fifteen or eighteen years ago, when telegraphic time and train time between the mentioned points was exactly the same, to wit, three hours and a half.

Six days ago—it was that raw day which provoked so much comment—my daughter was on her way up from New York, and at noon she telegraphed me from New Haven asking that I meet her with a cloak at Portsmouth. Her telegram reached me four hours and a quarter later—just 15 minutes too late for me to catch my train and meet her.

I judge that the telegram traveled about 200 miles. It is the best telegraphic work I have seen since I have been here, and I am mentioning it in this place not as a complaint but as a compliment. I think a compliment ought always to precede a complaint, where one is possible, because it softens resentment and insures for the complaint a courteous and gentle reception.

Still, there is a detail or two connected with this matter which ought perhaps to be mentioned. And now, having smoothed the way with the compliment, I will venture them.

The head corpse in the York Harbor office sent me that telegram although (1) he knew it would reach me too late to be of any value; (2) also, that he was going to send it to me by his boy; (3) that the boy would not take the trolley and come the 2 miles in 12 minutes, but would walk; (4) that he would be two hours and a quarter on the road; (5) and that he would collect 25 cents for transportation for a telegram which the h. c. knew to be worthless before he started it.

From these data I infer that the Western Union owes me 75 cents; that is to say, the amount paid for combined wire and land transportation—a recoup provided for in the printed paragraph which heads the telegraph blank.

By these humane and Christian stages we now arrive at the complaint proper. We have had a grave case of illness in the family, and a relative was coming some six hundred miles to help in the sick room during the convalescing period. It was an anxious time, of course, and I wrote and asked to be notified as to the hour of the expected arrival of this relative in Boston or in York Harbor. Being afraid of the telegraph, which I think ought not to be used in times of hurry and emergency, I asked that the desired message be brought to me by some swift method of transportation. By the milk-man, if he was coming this way.

But there are always people who think they know more than you do, especially young people, so of course the young fellow in charge of this lady used the telegraph. And at Boston, of all places! Except York Harbor.

The result was as usual. Let me employ a statelier and exacter term, and say historical.

The dispatch was handed to the h. c. of the Boston office at 9 this morning. It said, "Shall bring A. S. to you eleven forty-five this morning."

The distance traveled by the dispatch is forty or fifty miles, I suppose, as the train time is five minutes short of two hours, and the trains are so slow that they can't give a W. U. telegram two hours and twenty minutes start and overtake it.

As I have said, the dispatch was handed in at Boston at 9. The expected visitors left Boston at 9:40 and reached my house at 12 noon, beating the telegram 2 solid hours, and 5 minutes over.

The boy brought the telegram. It was baldheaded with age but still legible. The boy was prostrate with travel and exposure but still alive, and I went out to condole with him and get his last wishes and send for the ambulance. He was waiting to collect transportation before turning his passing spirit to less serious affairs. I found him strangely intelligent, considering his condition and where he is get-ting his training.

I asked him at what hour the telegram was handed to the h. c. in Boston.

He answered brightly that he didn't know.

I examined the blank, and sure enough the wary Boston h. c. had thoughtfully concealed that statistic.

I asked him at what hour it had started from Boston.

He answered up as brightly as ever, and said he didn't know.

I examined the blank, and sure enough the Boston h. c. had left that statistic out in the cold too. In fact it turned out to be an official concealment—no blank was provided for its exposure. And none required by the law, I suppose.

"It is a good one-sided idea," I remarked. "They can take your money and ship your telegram next year if they want to—you've no redress. The law ought to extend the privilege to all of us."

The boy looked upon me coldly.

I asked him when the telegram reached York Harbor.

He pointed to some figures following the signature at the bottom of the blank—"12:14."

I said it was now 1:45 and asked, "Do you mean that it reached your morgue an hour and a half ago?"

He nodded assent.

"It was at that time half an hour too late to be of any use to me if I wanted to go and meet my people, which was the case, for by the wording of the message you can see that they were to arrive at the station at 11:45. Why did your h. c. send me this useless message? Can't he read? Is he dead?"

"It's the rules."

"No, that does not account for it. Would he have sent it if it had been three years old, I in the meantime deceased, and he aware of it?"

The boy didn't know.

"Because, you know, a rule which required him to forward to the cemetery today a dispatch due three years ago would be as good a rule as one which should require him to forward a telegram to me today which he knew had lost all its value an hour or two before he started it. The construction of such a rule would discredit an idiot. In fact, an idiot—I mean a common ordinary Christian idiot, you understand—would be ashamed of it, and for the sake of his reputation wouldn't make it. What do you think?"

He replied with much natural brilliancy that he wasn't paid for thinking.

This gave me a better opinion of the commercial intelligence pervading his morgue than I had had before. It also softened my feelings toward him, and also my tone, which had hitherto been tinged with bitterness.

"Let bygones be bygones," I said gently. "We are all erring creatures, and mainly idiots, but God made us so and it is dangerous to criticise."

Sincerely
S. L. Clemens

August 1902 was a fateful month for the Clemenses. It was to change the course of their lives dramatically, for it marked the beginning of Livy's final and fatal illness, which lasted twenty-two months and which kept her and Clemens almost entirely apart even though they lived in close proximity. Her health, never strong, had seemed to Clemens fragile earlier in the year. Some years later he wrote of her in his autobiography, "Under a grave and gentle exterior burned inextinguishable fires of sympathy, energy, devotion, enthusiasm and absolutely limitless affection. She was *always* frail in body and she lived upon her spirit, whose hopefulness and courage were indestructible."

Her health improved for several weeks with the move to York Harbor but by early July she became worried about her heart.

"Her alarm increased rapidly," Clemens wrote. "Within a fortnight she began to dread driving out. Anything approaching swift motion terrified her. She was afraid of descending grades, even such slight ones as to be indeterminable and imperceptible in the summer twilights. She would implore the coachman not only to walk his horses down those low and imperceptible hills, but she watched him with fear and distress, and if the horses stepped out of a walk for only a moment she would seize me on one side and the carriage on the other, in an ecstasy of fright. This was the condition of things all through July."

According to Clemens, during the early part of August there were local celebrations to mark the 250th anniversary "of municipal self-constituted government on the continent of America." For two or three days "there were quaint back-settlement processions, mass meetings, orations and so on, by day, and fireworks by night." Despite his warnings, Livy became increasingly involved. "She could not rest. She never was intended to rest. She had the spirit of a steam engine in a frame of flesh. It was always racking that frame with its tireless energy; it was always exacting of it labors that were beyond its strength."

At 7 A.M. of August 12th he was awakened by a cry.

She was standing on the opposite side of the bedroom, leaning against a wall and panting. She was having great trouble breathing, and she had severe palpitations.

"I am dying," she said.

He too thought she was dying.

He helped her back to bed and summoned a Dr. Leonard, a New York physician who was living nearby. The doctor came within a half-hour. He said it was a nervous breakdown and prescribed absolute rest, seclusion and careful nursing. Nurses were employed and relatives notified. Leonard's diagnosis was supported in September by a Boston doctor who said she was suffering from "nervous prostration" and ordered her to be isolated from most members of her family, including Clemens. Later Clemens wrote, "During the twenty-two succeeding months she had for society physicians and trained nurses only, broadly speaking."

Howells thought she was suffering from heart disease. In later times there was speculation that she had an attack of asthma, with a consequent strain on her heart, and that her illnesses were at least to some extent psychomatic in origin.

When she was sixteen she fell on the ice and was partially paralyzed. For the next two years she kept to her bed in a darkened room, unable to sit up or to lie in any position except on her back. The doctors who were called failed to help her.

In Clemens's account, a relative of the Langdon family said one day, "You have tried everybody else. Now try Doctor Newton, the quack. He is downtown at the Rathbun House, practicing upon the well-to-do at war prices and upon the poor for nothing. I *saw him* wave his hands over Jake Brown's head and take his crutches away from him and send him about his business as good as new. *I saw him* do the like with some other cripples. *They* may have been 'temporaries' instituted for advertising purposes, and not genuine. But Jake is genuine. Send for Newton."

Newton was sent for. Clemens described him as moving "through the land in state, in magnificence, like a potentate, like a circus. Notice of his coming was spread upon the dead walls in vast colored posters, along with his formidable portrait, several weeks beforehand."

Previously, attempts to raise Livy to a sitting position had resulted in nausea and exhaustion for her. Now Newton lifted the shades of her room, opened the windows, delivered "a short fervent prayer." Putting an arm behind her shoulders, he said,

"Now we will sit up, my child."

She sat without nausea or discomfort. Then he said,

"Now we will walk a few steps, my child."

And he helped her out of bed and supported her while she walked several steps.

Then he said,

"I have reached the limit of my art. She is not cured. It is not likely that she will *ever* be cured. She will never be able to walk far, but after a little daily practice she will be able to walk one or two hundred yards, and she can depend on being able to do *that* for the rest of her life."

His fee was $1500. Clemens thought it was easily worth $100,000. In later years Clemens met Newton once and asked him what his secret was. Newton said he didn't know but he guessed that possibly "some subtle form of electricity proceeded from his body and wrought the cures."

It was not until October of 1902 that Livy was able to return to River-dale, to which she was taken in a specially arranged railroad invalid car. The butler carried her into the house. During the fall and winter of that year she was isolated in her room. On December 30 Clemens saw her for five minutes. It was their first meeting in three months.

To Twichell, Hartford

Riverdale, N. Y., *Oct. 31, '02*

Dear Joe,

It is ten days since Susy [Twichell] wrote that you were laid up with a sprained shoulder, since which time we have had no news about it. I hope that no news is good news, according to the proverb. Still, authoritative confirmation of it will be gladly received in this family if some of you will furnish it. Moreover, I should like to know how and where it happened. In the pulpit, as like as not, otherwise you would not be taking so much pains to conceal it. This is not a malicious suggestion and not a personally invented one. You told me yourself once that you threw artificial power and impressiveness into places in your sermons, where needed, by "banging the bible" (your own words). You have reached a time of life when it is not wise to take these risks. You would better jump around. We all have to change our methods as the infirmities of age creep upon us. Jumping around will be impressive now, whereas before you were gray it would have excited remark.

Poor Livy drags along drearily. It must be hard times for that turbulent spirit. It will be a long time before she is on her feet again. It is a most pathetic case. I wish I could transfer it to myself. Between ripping and raging and smoking and reading, I could get a good deal of a holiday out of it.

Clara runs the house smoothly and capably. She is discharging a trial cook today and hiring another.

A power of love to you all!

Mark

While Livy was so ill, Jean Clemens came down with pneumonia, which added to Clara's house-managing burdens. Clemens spent much time alone. Eventually he himself showed the physical strain. He spent most of April 1903 in bed with "bronchitis, rheumatism, two sets of teeth aching."

To Brander Matthews, New York

New York City, *May 4, '03*

Dear Brander,

I haven't been out of my bed for four weeks but—well, I have been reading a good deal and it occurs to me to ask you to sit down some time or other when you have 8 or 9 months to spare, and jot me down a certain few literary particulars for my help and elevation. Your time need not be thrown away, for at your further leisure you can make Columbian lectures out of the results and do your students a good turn.

1. Are there in Sir Walter's novels passages done in good English, English which is neither slovenly or involved?

2. Are there passages whose English is not poor and thin and commonplace, but is of a quality above that?

3. Are there passages which burn with real fire—not punk, fox-fire, make believe?

4. Has he heroes and heroines who are not cads and cadesses?

5. Has he personages whose acts and talk correspond with their characters as described by him?

6. Has he heroes and heroines whom the reader admires, admires and knows *why?*

7. Has he funny characters that are funny, and humorous passages that are humorous?

8. Does he ever chain the reader's interest and make him reluctant to lay the book down?

9. Are there pages where he ceases from posing, ceases from admiring the placid flood and flow of his own dilutions, ceases from being artificial, and is for a time, long or short, recognizably sincere and in earnest?

10. Did he know how to write English and didn't do it because he didn't want to?

11. Did he use the right word only when he couldn't think of another one, or did he run so much to wrong because he didn't know the right one when he saw it?

12. Can you read him and keep your respect for him? Of course a person could in *his* day—an era of sentimentality and sloppy romantics—but land! can a body do it today?

Brander, I lie here dying, slowly dying, under the blight of Sir Walter. I have read the first volume of *Rob Roy*, and as far as chapter XIX of *Guy Mannering*, and I can no longer hold my head up nor take my nourishment. Lord, it's all so juvenile! So artificial, so shoddy. And such wax figures and skeletons and spectres. Interest? Why, it is impossible to feel an interest in these bloodless shams, these milk-and-water humbugs. And oh, the poverty of the invention! Not poverty in inventing situations, but poverty in furnishing reasons for them. Sir Walter usually gives himself away when he arranges for a situation—elaborates, and elaborates, and elaborates, till if you live to get to it you don't believe in it when it happens.

I can't find the rest of *Rob Roy*, I can't stand any more *Mannering*. I do not know just what to do but I will reflect and not quit this great study rashly. He *was* great in his day and to his proper audience. And so was God in Jewish times, for that matter, but why should either of them rank high now? And *do* they? Honest, now, *do* they? Damned if I believe it.

My, I wish I could see you and Leigh Hunt!

Sincerely Yours
S. L. Clemens

Preparations were proceeding for a World's Fair to be held in St. Louis. One of the proposed features was a World's Literary Convention containing a Mark Twain Day.

To T. F. Gatts of Missouri

New York, *May 30, 1903*

Dear Mr. Gatts,

It is indeed a high compliment which you offer me in naming an association after me and in proposing the setting apart of a Mark Twain day at the great St. Louis fair, but such compliments are not proper for the living. They are proper and safe for the dead only. I value the impulse which moves you to tender me these honors. I value it as highly as anyone can and am grateful for it but I should stand in a sort of terror of the honors themselves. So long as we remain alive we are not safe from doing things which, however righteously and honorably intended, can wreck our repute and extinguish our friendships.

I hope that no society will be named for me while I am still alive, for I might at some time or other do something which would cause its members to regret having done me that honor. After I shall have joined the dead I shall follow the customs of those people and be guilty of no conduct that can wound any friend. But until that time shall come I shall be a doubtful quantity like the rest of our race.

Very truly yours,
S. L. Clemens

If the National Mark Twain Association was persistent, so was Clemens, who responded with the following to Gatts's second letter.

To T. F. Gatts of Missouri

New York, *June 8, 1903*

Dear Mr. Gatts,

While I am deeply touched by the desire of my friends of Hannibal to confer these great honors upon me, I must still forbear to accept them. Spontaneous and unpremeditated honors, like those which came to me at Hannibal, Columbia, St. Louis and at the village stations all down the line, are beyond all price and are a treasure for life in the memory, for they are a free gift out of the heart and they come without solicitations. But I am a Missourian and so I shrink from distinctions which have to be arranged beforehand and with my privity, for I then become a party to my own exalting. I am humanly fond of honors that happen, but chary of those that come by canvass and intention. With sincere thanks to you and your associates for this high compliment which you have been minded to offer me, I am,

Very truly yours,
S. L. Clemens

SIXTEEN

[1903–05]

Florence, Italy — Livy's illness — her seeming improvement — her death — "I am as one who wanders and has lost his way" — party politics — "Those were the days!"

On April 7, 1903, Clemens wrote to MacAlister from Riverdale, New York, that his daughter Clara was spelling the trained nurse in the afternoons and that he himself was allowed to see Livy only twenty minutes twice a day and to write her only two letters a day provided they excluded any news—almost any news might upset her and possibly cause a relapse. The only other people who saw her at this time were her physician and occasionally a nerve specialist from New York. Five days earlier the doctor and the specialist had ordered Livy to spend the next winter in Italy, so Clara was now writing to a friend in Florence in the hope of finding a suitable villa near the city.

Livy was able to leave Riverdale by the end of June, at which time the Clemens family traveled to Quarry Farm in Elmira. The Hartford house had been sold. The Tarrytown, New York, house, which Clemens had purchased prior to Livy's breakdown, had been rented. Clemens now worked in the study which Susy Crane had built for him three decades ago.

To Twichell, Hartford

Quarry Farm, Elmira, N. Y.
July 21, '03

Dear Joe,

That love letter delighted Livy beyond any like utterance received by her these thirty years and more. I was going to answer it for her right away and said so but she reserved the privilege to herself. I judge she is accumulating Hot Stuff, as George Ade would say. . . .

Livy is coming along. Eats well, sleeps some, is mostly very gay, not very often depressed. Spends all day on the porch, sleeps there a part of the night, makes excursions in carriage and in wheel-chair. And in the matter of superintending everything and everybody, has resumed business at the old stand.

Did you ever go house hunting 3,000 miles away? It costs three months of writing and telegraphing to pull off a success. We finished 3 or 4 days ago and took the Villa Papiniano (damn the name, I have to look at it 2 minutes after writing it and *then* am always in doubt) for a year by cable. Three miles outside of Florence, under Fiesole— a darling location, and apparently a choice house, near Fiske.

There's 7 in our gang. All women but me. It means trunks and things. But thanks be! Today (this is private) comes a most handsome voluntary document with seals and escutcheons on it from the Italian Ambassador (who is a stranger to me) commanding the Customs people to keep their hands off the Clemens's things. Now wasn't it lovely of him? And wasn't it lovely of me to let Livy take a pencil and edit my answer and knock a good third of it out?

And that's a nice ship—the *Irene,* new, swift, 13,000 tons, rooms up in the sky, open to sun and air, and all that. I was desperately troubled—for Livy—about the down-cellar cells in the ancient *Lahn.*

The cubs are in Riverdale yet. They come to us the first week in August.

With lots and lots of love to you all,

Mark

The plan to rent the Villa Papiniano miscarried. Clemens rented instead the Villa Reale di Quarto in the hills west of Florence. He did this with the help of George Gregory Smith, a friend and a Florence resident, who wrote that the Villa Quarto was a beautiful place with a southeastern exposure and with views of Valombrosa and the Chianti hills. Smith reported that the villa had extensive grounds and stables. The annual rental was $2,000.

Clemens and his family left Elmira on October 5th for New York, where they stayed at the Hotel Grosvenor until the 24th, the day they sailed in the *Princess Irene* for Genoa. Livy, carried aboard the ship, was accompanied by a trained nurse. She withstood the voyage and the overland travel to the villa without a mishap.

For a while Clemens was unhappy with the place, which had more than sixty rooms, many of them unused, and which lacked much of the plumbing he was accustomed to. And he was irritated by his landlady, the American wife of an Italian count. Even the weather bothered him at first. When MacAlister congratulated him on basking in the Florentine sunshine, he replied, "Florentine sunshine? Bless you, there isn't any. We have heavy fogs every morning, and rain all day. This house is not merely large, it is vast, therefore I think it must always lack the home feeling."

Nevertheless his work was going well.

To Twichell, Hartford

Villa di Quarto
Florence, *Jan. 7, '04*

Dear Joe,

. . . I have had a handsome success in one way here. I left New York under a sort of half promise to furnish to the Harper magazines 30,000 words this year. Magazining is difficult work because every third page represents 2 pages that you have put in the fire (because you are nearly sure to *start* wrong twice), and so when you have finished an article and are willing to let it go to print it represents only 10 cents a word instead of 30.

But this time I had the curious (and unprecedented) luck to start right in each case. I turned out 37,000 words in 25 working days, and the reason I think I started right every time is that not only have I approved and accepted the several articles, but the court of last resort (Livy) has done the same.

On many of the between-days I did some work, but only of an idle and not necessarily necessary sort, since it will not see print until I am dead. I shall continue this (an hour per day) but the rest of the year I expect to put in on a couple of long books (half-completed ones.) No more magazine work hanging over my head.

This secluded and silent solitude, this clean, soft air and this enchanting view of Florence, the great valley and the snow mountains that frame it, are the right conditions for work. They are a persistent inspiration. Today is very lovely. When the afternoon arrives there will be a new picture every hour till dark, and each of them divine, or progressing from divine to diviner and divinest. On this (second) floor Clara's room commands the finest. She keeps a window ten feet high wide open all the time and frames it in. I go in from time to time every day and trade sass for a look. The central detail is a distant and stately snow hump that rises above and behind black-forested hills, and its sloping vast buttresses, velvety and sun-polished with purple shadows between, make the sort of picture we knew that time we walked in Switzerland in the days of our youth.

I wish I could show your letter to Livy, but she must wait a week or so for it. I think I told you she had a prostrating week of tonsilitis a month ago. She has remained very feeble ever since and confined to the bed, of course, but we allow ourselves to believe she will regain the lost ground in another month. Her physician is Professor Grocco. She could not have a better. And she has a very good trained nurse.

Love to all of you from all of us. And to all of our dear Hartford friends.

Mark

P. S. *3 days later.*

Livy is as remarkable as ever. The day I wrote you—that night, I mean—she had a bitter attack of gout or rheumatism occupying the whole left arm from shoulder to fingers, accompanied by fever. The pains racked her 50 or 60 hours. They have departed now, and already she is planning a trip to Egypt next fall and a winter's sojourn there! There is life in her yet.

You will be surprised that I was willing to do so much magazine writing, a thing I have always been chary about, but I had good reasons. Our expenses have been so prodigious for a year and a half, and are still so prodigious, that Livy was worrying altogether too much about them and doing a very dangerous amount of lying awake on their account. It was necessary to stop that, and it is now stopped.

Yes, she is remarkable, Joe. Her rheumatic attack set me to cursing and swearing without limit as to time or energy but it merely concentrated her patience and her unconquerable fortitude. It is the difference between us. I can't count the different kinds of ailments which have assaulted her in this fiendish year and a half—and I forgive none of them—but here she comes up again as bright and fresh and enterprising as ever and goes to planning about Egypt with a hope and a confidence which are to me amazing.

Clara is calling for me. We have to go into town and pay calls.

Mark

That winter in Florence, Clemens began dictating some chapters of his autobiography. Presently the news reached him of the death of Henry M. Stanley, the English explorer and one of his oldest friends. He believed he had met Stanley as long ago as 1867, just before the *Quaker City* excursion. Meanwhile Livy's health fluctuated considerably, profoundly affecting Clemens's mood as well as those of his daughters.

By the end of March the villa had a homelike feeling for Clemens. "Under certain conditions I should like to go on living in it indefinitely. I should wish the Countess to move out of Italy, out of Europe, out of the planet. I should want her bonded to retire to her place in the next world and inform me which of the two it was, so that I could arrange for my own hereafter."

To Twichell, Hartford

Villa di Quarto, *May 11, '04*

Dear Joe,

Yours has this moment arrived—just as I was finishing a note to poor Lady Stanley. I believe the last country house visit we paid in England was to Stanley's. Lord, how my friends and acquaintances fall about me now in my gray-headed days! Vereschagin, Mommsen, Dvorak, Lenbach, Jokai—all so recently, and now Stanley. I had known Stanley 37 years. Goodness, who is it I *haven't* known! As a rule the necrologies find me personally interested—when they treat of old stagers. Generally when a man dies who is worth cabling, it happens that I have run across him somewhere, some time or other.

Oh, say! Down by the Laurentian Library there's a marble image that has been sitting on its pedestal some 450 years, if my dates are right—Cosimo I. I've seen the back of it many a time but not the front, but yesterday I twisted my head around after we had driven by, and the profane exclamation burst from my mouth before I could think: "—there's Chauncey Depew!"

I mean to get a photo of it and use it if it confirms yesterday's conviction. That's a very nice word from the *Catholic Magazine* and I am glad you sent it. I mean to show it to my priest. We are very fond of him. He is a sterling man and is also learnedly scientific. He invented the thing which records the seismatic disturbances, for the peoples of the earth. And he's an astronomer and has an observatory of his own.

Ah, many's the cry I have over reflecting that maybe we could have had Young Harmony for Livy, and didn't have wit enough to think of it.

Speaking of Livy reminds me that your inquiry arrives at a good time (unberufen). It has been weeks (I don't know how many!) since we could have said a hopeful word, but this morning Katy came the minute the day-nurse came on watch and said words of a strange and long-forgotten sound: "Mr. Clemens, Mrs. Clemens is really and truly *better!* Anybody can see it. She sees it herself. And last night at 9 o'clock she *said* it."

There—it is heart-warming, it is splendid, it is sublime. Let us enjoy it, let us make the most of it today—and bet not a farthing on tomorrow. The tomorrows have nothing for us. Too many times they have breathed the word of promise to our ear and broken it to our hope. We take no tomorrow's word any more.

You've done a wonder, Joe. You've written a letter that can be sent in to Livy. That doesn't often happen when either a friend or a stranger writes. You *did* whirl in a P. S. that wouldn't do, but you wrote it on a margin of a page in such a way that I was able to clip off the margin clear across both pages, and now Livy won't perceive that the sheet isn't the same size it used to was. It was about Aldrich's son, and I came near forgetting to remove it. It should have been written on a loose strip and enclosed. That son died on the 5th of March, and Aldrich wrote me on the night before that his minutes were numbered. On the 18th Livy asked after that patient, and I was prepared, and able to give her a grateful surprise by telling her "the Aldriches are no longer uneasy about him."

I do wish I could have been present and heard Charley Clark. When he can't light up a dark place nobody can.

With lots of love to you all.
Mark

To Richard Watson Gilder, New York

Villa di Quarto, Florence
May 12, '04

Dear Gilder,

A friend of ours (the Baroness de Nolda) was here this afternoon and wanted a note of introduction to the *Century*, for she has something to sell to you in case you'll want to make her an offer after seeing a sample of the goods.

I said, "With pleasure. Get the goods ready. Send the same to me. I will have Jean typewrite them. Then I will mail them to the *Century* and tonight I will write the note to Mr. Gilder and start it along. Also write me a letter embodying what you have been saying to me about the goods, and your proposed plan of arranging and explaining them, and I will forward that to Gilder too."

As to the Baroness. She is a German. 30 years old. Was married at 17. Is very pretty—indeed I might say *very* pretty. Has a lot of sons (5) running up from seven to 12 years old. Her husband is a Russian. They live half the time in Russia and the other half in Florence, and supply population alternately to the one country and then to the other.

Of course it is a family that speaks languages. This occurs at their table. I know it by experience. It is Babel come again. The other day, when no guests were present to keep order, the tribes were all talking at once, and 6 languages were being traded in. At last the littlest boy lost his temper and screamed out at the top of his voice, with angry sobs: "Mais, vraiment, io non capisco *gar* nichts."

The Baroness is a little afraid of her English, therefore she will write her remarks in French. I said there's a plenty of translators in New York. Examine her samples and drop her a line.

For two entire days now we have not been anxious about Mrs. Clemens (unberufen). After 20 months of bedridden solitude and bodily misery she all of a sudden ceases to be a pallid shrunken shadow and looks bright and young and pretty. She remains what she always was, the most wonderful creature of fortitude, patience, endurance and recuperative power that ever was. But ah, dear, it won't last. This fiendish malady will play new treacheries upon her, and I shall go back to my prayers again—unutterable from any pulpit!

With love to you and yours,
S.L.C.

May 13, 10 A.M. I have just paid one of my pair of permitted 2 minutes visits per day to the sick room. And found what I have learned to expect—retrogression, and that pathetic something in the eye which betrays the secret of a waning hope.

Clemens was invited to attend the World's Fair in St. Louis and take first prize.

To Governor Francis of Missouri

Villa di Quarto, Firenze
May 26, 1904

Dear Governor Francis,

It has been a dear wish of mine to exhibit myself at the Great Fair and get a prize, but circumstances beyond my control have interfered and I must remain in Florence. Although I have never taken prizes anywhere else I used to take them at school in Missouri half a century ago, and I ought to be able to repeat now if I could have a chance. I used to get the medal for good spelling every week, and I could have had the medal for good conduct if there hadn't been so much curruption in Missouri in those days. Still, I got it several times by trading medals and giving boot. I am willing to give boot now if—however, those days are forever gone by in Missouri and perhaps it is better so. Nothing ever stops the way it was in this changeable world. Although I cannot be at the Fair, I am going to be represented there anyway, by a portrait by Professor Gelli. You will find it excellent. Good judges here say it is better than the original. They say it has all the merits of the original and keeps still, besides. It sounds like flattery but it is just true.

I suppose you will get a prize, because you have created the most prodigious and in all ways most wonderful Fair the planet has ever seen. Very well, you have indeed earned it, and with it the gratitude of the State and the nation.

Sincerely yours,
Mark Twain

In the first days of June, Livy's health seemed to improve, or at least the household, including her nurse, thought so. For the past five months Clemens had tried to find another villa, hoping to improve Livy both in mind and body if he could move her out of "the odious Villa di Quarto," as he referred to it in his autobiography, with "its fiendish associations." At last, on Saturday, June 4th, he heard of one which seemed to meet all his requirements. He and his daughter Jean examined it the following afternoon and were delighted with it. The price was $30,000 in cash, and he could take possession at once.

At this time he was permitted to have fifteen minutes in Livy's room two or three times a day, the last one being at 7 P.M. In addition, he was allowed to see her for a moment between 9:15 and 9:30 to say good night.

He and Jean returned to the Villa di Quarto at 5 P.M. on Sunday. At seven he described the prospective new villa for Livy.

"She was pleased. She was satisfied. And her face—snow white, marble white, these latter weeks—was radiant," he wrote in his autobiography.

As he was leaving, she asked, "Will you come back?"

"Yes, to say good night," he said.

He paused a minute at the door. They threw kisses at each other.

He sat awhile in his room, "my spirit at peace for the first time in so many heavy months." Then he went to the piano and sang *Swing Low, Sweet Chariot* and *My Lord He Calls Me*, songs which Susy had liked to hear him sing. Jean entered and listened. Noticing her, he stopped, embarrassed. She asked him to continue.

Livy, hearing him, said to her nurse, "He's singing a good night carol for me."

Presently a servant called Jean away.

Clemens returned to his room, staying there until it was time to go downstairs and say good night to Livy.

He entered her room at around 9:20. She was sitting up in bed. She had been unable to lie down the past seven months. Her head was bent forward. She was supported by Katy Leary, the maid, on one side, and by the nurse on the other. Clara and Jean were near the foot of the bed, looking dazed. He bent over Livy, said something, stared into her face and was puzzled because she didn't answer.

"But is it *true?* Katy, *is* it true? It can't be true!" Clara cried.

Katy Leary burst into sobs. Then Clemens knew that Livy was dead.

Two hours later he was writing an account of her death, which appeared in my edition of his autobiography.

"*Sunday Evening, June 5, 1904—11:15 o'clock*. She has been dead two hours. It is impossible. The words have no meaning. But they are true; I know it, without realizing it. She was my life, and she is gone; she was my riches, and I am a pauper. . . . How grateful I was that she had been spared the struggle she had so dreaded. And that I, too, had so dreaded for her. Five times in the last four months she spent an hour and more fighting violently for breath, and she lived in the awful fear of death by strangulation. Mercifully she was granted the gentlest and swiftest of deaths—by heart-failure—and she never knew, she never knew! She was the most beautiful spirit, and the highest and the noblest I have known. And now she is dead."

Livy was fifty-eight and a half at her death. She had been married thirty-four years. Clemens, ten years older, had six more years to live.

To Howells, New York

Villa di Quarto, Florence, *June 6, '04*

Dear Howells,

Last night at 9:20 I entered Mrs. Clemens's room to say the usual goodnight—and she was dead—though no none knew it. She had been cheerfully talking a moment before. She was sitting up in bed. She had not lain down for months. And Katie and the nurse were supporting her. They supposed she had fainted, and they were holding the oxygen pipe to her mouth, expecting to revive her. I bent over her and looked in her face and I think I spoke. I was surprised and troubled that she did not notice me. Then we understood, and our hearts broke. How poor we are today!

But how thankful I am that her persecutions are ended. I would not call her back if I could.

Today, treasured in her worn old Testament, I found a dear and gentle letter from you, dated Far Rockaway, Sept. 13, 1896, about our poor Susy's death. I am tired and old. I wish I were with Livy.

I send my love—and hers—to you all.

S.L.C.

In a letter to Twichell he wrote, "How sweet she was in death; how young, how beautiful, how like her dear, girlish self of thirty years ago; not a gray hair showing."

To R. W. Gilder, New York

Villa di Quarto, Florence
June 7, '04

Dear Gilder Family,

I have been worrying and worrying to know what to do. At last I went to the girls with an idea: to ask the Gilders to get us shelter near their summer home. It was the first time they have not shaken their heads. So tomorrow I will cable to you and shall hope to be in time.

An hour ago the best heart that ever beat for me and mine went silent out of this house, and I am as one who wanders and has lost his way. She who is gone was our head, she was our hands. We are now trying to make plans—*we:* we who have never made a plan before, nor ever needed to. If she could speak to us she would make it all simple and easy with a word, and our perplexities would vanish away. If she had known she was near to death she would have told us where to go and what to do. But she was not suspecting. Neither were we. She had been chatting cheerfully a moment before, and in an instant she was gone from us and we did not know it. We were not alarmed. We did not know anything had happened. It was a blessed death. She passed away without knowing it. She was all our riches and she is gone. She was our breath. She was our life. And now we are nothing.

We send you our love—and with it the love of you that was in her heart when she died.

S. L. Clemens

To Howells, New York

Villa di Quarto, '04
June 12, 6 p.m.

Dear Howells,

We have to sit and hold our hands and wait in the silence and solitude of this prodigious house, wait until June 25. Then we go to Naples and sail in the *Prince Oscar* the 26th. There is a ship 12 days earlier (but we came in that one). I see Clara twice a day—morning and evening—greeting—nothing more is allowed. She keeps her bed and says nothing. She has not cried yet. I wish she could cry. It would break Livy's heart to see Clara. We excuse ourselves from all the friends that call, though of course only intimates come. Intimates—but they are not the old old friends, the friends of the old, old times when we laughed.

Shall we ever laugh again? If I could only see a dog that I knew in the old times! and could put my arms around his neck and tell him all, everything, and ease my heart.

Think—in 3 hours it will be a week!—and soon a month; and by and by a year. How fast our dead fly from us.

She loved you so, and was always as pleased as a child with any notice you took of her.

Soon your wife will be with you, oh fortunate man! And John, whom mine was so fond of. The sight of him was such a delight to her. Lord, the old friends, how dear they are.

S.L.C.

To Twichell, Hartford

Villa di Quarto, Florence
June 18, '04

Dear Joe,

It is 13 days. I am bewildered and must remain so for a time longer. It was so sudden, so unexpected. Imagine a man worth a hundred millions who finds himself suddenly penniless and fifty million in debt in his old age.

I was richer than any other person in the world, and now I am that pauper without peer. Some day I will tell you about it, not now.

Mark

In his autobiography Clemens wrote, "Mrs. Clemens was doomed from the beginning but she never suspected it—*we* never suspected it. She had been ill many times in her life but her miraculous recuperative powers always brought her out of these perils safely. We were full of fears and anxieties and solicitudes all the time but I do not think we ever really lost hope. At least, not until the last two or three weeks. It was not like *her* to lose hope. We never expected her to lose it—and so at last when she looked me pathetically in the eyes and said, 'You believe I shall get well?' it was a form which she had never used before and it was a betrayal. Her hope was perishing and I recognized it."

Clemens and his entourage returned to the U.S. in July. Accompanied by Twichell, they went to Elmira, where Livy was buried beside Susy and Langdon on the 14th. They spent the summer in a cottage on Gilder's place in Tyringham, Mass., in the Berkshires. By November, Clemens was staying at the Grosvenor in New York and preparing to establish himself in a house at the corner of Fifth Avenue and Ninth Street: 21 Fifth Avenue.

To F. N. Doubleday, New York

Dear Doubleday,

I did not know you were going to England. I would have freighted you with such messages of homage and affection to Kipling. And I would have pressed his hand, through you, for his sympathy with me in my crushing loss, as expressed by him in his letter to Gilder. You know my feeling for Kipling and that it antedates that expression.

I was glad that the boys came here to invite me to the house-warming and I think they understood why a man in the shadow of a calamity like mine could not go.

It has taken three months to repair and renovate our house— corner of 9th and 5th Avenue—but I shall be in it in 10 or 15 days hence. Much of the furniture went into it today (from Hartford). We have not seen it for 13 years. Katy Leary, our old housekeeper, who has been in our service more than 24 years, cried when she told me about it today.

She said "I had forgotten it was so beautiful, and it brought Mrs. Clemens right back to me—in that old time when she was so young and lovely."

Jean and my secretary and the servants whom we brought from Italy because Mrs. Clemens liked them so well are still keeping house in the Berkshire hills—and waiting. Clara (nervously wrecked by her mother's death) is in the hands of a specialist in 69th St., and I shall not be allowed to have any communication with her, even telephone, for a year. I am in this comfortable little hotel and still in bed—for I dasn't budge till I'm safe from my pet devil, bronchitis.

Isn't it pathetic? One hour and ten minutes before Mrs. Clemens died I was saying to her, "Today, after five months search, I've found the villa that will content you. Tomorrow you will examine the plans and give it your consent and I will buy it."

Her eyes danced with pleasure, for she longed for a home of her own. And there on that morrow she lay white and cold. And unresponsive to my reverent caresses—a new thing to me and a new thing to her. *That* had not happened before in five and thirty years.

I am coming to see you and Mrs. Doubleday by and by. She loved and honored Mrs. Doubleday and her work.

Always yours,
Mark

Paine has written: "It was a presidential year and the air was thick with politics. Mark Twain was no longer actively interested in the political situation. He was only disheartened by the hollowness and pretense of office-seeking, and the methods of office seekers in general. Grieved that Twichell should still pin his faith to any party when all parties were so obviously venal and time-serving, he wrote in outspoken and rather somber protest."

To Twichell, Hartford

The Grosvenor, *Nov. 4, '04*

Oh, dear! Get out of that sewer—party politics—dear Joe. At least with your mouth. We had only two men who could make speeches for their parties and preserve their honor and their dignity. One of them is dead. Possibly there were four. I am sorry for John Hay, sorry and ashamed. And yet I know he couldn't help it. He wears the collar and he had to pay the penalty. Certainly he had no more desire to stand up before a mob of confiding human incapables and debauch them than you had. Certainly he took no more real pleasure in distorting history, concealing facts, propagating immoralities and appealing to the sordid side of human nature than did you. But he was his party's property and he had to climb away down and do it.

It is interesting, wonderfully interesting, the miracles which party politics can do with a man's mental and moral make-up. Look at McKinley, Roosevelt and yourself: in private life spotless in character; honorable, honest, just, humane, generous; scorning trickeries, treacheries, suppressions of the truth, mistranslations of the meanings of facts, the filching of credit earned by another, the condoning of crime, the glorifying of base acts: in public political life the *reverse* of all this.

McKinley was a silverite—you concealed it. Roosevelt was a silverite—you concealed it. Parker was a silverite—you publish it. Along with a shudder and a warning: "He was unsafe then. Is he any safer now?"

Joe, even I could be guilty of such a thing as that—if I were in party politics. I really believe it.

Mr. Cleveland gave the country the gold standard. By implication you credit the matter to the Republican Party.

By implication you prove the whole annual pension scoop, concealing the fact that the bulk of the money goes to people who in no way deserve it. You imply that all the batteners upon this bribery fund are Republicans. An indiscreet confession, since about half of them must have been Democrats before they were bought.

You as good as praise Order 78. It is true you do not shout, and you do not linger, you only whisper and skip. Still, what little you *do* in the matter is complimentary to the crime.

It means, if it means anything, that our outlying properties will all be given up by the Democrats and our flag hauled down. *All* of them? Not only the properties stolen by Mr. McKinley and Mr. Roosevelt, but the properties honestly acquired? Joe, did you believe that hardy statement when you made it? Yet you made it, and there it stands in permanent print. Now what moral law would suffer if we should give up the stolen ones? But—

"You know our standard bearer. He will maintain all that we have gained"—by whatever process. Land, I believe you!

By George, Joe, you are as handy at the game as if you had been in training for it all your life. Your campaign Address is built from the ground upon the oldest and best models. There isn't a paragraph in it whose facts or morals will wash—not even a sentence, I believe.

But you will soon be out of this. You didn't *want* to do it—that is sufficiently apparent, thanks be!—but you couldn't well get out of it. In a few days you will be out of it and then you can fumigate yourself and take up your legitimate work again and resume your clean and wholesome private character once more and be happy—and useful.

I know I ought to hand you some guff now as propitiation and apology for these reproaches, but on the whole I believe I won't.

I have inquired, and find that Mitsikuri does not arrive here until tomorrow night. I shall watch out and telephone again, for I greatly want to see him.

Always Yours,
Mark

P. S. Nov. 4. I wish I could learn to remember that it is unjust and dishonorable to put blame upon the human race for any of its acts. For it did not make itself, it did not make its nature, it is merely a machine, it is moved wholly by outside influences, it has no hand in creating the outside influences nor in choosing which of them it will welcome or reject. Its performance is wholly automatic. It has no more mastership nor authority over its mind than it has over its stomach, which receives material from the outside and does as it pleases with it, indifferent to its proprietor's suggestions, even, let alone his commands; wherefore, whatever the machine does—so called crimes and infamies included—is the personal act of its Maker, and He, solely, is responsible.

I wish I could learn to pity the human race instead of censuring it and laughing at it. And I could if the outside influences of old habit were not so strong upon my machine. It vexes me to catch myself praising the clean private citizen Roosevelt and blaming the soiled President Roosevelt, when I know that neither praise nor blame is due to him for any thought or word or deed of his, he being merely a helplesss and irresponsible coffee mill ground by the hand of God.

1905 was Clemens's seventieth year. In the spring he received an invitation to attend a kind of pioneers' reunion on the West Coast.

To Robert Fulton, Reno, Nevada

In the Mountains
May 24, 1905

Dear Mr. Fulton,

I remember as if it were yesterday that when I disembarked from the overland stage in front of the Ormsby in Carson City in August, 1861, I was not expecting to be asked to come again. I was tired, discouraged, white with alkali dust and did not know anybody. And if you had said then, "Cheer up, desolate stranger, don't be downhearted. Pass on, and come again in 1905," you cannot think how grateful I would have been and how gladly I would have closed the contract. Although I was not expecting to be invited, I was watching out for it and was hurt and disappointed when you started to ask me and changed it to, "How soon are you going away?"

But you have made it all right now, the wound is closed. And so I thank you sincerely for the invitation, and with you all Reno, and if I were a few years younger I would accept it, and promptly. I would go. I would let somebody else do the oration but, as for me, I would talk—just talk. I would renew my youth. And talk—and talk—and talk—and have the time of my life! I would march the unforgotten and unforgettable antiques by and name their names and give them reverent Hail-and-farewell as they passed: Goodman, McCarthy, Gillis, Curry, Baldwin, Winters, Howard, Nye, Stewart, Neely Johnson, Hal Clayton, North, Root—and my brother, upon whom be peace! And then the desperadoes, who made life a joy and the "Slaughter-house" a precious possession: Sam Brown, Farmer Pete, Bill Mayfield, Six-fingered Jake, Jack Williams and the rest of the crimson discipleship—and so on and so on. Believe me, I would start a resurrection it would do you more good to look at than the next one will, if you go on the way you are doing now.

Those were the days!—those old ones. They will come no more. Youth will come no more. They were so full to the brim with the wine of life. There have been no others like them. It chokes me up to think of them. Would you like me to come out there and cry? It would not beseem my white head.

Goodbye. I drink to you all. Have a good time—and take an old man's blessing.

Mark Twain

Clemens spent the summer of 1905 in a rented house in the village of Dublin, N. H., where he wrote a new version of "The Mysterious Stranger," "Three Thousand Years Among the Microbes," and "Eve's Diary."

To Susy Crane, Quarry Farm, Elmira, N. Y.

Dublin, N. H., *Sept. 24, '05*

Susy dear,

I have had a lovely dream. Livy, dressed in black, was sitting up in my bed (here) at my right and looking as young and sweet as she used to do when she was in health.

She said, "What is the name of your sweet sister?"

I said, "Pamela."

"Oh yes, that is it. I thought it was"—(naming a name which has escaped me). "Won't you write it down for me?"

I reached eagerly for a pen and pad—laid my hands upon both—then said to myself, "It is only a dream," and turned back sorrowfully and there she was, still. The conviction flamed through me that our lamented disaster was a dream, and this a reality. I said, "How blessed it is, how blessed it is, it was all a dream, only a dream!"

She only smiled and did not ask what dream I meant, which surprised me. She leaned her head against mine and I kept saying, "I was perfectly sure it was a dream. I never would have believed it wasn't."

I think she said several things, but if so they are gone from my memory. I woke and did not know I had been dreaming. She was gone. I wondered how she could go without my knowing it, but I did not spend any thought upon that, I was too busy thinking of how vivid and real was the dream that we had lost her and how unspeakably blessed it was to find that it was not true and that she was still ours and with us.

S.L.C.

SEVENTEEN

[[1905–09]]

Dublin, N.H. and environs — New York — dictating for his autobiography — the tragedy of marriage — the new house, Redding, Conn. — postage due — Letters from the Earth — the death of Jean Clemens

The following was written for Frederick A. Duneka, former editor of the *New York World* and in 1905 secretary of Harper & Brothers, Clemens's publisher. The purpose was to satisfy the inquiries of newspaper reporters, which were very frequent, regarding Clemens's current activities and his plans for the coming year.

Memorandum for Frederick A. Duneka, New York

Dublin, N. H., *Oct. 9, 1905*

. . . As to the other matters, here are the details.

Yes, I have tried a number of summer homes, here and in Europe together.

Each of these homes had charms of its own, charms and delights of its own, and some of them, even in Europe, had comforts. Several of them had conveniences, too. They all had a "view."

It is my conviction that there should always be some water in a view—a lake or a river but not the ocean, if you are down on its level. I think that when you are down on its level it seldom inflames you with an ecstasy which you could not get out of a sandflat. It is like being on board ship, over again. Indeed it is worse than that, for there's three months of it. On board ship one tires of the aspects in a couple of days and quits looking. The same vast circle of heaving humps is spread around you all the time, with you in the center of it and never gaining an inch on the horizon, so far as you can see. For variety, a flight of flying fish, mornings. A flock of porpoises throwing summersaults afternoons. A remote whale spouting, Sundays. Occasional phosphorescent effects, nights. Every other day a streak of black smoke trailing along under the horizon. On the one single red letter day, the illustrious iceberg.

I have seen that iceberg thirty-four times in thirty-seven voyages. It is always the same shape. It is always the same size. It always throws up the same old flash when the sun strikes it. You may set it on any New York doorstep of a June morning and light it up with a mirror-flash, and I will engage to recognize it. It is artificial, and it is provided and anchored out by the steamer companies. I used to like the sea but I was young then, and could easily get excited over any kind of monotony, and keep it up till the monotonies ran out, if it was a fortnight.

Last January, when we were beginning to inquire about a home for this summer, I remembered that Abbott Thayer had said, three years before, that the New Hampshire highlands was a good place. He was right—it was a good place. Any place that is good for an artist in paint is good for an artist in morals and ink. Brush is here too. So is Col. T. W. Higginson. So is Raphael Pumpelly. So is Mr. Secretary Hitchcock. So is Henderson. So is Learned. So is Sumner. So is Franklin MacVeigh. So is Joseph L. Smith. So is Henry Copley Greene when I am not occupying his house, which I am doing this season.

Paint, literature, science, statesmanship, history, professorship, law, morals—these are all represented here, yet crime is substantially unknown.

The summer homes of these refugees are sprinkled a mile apart among the forest-clad hills, with access to each other by firm smooth country roads which are so embowered in dense foliage that it is always twilight in there and comfortable. The forests are spider-webbed with these good roads, they go everywhere. But for the help of the guideboards, the stranger would not arrive anywhere.

The village—Dublin—is bunched together in its own place but a good telephone service makes its markets handy to all those outliars. I have spelt it that way to be witty. The village executes orders on the Boston plan—promptness and courtesy.

The summer homes are high perched, as a rule, and have contenting outlooks. The house we occupy has one. Monadnock, a soaring double hump, rises into the sky at its left elbow—that is to say, it is close at hand. From the base of the long slant of the mountain the valley spreads away to the circling frame of the hills, and beyond the frame the billowy sweep of remote great ranges rises to view and flows, fold upon fold, wave upon wave, soft and blue and unwordly, to the horizon fifty miles away.

In these October days Monadnock and the valley and its framing hills make an inspiring picture to look at, for they are sumptuously splashed and mottled and betorched from skyline to skyline with the richest dyes the autumn can furnish. And when they lie flaming in the full drench of the midafternoon sun, the sight affects the spectator physically, it stirs his blood like military music.

These summer homes are commodious, well built and well furnished, facts which sufficiently indicate that the owners built them to live in themselves. They have furnaces and wood fireplaces and the rest of the comforts and conveniences of a city home and can be comfortably occupied all the year round.

We cannot have this house next season but I have secured Mrs. Upton's house, which is over in the law and science quarter two or three miles from here and about the same distance from the art, literary and scholastic groups. The science and law quarter has needed improving this good while.

The nearest railway station is distant something like an hour's drive. It is three hours from there to Boston over a branch line. You can go to New York in six hours per branch lines if you change cars every time you think of it, but it is better to go to Boston and stop over and take the trunk line next day. Then you do not get lost.

It is claimed that the atmosphere of the New Hampshire highlands is exceptionally bracing and stimulating, and a fine aid to hard and continuous work. It is a just claim, I think. I came in May and wrought 35 successive days without a break. It is possible that I could not have done it elsewhere. I do not know. I have not had any disposition to try it before. I think I got the disposition out of the atmosphere this time. I feel quite sure, in fact, that that is where it came from.

I am ashamed to confess what an intolerable pile of manuscript I ground out in the 35 days, therefore I will keep the number of words to myself. I wrote the first half of a long tale—"The Adventures of a

Microbe"—and put it away for a finish next summer, and started another long tale—"The Mysterious Stranger." I wrote the first half of it and put it with the other for a finish next summer. I stopped then. I was not tired but I had no books on hand that needed finishing this year except one that was seven years old. After a little I took that one up and finished it. Not for publication, but to have it ready for revision next summer.

Since I stopped work I have had a two months holiday. The summer has been my working time for 35 years. To have a holiday in it (in America) is new for me. I have not broken it except to write "Eve's Diary" and "A Horse's Tale"—short things occupying the mill 12 days.

This year our summer is 6 months long and ends with November and the flight home to New York, but next year we hope and expect to stretch it another month and end it the first of December.

[No signature]

It was widely known that Clemens was a devoted cigar smoker. Occasionally an admirer who was ignorant of his tobacco tastes would ask permission to send him some expensive cigars. Clemens had no use for them, including Havanas. He loved the cheap, fragrant, domestic stogies which he could buy by the barrel, the kind most of his male guests shunned in a sort of panic.

To Rev. L. M. Powers, Haverhill, Mass.

Nov. 9, 1905

Dear Mr. Powers,

I should accept your hospitable offer at once but for the fact I couldn't do it and remain honest. That is to say if I allowed you to send me what you believe to be good cigars it would distinctly mean that I meant to smoke them, whereas I should do nothing of the kind. I know a good cigar better than you do, for I have had 60 years experience.

No, that is not what I mean. I mean I know a bad cigar better than anybody else. I judge by the price only. If it costs above 5 cents I know it to be either foreign or half-foreign, and unsmokeable. By me. I have many boxes of Havana cigars, of all prices from 20 cts apiece up to 1.66 apiece. I bought none of them, they were all presents, they are an accumulation of several years. I have never smoked one of them and never shall. I work them off on the visitor. You shall have a chance when you come.

Pessimists are born, not made. Optimists are born, not made. But no man is born either pessimist wholly or optimist wholly, perhaps. He is pessimistic along certain lines and optimistic along certain others. That is my case.

Sincerely yours,
S. L. Clemens

Years earlier, a photographer named Sarony had photographed Clemens and had put a print on public sale, which admirers of Clemens often sent to him to be autographed. Clemens had strong feelings about both Sarony and his print, as is evidenced in the following reply to an inquiry regarding the photo.

To Mr. Row

21 Fifth Avenue, New York
November 14, 1905

Dear Mr. Row,

That alleged portrait has a private history. Sarony was as much of an enthusiast about wild animals as he was about photography, and when Du Chaillu brought the first gorilla to this country in 1819 he came to me in a fever of excitement and asked me if my father was of record and authentic. I said he was. Then Sarony, without any abatement of his excitement, asked if my grandfather also was of record and authentic. I said he was. Then Sarony, with still rising excitement and with joy added to it, said he had found my great grandfather in the person of the gorilla and had recognized him at once by his resemblance to me.

I was deeply hurt but did not reveal this, because I knew Sarony meant no offense, for the gorilla had not done him any harm and he was not a man who would say an unkind thing about a gorilla wantonly. I went with him to inspect the ancestor, and examined him from several points of view without being able to detect anything more than a passing resemblance.

"Wait," said Sarony with strong confidence, "let me show you."

He borrowed my overcoat and put it on the gorilla. The result was surprising. I saw that the gorilla, while not looking distinctly like me, was exactly what my great-grandfather would have looked like if I had had one.

Sarony photographed the creature in that overcoat and spread the picture about the world. It has remained spread about the world ever since. It turns up every week in some newspaper somewhere or other. It is not my favorite, but to my exasperation it is everybody else's. Do you think you could get it suppressed for me? I will pay the limit.

Sincerely yours,
S. L. Clemens

At the close of November of 1905 Clemens turned seventy. He resumed dictating portions of his autobiography. The work aroused strong feelings of nostalgia, which were intensified when he received an invitation to attend the golden anniversary of two old friends.

To Mr. and Mrs. Gordon

21 Fifth Avenue
Jan. 24, '06

Dear Gordons,

I have just received your golden wedding "At Home" and am trying to adjust my focus to it and realize how much it means. It is inconceivable! With a simple sweep it carries me back over a stretch of time measurable only in astronomical terms and geological periods. It brings before me Mrs. Gordon, young, round-limbed, handsome, and with her the Youngbloods and their two babies, and Laura Wright, that unspoiled little maid, that fresh flower of the woods and the prairies. Forty-eight years ago!

Life was a fairy tale then. It is a tragedy now. When I was 43 and John Hay 41 he said life was a tragedy after 40, and I disputed it.

Three years ago he asked me to testify again. I counted my graves and there was nothing for me to say.

I am old. I recognize it but I don't realize it. I wonder if a person ever really ceases to feel young—I mean, for a whole day at a time. My love to you both, and to all of us that are left.

Mark

That spring a Russian revolutionary named Tchaikowski was lecturing in the U.S. in the hope of arousing support for his cause. He invited Clemens to address one of the meetings.

Dear Mr. Tchaikowski,

I thank you for the honor of the invitation but I am not able to accept it because on Thursday evening I shall be presiding at a meeting whose object is to find remunerative work for certain classes of our blind who would gladly support themselves if they had the opportunity.

My sympathies are with the Russian revolution, of course. It goes without saying. I hope it will succeed, and now that I have talked with you I take heart to believe it will. Government by falsified promises, by lies, by treacheries and by the butcher knife for the aggrandizement of a single family of drones and its idle and vicious kin has been borne quite long enough in Russia, I should think, and it is to be hoped that the roused nation, now rising in its strength, will presently put an end to it and set up the republic in its place. Some of us, even of the white headed, may live to see the blessed day when Czars and Grand Dukes will be as scarce there as I trust they are in heaven.

Most sincerely yours,
Mark Twain

Clemens spent that summer in a rented house in Dublin, N.H., where in June he dictated five chapters of his autobiography, which I titled "Reflections on Religion" and which have appeared in print only once, in the Autumn 1963 issue of *The Hudson Review*.

In his official biography of Clemens, issued in 1912, Paine quoted from the chapters but did not identify them. He offered a few fragments as musings or table talk and scattered them about, abridging, rewriting and rearranging. His edition of the Autobiography (*Mark Twain's Autobiography*, 1924) omitted the chapters although he could have printed them if he had wished inasmuch as he was Clemens's literary executor and the editor of the Mark Twain Estate.

Bernard DeVoto made an effort to publish them in 1940 in *Mark Twain in Eruption*, which culled materials from the unpublished sections of the Autobiography. It was at the request of Clemens's daughter, then Mrs. Clara Gabrilowitsch, that DeVoto withheld them from the public. Three of the chapters have penciled on their title pages, "Edited, for publication in *Mark Twain in Eruption*, but omitted at the request of Mme. Gabrilowitsch." In his introduction to *Mark Twain in Eruption*, DeVoto made the surprising mistake of assuming responsibility not only for what he had included in the volume, but also for everything he had omitted, a sweeping gesture which necessarily included the chapters which had been refused him.

While I was preparing my own edition of the Autobiography (*The Autobiography of Mark Twain*, 1959) I asked Clemens's daughter, now Mrs. Clara Samossoud, to reconsider the matter after the lapse of eighteen years. Her decision was that no good could come from the publication of the chapters, which attacked religion in general and Christianity in particular. She and her husband, Jacques Samossoud, of Russian birth, felt especially that to publish them would be to give aid and comfort to the anti-religious Soviet Union.

There was perhaps another reason for her suppressing the chapters, one which she did not mention to me: the offense she must have taken because of her father's comments on Mary Baker Eddy. Mrs. Samossoud was a Christian Scientist. Also, she was old and her health was precarious. Her husband feared that the publication of the chapters would release a deluge of fanatical mail upon her.

Unlike DeVoto, in the introduction to my edition I expressly divorced myself from responsibility in the matter of suppressing the chapters. This did not prevent the *Literary Gazette* of Moscow from accusing me of willful censorship, as well as crying out that Mark Twain was being censored officially in his own country.

From time to time in my correspondence with Mrs. Samossoud I urged that the chapters be released, pointing out, among other things, that their suppression was giving the very aid and comfort to the Russians which she had feared their publication would give them. On the occasion of the appearance of the English edition of *The Autobiography of Mark Twain* in 1960, shortly before the 125th anniversary of Clemens's birth on November 30th of that year, I once again asked her to change her mind.

This time she consented. She went even further and lifted the ban on all her father's unpublished work. Still other (although relatively minor) obstacles presented themselves, which is why the chapters did not make their public appearance until 1963. A direct consequence of her change of mind was the release for publication of the hitherto suppressed *Letters from the Earth*, which DeVoto had edited.

Clemens dictated the chapters in the rented house a couple of miles from the village of Dublin. This was the Upton House, located on a slope of Mt. Monadnock. With him during that summer were his daughter Jean, a stenographer (Miss Josephine Hobby) and Paine. Clara Clemens lived at this time under her physician's care in a retreat in Norfolk, Conn.

It was a pleasant summer environment outside of Dublin, although Paine found it somewhat spectral, perhaps because of a westerly that never seemed to relent. Clemens's mornings were chiefly devoted to dictating his Autobiography. Paine, who lodged in the village for the summer, would drive up to the house each morning to be present for the session, sometimes returning in the afternoon to interview Clemens.

Whenever the weather permitted, Clemens dictated while pacing a long colonnaded veranda open to the country views, or while sitting in a rocker. These are the veranda and rocker pictured in the famous series of seven photographs of Clemens which Paine, a former photographer, took that August and which Clemens inserted in his Autobiography. On rainy days Clemens worked indoors, pacing constantly. After work there would be relaxation with music, usually Beethoven, Chopin or Schubert.

Writing to Howells, as he did in the following letter, Clemens dared his heirs and assigns to print the chapters on religion a century thence. But on his own manuscripts he specifically prohibited them from publishing the chapters until five centuries had elapsed. His injunction is penned in his own hand on the title pages of two of the chapters; "Not to be exposed to any eye until the edition of A.D. 2406. S.L.C."

To Howells, Maine

Dublin, N. H. *Sunday, June 17, '06*

Dear Howells,

. . . . The dictating goes lazily and pleasantly on. With intervals. I find that I have been at it off and on nearly two hours a day for 155 days since Jan. 9. To be exact I've dictated 75 hours in 80 days and loafed 75 days. I've added 60,000 words in the month that I've been here, which indicates that I've dictated during 20 days of that time—40 hours, at an average of 1,500 words an hour. It's a plenty, and I am satisfied.

There's a good deal of "fat." I've dictated (from Jan. 9) 210,000 words, and the "fat" adds about 50,000 more.

The "fat" is old pigeonholed things of the years gone by, which I or editors didn't das't to print. For instance, I am dumping in the little old book which I read to you in Hartford about 30 years ago and which you said, "Publish—and ask Dean Stanley to furnish an introduction. He'll do it." ("Captain Stormfield's Visit to Heaven.") It reads quite to suit me, without altering a word, now that it isn't to see print until I am dead.

Tomorrow I mean to dictate a chapter which will get my heirs and assigns burnt alive if they venture to print it this side of 2006 A.D.—which I judge they won't. There'll be lots of such chapters if I live 3 or 4 years longer. The edition of A.D. 2006 will make a stir when it comes out. I shall be hovering around taking notice, along with other dead pals. You are invited.

Mark

According to Paine, Clemens had a passion for billiards "but had played comparatively little since the old Hartford days of fifteen years before, when a group of his friends used to assemble on Friday nights in the room at the top of the house for long, strenuous games and much hilarity. Now the old fever all came back; the fascinations of the game superseded even his interest in the daily dictations."

To Mrs. H. H. Rogers, New York

21 Fifth Avenue, Monday, Nov., 1906

Dear Mrs. Rogers,

The billiard table is better than the doctors. It is driving out the heartburn in a most promising way. I have a billiardist on the premises, and I walk not less than ten miles every day with the cue in my hand. And the walking is not the whole of the exercise, nor the most health-giving part of it, I think. Through the multitude of the positions and attitudes, it brings into play every muscle in the body and exercises them all.

The games begin right after luncheon daily and continue until midnight, with 2 hours intermission for dinner and music. And so it is 9 hours exercise per day, and 10 or 12 on Sunday. Yesterday and last night it was 12, and I slept until 8 this morning without waking. The billiard table, as a Sabbath breaker, can beat any coal breaker in Pennsylvania, and give it 30 in the game. If Mr. Rogers will take to daily billiards, he can do without doctors and the massageur, I think.

We are really going to build a house on my farm an hour and a half from New York. It is decided. It is to be built by contract and is to come within $25,000.

With love and many thanks.
S.L.C.

P. S. Clara is in the sanitarium till January 28, when her western concert tour will begin. She is getting to be a mighty competent singer. You must know Clara better. She is one of the very finest and completest and most satisfactory characters I have ever met. Others knew it before, but I have always been busy with other matters.

The "billiardist on the premises" was Paine, who earlier in the year had become Clemens's official biographer and by now was his daily companion. The farm was in Redding, Conn., where Clemens later built a large house known as Stormfield.

Henry Mills Alden was for a great many years editor of *Harper's Magazine*. Harper & Brothers arranged to give him a great seventieth birthday dinner in their offices at Franklin Square in New York. Clemens was invited but he did not feel up to attending.

To Henry Alden

Alden,

Dear and ancient friend, it is a solemn moment. You have now reached the age of discretion. You have been a long time arriving. Many years ago you docked me on an article because the subject was too old. Later you docked me on an article because the subject was too new. Later still you docked me on an article because the subject was betwixt and between.

Once, when I wrote a Letter to Queen Victoria, you did not put it in the respectable part of the Magazine but interred it in that potter's field, the Editor's Drawer. As a result, she never answered it.

How often we recall with regret that Napoleon once shot at a magazine editor and missed him and killed a publisher. But we remember with charity that his intentions were good.

You will reform now, Alden. You will cease from these economies, and you will be discharged. But in your retirement you will carry with you the admiration and earnest good wishes of the oppressed and toiling scribes. This will be better than bread. Let this console you when the bread fails.

You will carry with you another thing too—the affection of the scribes, for they all love you in spite of your crimes. For you bear a kind heart in your breast, and the sweet and winning spirit that charms away all hostilities and animosities, and makes of your enemy your friend and keeps him so. You have reigned over us thirty-six years, and, please God, you shall reign another thirty-six—"and peace to Mahmoud on his golden throne!"

Always yours
Mark

After Livy's death the news of any approaching wedding tended to sadden Clemens, arousing in him his profound bereavement and at times coloring his congratulations.

To Father Fitz-Simon, Washington

June 5, '08

Dear Father Fitz-Simon,

Marriage—yes, it *is* the supreme felicity of life. I concede it. And it is also the supreme tragedy of life. The deeper the love, the surer the tragedy. And the more disconsolating when it comes.

And so I congratulate you. Not perfunctorily, not lukewarmly, but with a fervency and fire that no word in the dictionary is strong enough to convey. And in the same breath and with the same depth and sincerity, I grieve for you. Not for both of you and not for the one that shall go first, but for the one that is fated to be left behind. For that one there is no recompense. For that one no recompense is possible.

There are times—thousands of times—when I can expose the half of my mind and conceal the other half. But in the matter of the tragedy of marriage I feel too deeply for that, and I have to bleed it all out or shut it all in. And so you must consider what I have been through, and am passing through, and be charitable with me.

Make the most of the sunshine! And I hope it will last long—ever so long.

I do not really want to be present. Yet, for friendship's sake and because I honor you so, I would be there if I could.

Most sincerely your friend,
S. L. Clemens

Clemens's last home, Stormfield, which at first he called Innocence at Home, was completed in the spring of 1908. It was designed by Howells's son, John. Clemens did not see it until June 18, by which time it was entirely furnished. As Paine put it, "He preferred the surprise of it, and the general avoidance of detail."

To Mrs. H. H. Rogers, Fair Haven, Mass.

Redding, Conn., *Aug. 12, 1908*

Dear Mrs. Rogers,

I believe I am the wellest man on the planet today and good for a trip to Fair Haven (which I discussed with the Captain of the New Bedford boat, who pleasantly accosted me in the Grand Central August 5) but the doctor came up from New York day before yesterday and gave positive orders that I must not stir from here before frost. It is because I was threatened with a swoon 10 or 12 days ago and went to New York a day or two later to attend my nephew's funeral and got horribly exhausted by the heat and came back here and had a bilious collapse. In 24 hours I was as sound as a nut again but nobody believes it but me.

This is a prodigiously satisfactory place, and I am so glad I don't have to go back to the turmoil and rush of New York. The house stands high and the horizons are wide, yet the seclusion is perfect. The nearest *public* road is half a mile away, so there is nobody to look in, and I don't have to wear clothes if I don't want to. I have been downstairs in nightgown and slippers a couple of hours and have been photographed in that costume. But I will dress now and behave myself.

That doctor had half an idea that there is something the matter with my brain. . . . Doctors do know so little and they do charge so much for it. I wish Henry Rogers would come here, and I wish you would come with him. You can't rest in that crowded place but you could rest here, for sure! I would learn bridge, and entertain you, and rob you.

With love to you both,

Ever yours,
S.L.C.

The nephew mentioned above was Pamela Clemens's son, Samuel E. Moffett, a journalist. He had drowned off a New Jersey beach.

To Howells, Kittery Point, Maine

Aug. 12, '08

Dear Howells,

Won't you and Mrs. Howells and Mildred come and give us as many days as you can spare, and examine John's triumph? It is the most satisfactory house I am acquainted with and the most satisfactorily situated.

But it is no place to work in, because one is outside of it all the time while the sun and the moon are on duty. Outside of it in the loggia, where the breezes blow and the tall arches divide up the scenery and frame it.

It's a ghastly long distance to come, and I wouldn't travel such a distance to see anything short of a memorial museum, but if you can't come now you can at least come later when you return to New York, for the journey will be only an hour and a half per express train. Things are gradually and steadily taking shape inside the house, and nature is taking care of the outside in her ingenious and wonderful fashion—and she is competent and asks no help and gets none. I have retired from New York for good. I have retired from labor for good. I have dismissed my stenographer and have entered upon a holiday whose other end is in the cemetery.

Yours ever,
Mark

One day Clemens received a letter enclosing an incomplete list of the world's "One Hundred Greatest Men," who had exerted "the largest visible influence on the life and activities of the race." He was asked to examine the list and suggest candidates for it. Clemens offered Thomas Paine, Thomas Edison and Alexander Graham Bell. The writer of the letter asked, "Would you include Jesus, as the founder of Christianity, in the list?"

To_____, Buffalo, N. Y.

Private.   Redding, Conn., *Aug. 28, '08*

Dear Sir,

By "private," I mean don't print any remarks of mine.

I like your list.

The *"largest visible influence."*

These terms *require* you to add Jesus. And they doubly and trebly require you to add Satan. From A.D. 350 to A.D. 1850 these gentlemen exercised a vaster influence over a fifth part of the human race than was exercised over that fraction of the race by all other influences combined. Ninety-nine hundredths of this influence proceeded from Satan, the remaining fraction of it from Jesus. During those 1500 years the fear of Satan and Hell made 99 Christians where love of God and Heaven landed *one*. During those 1500 years Satan's influence was worth very nearly a hundred times as much to the business as was the influence of all the rest of the Holy Family put together.

You have asked me a question and I have answered it seriously and sincerely. You have put in Buddha—a god with a following at one time greater than Jesus ever had, a god with perhaps a little better evidence of his godship than that which is offered for Jesus's. How then in fairness can you leave Jesus out? And if you put him in, how can you logically leave Satan out? Thunder is good, thunder is impressive, but it is the lightning that does the work.

Very truly yours,
S. L. Clemens

Clemens spent that winter at Stormfield. Mostly he was content with staying at home and occasionally entertaining weekend guests from New York. According to Paine, "if he ever was restless or lonely he did not show it." He was often invited to private or public gatherings. One invitation came from Gen. O. O. Howard, who asked him to preside at a meeting to raise an endowment fund for a Lincoln Memorial University at Cumberland Gap, Tenn. Howard closed his invitation with, "Never mind if you did fight on the other side."

To General O. O. Howard

Stormfield, Redding, Connecticut
Jan. 12, '09

Dear General Howard,

You pay me a most gratifying compliment in asking me to preside, and it causes me very real regret that I am obliged to decline, for the object of the meeting appeals strongly to me, since that object is to aid in raising the $500,000 Endowment Fund for Lincoln Memorial University. The Endowment Fund will be the most fitting of all the memorials the country will dedicate to the memory of Lincoln, serving, as it will, to uplift his very own people.

I hope you will meet with complete success, and I am sorry I cannot be there to witness it and help you rejoice. But I am older than people think, and besides I live away out in the country and never stir from home except at geological intervals to fill left-over engagements in mesozoic times when I was younger and indiscreeter.

You ought not to say sarcastic things about my "fighting on the other side." General Grant did not act like that. General Grant paid me compliments. He bracketed me with Zenophon—it is there in his *Memoirs* for anybody to read. He said if all the Confederate soldiers had followed my example and adopted my military arts he could never have caught enough of them in a bunch to inconvenience the Rebellion. General Grant was a fair man and recognized my worth. But you are prejudiced, and you have hurt my feelings.

But I have an affection for you anyway.

Mark Twain

J. Henniker Heaton, a friend of Clemens, was the so-called "Father of Penny Postage" between England and the U.S. He was now lobbying for cheap cable service.

To J. Henniker Heaton, London

Stormfield, Redding, Connecticut
Jan. 18, 1909

Dear Henniker Heaton,

I do hope you will succeed to your heart's desire in your cheap-cablegram campaign, and I feel sure you will. Indeed your cheap-postage victory, achieved in spite of a quarter-century of determined opposition, is good and rational prophecy that you will. Wireless, not being as yet imprisoned in a Chinese wall of private cash and high-placed and formidable influence, will come to your aid and make your new campaign briefer and easier than the other one was.

Now then, after uttering my serious word, am I privileged to be frivolous for a moment? When you shall have achieved cheap telegraphy, are you going to employ it for just your own selfish profit and other people's pecuniary damage, the way you are doing with your cheap postage? You get letter postage reduced to 2 cents an ounce, then you mail me a 4-ounce letter with a 2-cent stamp on it, and I have to pay the extra freight at this end of the line. I return your envelope for inspection. Look at it. Stamped in one place is a vast "T," and under it the figures "40." And under those figures appears an "L," a sinister and suspicious and mysterious L. In another place, stamped within a circle in offensively large capitals, you find the words "DUE 8 CENTS."

Finally, in the midst of a desert space up nor-noreastard from that circle you find a figure "3" of quite unnecessarily aggressive and insolent magnitude—and done with a blue pencil, so as to be as conspicuous as possible. I inquired about these strange signs and symbols of the postman. He said they were P. O. Department signals for his instruction.

"Instruction for what?"

"To get extra postage."

"Is it so? Explain. Tell me about the large T and the 40."

"It's short for *Take* 40—or as we postmen say, grab 40."

"Go on, please, while I think up some words to swear with."

"Due 8 means, grab 8 more."

"_____. Continue."

"The blue-pencil 3 was an afterthought. There aren't any stamps for afterthoughts. The sums vary according to inspiration, and they whirl in the one that suggests itself at the last moment. Sometimes they go several times higher than this one. This one only means hog 3 cents more. And so if you've got 51 cents about you, or can borrow it—"

"Tell me. Who gets this corruption?"

"Half of it goes to the man in England who ships the letter on short postage, and the other half goes to the P.O.D. to protect cheap postage from inaugurating a deficit."

"_____!"

"I can't blame you. I would say it myself in your place if these ladies were not present. But you see I'm only obeying orders, I can't help myself."

"Oh, I know it. I'm not blaming you. Finally, what does that L stand for?"

"Get the money or give him L. It's English, you know."

"Take it and go. It's the last cent I've got in the world_____."

After seeing the Oxford pageant file by the grand stand, picture after picture, splendor after splendor, three thousand five hundred strong, the most moving and beautiful and impressive and historically-instructive show conceivable, you are not to think I would miss the London pageant of next year, with its shining host of 15,000 historical English men and women dug from the misty books of all the vanished ages and marching in the light of the sun—all alive and looking just as they were used to look!

Mr. Lascelles spent yesterday here on the farm and told me all about it. I shall be in the middle of my 75th year then and interested in pageants for personal and prospective reasons.

I beg you to give my best thanks to the Bath Club for the offer of its hospitalities but I shall not be able to take advantage of it, because I am to be a guest in a private house during my stay in London.

Sincerely yours,
S. L. Clemens

To Howells, New York

Stormfield, Redding, Conn.
Jan. 18, '09

Dear Howells,

I have to write a line, lazy as I am, to say how your Poe article delighted me, and to say that I am in agreement with substantially all you say about his literature. To me his prose is unreadable—like Jane Austen's. No there is a difference. I could read his prose on salary, but not Jane's. Jane is entirely impossible. It seems a great pity that they allowed her to die a natural death.

Another thing. You grant that God and circumstances sinned against Poe, but you also grant that he sinned against himself—a thing which he couldn't do and didn't do.

It is lively up here now. I wish you could come.

Yrs ever,
Mark

The following is to Elizabeth Wallace, a Bermuda friend who after Clemens's death published a small volume titled *Mark Twain in the Happy Island*.

"Stormfield," Redding, Connecticut
Nov. 13, '09

Dear Betsy,

... I've been writing *Letters from the Earth,* and if you will come here and see us I will—what? Put the MS in your hands, with the places to skip marked? No. I won't trust you quite that far. I'll read messages to you. This book will never be published—in fact it couldn't be, because it would be felony to soil the mails with it, for it has much Holy Scripture in it of the kind that . . . can't properly be read aloud except from the pulpit and in family worship. Paine enjoys it but Paine is going to be damned one of these days, I suppose.

The autumn splendors passed you by? What a pity. I wish you had been here. It was beyond words! It was heaven and hell and sunset and rainbows and the aurora all fused into one divine harmony, and you couldn't look at it and keep the tears back. All the hosannahing strong gorgeousnesses have gone back to heaven and hell and the pole now, but no matter. If you could look out of my bedroom window at this moment you would choke up, and when you got your voice you would say: This is not real, this is a dream. Such a singing together, and such a whispering together, and such a snuggling together of cosy soft colors, and such kissing and caressing, and such pretty blushing when the sun breaks out and catches those dainty weeds at it—you remember that weed garden of mine!—and then—then the far hills sleeping in a dim blue trance—oh, hearing about it is nothing, you should be here to see it.

Good! I wish I could go on the platform and read. And I could, if it could be kept out of the papers. There's a charity school of 400 young girls in Boston that I would give my ears to talk to, if I had some more. But—oh, well, I can't go and it's no use to grieve about it.

This morning Jean went to town. Also Paine. Also the butler. Also Katy. Also the laundress. The cook and the maid and the boy and the roustabout and Jean's coachman are left—just enough to make it lonesome, because they are around yet never visible. However, the Harpers are sending Leigh up to play billiards, therefore I shall survive.

Affectionately,
S. L. Clemens

Jean is Clemens's daughter. Katy is Katy Leary, who had worked for him for twenty-nine years. Leigh is Frederick T. Leigh, an employee of Harper & Brothers.

Paine has written:

"Early in June that year Clemens had developed unmistakable symptoms of heart trouble of a very serious nature. It was angina pectoris, and while to all appearances he was as well as ever and usually felt so, he was periodically visited by severe attacks of acute 'breast pains' which, as the months passed, increased in frequency and severity. He was alarmed and distressed, not on his own account but because of his daughter Jean, a handsome girl who had long been subject to epileptic seizures. In case of his death he feared that Jean would be without permanent anchorage, his other daughter, Clara, following her marriage to Ossip Gabrilowitsch [a concert pianist] in October, having taken up residence abroad."

At 7:30 A.M. of December 24th Clemens was awakened by voices outside his door. Jean was the only person in the house who was used to entering his room without knocking. She had been named Jane Lampton after his mother but had always been called Jean. She was twenty-nine.

Katy Leary entered abruptly. Clemens thought it was his daughter.

"Miss Jean is dead!" Katy Leary gasped.

Jean had been found in her bathtub. She was later reported to have drowned as a result of a seizure. Paine wrote that this was incorrect, that she died of "heart exhaustion" caused by her malady and "the shock of cold water."

Clemens and the servants tried to revive her. A doctor traveled several miles and tried too.

The previous evening Jean and her father had chatted in the library until nine, a late hour for them.

She said at his door, "I can't kiss you good night, father. I have a cold and you could catch it."

He bent over and kissed her hand. She impulsively kissed his. Then with the usual "Sleep well, dear!" they parted.

Four days ago he had returned from a month's holiday in Bermuda and had considered himself to be in restored health. Friends, however, thought him to be dangerously ill. Jean was at the dock in New York when his ship came in, and she was at the door of Stormfield when he reached the house the following evening. She had not had a seizure for months.

Clemens had received hard blows in recent times. Seven months ago H. H. Rogers had died. Within the past six weeks two other friends, Richard W. Gilder and William M. Laffan, had passed away.

Jean had been worried that Clara, in Europe, would hear the rumors of her father's serious illness. According to Clemens, Clara had been nursing her husband "day and night for four months" and was worn out. She might see the accounts of his illness in the German papers, "with disastrous results."

Jean had urged him to explain his situation through the Associated Press. So he had telephoned the AP and had denied the charge that he was dying, adding, "I would not do such a thing at my time of life." He was seventy-four.

He had the extraordinary ability to write powerfully and in depth about a personal tragedy almost immediately after learning about it. He began writing a remarkable essay, "The Death of Jean," at 11 A.M., less than four hours after being told that she was dead. That morning he sent Clara a cablegram informing her of the event and urging her not to come home.

"She lies there, and I sit here—writing, busying myself, to keep my heart from breaking. How dazzlingly the sunshine is flooding the hills around! It is like a mockery. . . . I saw her mother buried. I said I would never endure that horror again; that I would never again look into the grave of any one dear to me. I have kept to that. They will take Jean from this house tomorrow and bear her to Elmira, New York, where lie those of us that have been released, but I shall not follow. . . . I was getting acquainted with Jean in these last nine months. She had been long an exile from home when she came to us three-quarters of a year ago. She had been shut up in sanitariums, many miles from us. How eloquently glad and grateful she was to cross her father's threshold again!"

Two days later Clemens showed Paine the essay and said, "If you think it worthy, some day—at the proper time—it can end my autobiography. It is the final chapter."

The essay first appeared in print in *Harper's Magazine* December 1910. It concludes my edition of the Autobiography, *The Autobiography of Mark Twain.*

To Clara Clemens Gabrilowitsch, in Europe

Redding, Conn.
Dec. 29, '09

O, Clara, Clara dear, I am so glad she is out of it and safe—safe! I am not melancholy. I shall never be melancholy again, I think. You see, I was in such distress when I came to realize that you were gone far away and no one stood between her and danger but me—and I could die at any moment, and *then*—oh then what would become of her! For she was wilful, you know, and would not have been governable.

You can't imagine what a darling she was, that last two or three days. And how *fine*, and good, and sweet, and noble—and *joyful*, thank Heaven!—and how intellectually brilliant. I had never been acquainted with Jean before. I recognized that.

But I mustn't try to write about her—I *can't*. I have already poured my heart out with the pen, recording that last day or two. I will send you that—and you must let no one but Ossip read it.

Goodbye. I love you so! And Ossip.

Father

On the afternoon of April 21, 1910, Clemens sank into a coma at Stormfield. He died "just at sunset," according to Paine. Three days later he was buried in Elmira.

Index

Note: Names in SMALL CAPITALS are recipients of letters. Titles without an author's name pertain to works by Mark Twain. Abbreviation used: SC for Samuel Clemens, Mark Twain

OTHER COOPER SQUARE PRESS TITLES OF INTEREST

THE LANTERN-BEARERS AND OTHER ESSAYS
Robert Louis Stevenson
Edited by Jeremy Treglown
320 pp.
0-8154-1012-3
$16.95

TOLSTOY
Tales of Courage and Conflict
Count Leo Tolstoy
Edited by Charles Neider
576 pp.
0-8154-1010-7
$19.95

THE WAR OF 1812
Henry Adams
New introduction by Col. John R. Elting
392 pp., 27 maps
0-8154-1013-1
$16.95

MARGARET SANGER
An Autobiography
New introduction by Kathryn Cullen-DuPont
516 pp., 1 b/w photo
0-8154-1015-8
$17.95

Available at bookstores; or call 1-800-462-6420

 Cooper Square Press

150 Fifth Avenue
Suite 911
New York, NY 10011